T0243263

SUDDENLY SOLDIERS

SUDDENLY SOLDIERS

THE 166TH
INFANTRY REGIMENT
IN WORLD WAR I

ROBERT THOMPSON

WESTHOLME
Yardley

Westholme Publishing, LLC
904 Edgewood Road
Yardley, Pennsylvania 19067
Visit our Web site at www.westholmepublishing.com

ISBN: 978-1-59416-350-0
Also available as an eBook.

Printed in the United States of America.

In memory of my great uncle, Private Robert L. Thorn, E Company, 166th Infantry Regiment, who was killed in action in the wheat fields above the Ourcq River on July 29, 1918.

Contents

Illustrations

Preface

Dᴜʀɪɴɢ ᴛʜᴇ ɴᴇᴀʀʟʏ four-and-a-half years from July 28, 2014, until November 11, 2018, much of the Western world commemorated the one-hundredth anniversary of World War I. It is noteworthy that most of the official ceremonies marking this centennial were appropriately somber and subdued. There were almost no outward celebrations of heroism, courage, or the eventual victory of the Allied powers, Great Britain, France, Italy, and the United States. This war had simply been too awful, too bloody, and too stupid. It was a catastrophe that never should have happened.

However, while Western Europe and Australia took particular care to remember the war and its dead, the commemorations in the United States were more than a little muted. The government established an official centennial commission in 2013 that planned, developed, and executed various programs, projects, and activities to commemorate the country's part in the war. However, none of those efforts came close to being as noteworthy as those in Europe, particularly in Great Britain, where the painful losses from the war are still keenly felt. In the United States, one could arguably state that World War I has become something of a forgotten conflict.

Even for those Americans who do remember the war, their mental image of it is limited to rousing songs like George M. Cohan's "Over There" and scenes from grainy films showing smiling doughboys boarding ships bound for France. They do not see, however, the mud, rats, and body lice of the trenches, the dead men laying hideously prone across tangled barbed wire, nor the thousands forever damaged mentally and emotionally by what people referred to as "shell shock."

This lack of knowledge and understanding is tragic given that almost five million Americans served in the war, and the nation suffered over four hundred thousand killed, wounded, and missing during barely a year of combat operations. This conflict was America's first entry into a major foreign war and the first that demanded a massive, nationwide mobilization. Moreover, a crucial part of that mobilization included something new: the activation of state National Guard units into federal service and their incorporation into the US Army. To be sure, militia-type military organizations and their citizen-soldiers had always played a prominent role in providing American military manpower. However, before the Militia Act of 1903 and the National Defense Act of 1916, there was no formal relationship between state militia organizations like the National Guard and the Regular Army. By the time war was declared on Germany in April 1917, that had changed and, as a result, the lives of millions of men who had enlisted in their local National Guard units in peacetime would be altered forever.

In April 1917, no one had ever seriously considered the idea of sending the US Army across the ocean to fight a war against a major European power. Now, suddenly, the nation needed men to do just that. The Regular Army was very small at the time and, therefore, the only organization capable of providing an immediate source of manpower was the National Guard. They were not ready for a war of any kind, and neither they nor their Regular Army counterparts were prepared to fight the kind of war that had been raging on the Western Front in France since the summer of 1914.

In June 1917, just a few months after war was declared, the first division of Regular Army infantrymen left for France. Initially, that was the best America could do. The next men to deploy overseas would have to be from the National Guard. The War Department and its Militia Bureau determined which National Guard units had the highest state of readiness, as low as that state might actually be. The first National Guard division to go to France was the 26th Division, which was formed from units in the New England states. Next, the War Department decided to mobilize the remaining National Guard units deemed ready into a single organization, the 42nd Division, and sent them to France only a few weeks after the departure of the 26th Division. Because this new division had National Guard units from twenty-six different states and stretched across the nation "like a rainbow," it became known as the Rainbow Division. It would be one of the most famous American military units to fight in World War I.

One of the National Guard units picked by the War Department for the Rainbow Division was the 4th Ohio Infantry Regiment, which they redesignated as the 166th Infantry Regiment of the US Army. The companies that made up the regiment came from ten towns across Ohio, and the men who went to fight were very ordinary, the sort of people all of us know even today, who do everyday jobs and live unremarkable lives. But now, they would be asked to do something so extraordinary that they would have never considered it in their wildest dreams, or perhaps, one should say, their worst nightmares. That is what I found so compelling about their story, and that is why I decided to write it down for everyone to read.

In collecting source material, I was greatly aided by two previous histories written about the 166th. The first was *Ohio in the Rainbow: Official Story of the 166th Infantry Regiment, 42nd Division, in the World War*, which was written in 1924 by a former captain in the regiment, Raymond Cheseldine. The second history was authored by another officer from the regiment, Alison Reppy, in 1919 and was titled *Rainbow Memories: Character Sketches and History of the First Battalion, 166th Infantry, 42nd Division, American Expeditionary Force*. Both offered excellent starting points for my research, providing a wealth of material and an excellent chronological basis for the regiment's story. But, at the same time, they both suffered from one understandable failing.

Written shortly after the war for an audience that was made up primarily of the regiment's veterans and their families, both books tended to take a somewhat romantic approach to the war, deemphasizing the pain, suffering, and loss experienced by the men of the regiment. That shortcoming left me needing sources that were more intimate, grittier, and a bit more honest and forthright.

Luckily, I was able to find those sources in the form of journals, diaries, and letters from soldiers in the 166th, and they were critical in producing the final product. Some of these were published, but most were not. Most of the unpublished documents were made available online by descendants of the soldiers who wrote them. Meanwhile, others could be found in the archives of the Ohio Historical Society, now known as the Ohio History Connection. The information in these documents helped tell the soldiers' real stories, providing not just personal details but also color and texture.

Also, they helped fill blanks in the official versions of the regiment's history, as well as provide essential information missing in the other two books, as well as important clarifications of some issues.

As I read the various accounts detailed in the memoirs, letters, journals, and diaries written by the men of the 166th Infantry, several things struck me and made a particularly strong impression. The first is the human capacity for enduring suffering that can only be described as a doggedly persistent form of courage. Despite not being professionals, these soldiers were remarkably resilient. Thrown into a savage European conflict for which they were totally unprepared, they met both the physical and mental challenges posed by heavy German artillery shelling, poison gas, and the presence of sudden death and horrific maiming all around them. And they did this despite the almost constant presence of rats, unimaginable filth, mud, and body lice. Further, they battled a determined enemy while often living in a hole in the ground as rain poured down on them, forcing them to wear the same worn, dirty, soaked clothing for weeks at a time while subsisting on a diet of canned beef, hard bread, and coffee.

At the same time, I also could not help but be impressed by the high quality of leadership exhibited at every command level of the regiment. First and foremost, there was the regiment's commander, Benson W. Hough, who was the epitome of an outstanding combat commander. Next, there were the officers and noncommissioned officers at the battalion, company, platoon, and squad levels, leaders who seemed to make up for a lack of experience and training with common sense, intense dedication to their men, and an often innovative approach to every challenge, no matter how daunting or dangerous that challenge might have been.

Lastly, there was the compassion and love these men demonstrated for one another. This is particularly evident in their attitudes toward those in their ranks struck down by shell shock. While the primary sources I used certainly did not provide anything close to a comprehensive survey on the subject, the ones I was able to review did not contain a single opinion that expressed a view of those afflicted by shell shock as being either cowards or men who shirked their duty. Rather, they demonstrated a spirt of empathy and emotional generosity that is truly noteworthy. In this way, these soldiers seem to have been generations ahead of the US Army and American society in general. Perhaps that is because the others in the regiment realized the line between their own emotional and mental health and that of those broken by the strain of combat was very, very thin.

As I was writing this manuscript, I tried to add a few details about the men who were part of this story. In most cases, this was only information on their age, their hometown, and, sometimes, their peacetime occupation. If I was fortunate, genealogical sources such as their military records, hometown newspaper, or even census data might tell me whether they were married or had children. I wanted, somehow, to make them as real as possible to the reader and not merely a name. I was assisted greatly in this process by online sources such as Ancestry.com, Fold3.com, and Newspapers.com.

I was also fortunate to find excellent sources of photographs for use in illustrating the book. I have to thank the Ohio History Connection, Union County Historical Society, Library of Congress and, in particular, the National Archives and Records Administration for the availability of digital copies of photos from the war. Luckily, the National Archives and Records Administration had even created a special online collection of documents, photos, and films from World War I for use by researchers such as myself. I cannot say how grateful I am for their work on that project.

Introduction: The Great War

"The lamps are going out all over Europe: we shall not see them lit again in our lifetime."—Sir Edward Grey, British foreign secretary, August 3, 1914, *Twenty-Five Years, 1892-1916*

It was a massive cataclysm called the Great War.

More often than not, people also referred to it as the World War, because it had a global scope that had never been seen before. It would create a new and horrific standard for carnage, destruction, cruelty, and human misery that would not be surpassed until a second world war began twenty-one years after this first one had ended. The causes of the Great War are too numerous to recount and debate here, but suffice to say, rising nationalism among vassal states within the Austro-Hungarian Empire and rapid military mobilization by three of Europe's ruling monarchies were crucial factors. The petty jealousies among the Hapsburgs of Austro-Hungary, the Hohenzollerns of Germany, and the Romanovs of Russia resulted in tangled alliances and automatic mobilization plans that would also draw Great Britain, Italy, and France into a war no sane person would have ever contemplated.

As a result, in August 1914, a war that would kill millions and topple ancient monarchies started before anyone seemed to think about taking a step back from the brink and pausing to consider if the conflict that was coming was truly the only option available. It is ironic, therefore, that, of the five major European monarchies involved in the war, only two, the Windsors of Great Britain and the Savoys of Italy, would survive it. At the same time, the war would unleash progressive social forces across Europe, while the nature of its eventual conclusion facilitated the rise of the militant fascism that caused the coming of a second and even more horrific world war.

By 1917, the fighting had taken on a form that was, in the understated words of one historian, "quite rigid in nature and unimaginative in practice."[1] The opening campaigns that started in the late summer of 1914 along what became known as the Western Front quickly lost all momentum amid casualties of an unimaginable scale. Here, the opposing armies dug an elaborate line of trenches four hundred seventy miles long through Belgium and northern France from the English Channel to the Swiss border. The pattern of combat became one of constant artillery barrages, attacks with poison gases, and infantry assaults across the deadly "no man's land" between the trenches, a nightmarish place riddled with thousands of deep shell holes, tangled barbed wire, broken equipment, and dead men. More often than not, the infantry attacks across this no man's land gained absolutely nothing except for an appreciation of the human capacity for courageous but utterly meaningless sacrifice, suffering, and death.

The casualties that resulted from the use of modern weapons such as heavy artillery and the machine gun were far beyond staggering—they were incomprehensible. For example, on the first day of the Somme Offensive in July 1916, the British army suffered more than fifty-seven thousand dead or wounded, with almost nineteen thousand men killed within the first hour.[2] The machine gun was responsible for much of the carnage. Even though the British, French, and Germans had been using machine guns since the late nineteenth century, they failed to appreciate the weapon's ability to inflict a deadly toll on infantrymen. This was primarily because, while they all had experienced great success in using the machine gun, they had used the machine gun mostly against Asian and African colonial insurgents. Therefore, they discounted the weapon's potential because, first, their own armies had not been subject to machine-gun fire and, second, they had no respect for their colonial opponents—the machine gun might be effective against mere "native" combatants, but it could not possibly stand up to a determined bayonet charge by white, European infantry.[3]

As casualties mounted in the face of withering firepower, tactics from the late nineteenth century were not significantly altered. Infantrymen still charged across hundreds of yards of open ground with fixed bayonets.

So, instead of evolving tactics to the times, men like Field Marshal Douglas Haig, the commander of the British Expeditionary Force, made high casualties a measure of success and referred to them as "normal wastage."[4] The perverse logic that Haig and other generals applied was that, if their own losses were high, surely the enemy's must be worse. While he had no intelligence or empirical data to support this bizarre conclusion, Haig would berate his field commanders if their losses were lower than anticipated. In one instance, after reading a casualty report, Haig complained in his diary that "the total losses of this division are under a thousand!"[5] It is, therefore, no surprise that Great Britain lost much of an entire generation of young men in what was a mindless slaughter.

As 1916 came to an end, the British, French, and German armies were all worn down from what had become a steady battle of attrition. Morale was low, their soldiers' appetite for combat was almost nonexistent, and it was starting to become a question of whose army would crumble first. Little wonder then that people in the United States had no appetite for joining in the fight and allowing their young men to become "normal wastage."

AS THE BLOODLETTING on the Western Front continued into early 1917, America remained officially neutral. President Woodrow Wilson had been reelected in 1916 using the slogan, "He kept us out of war!" While the United States had continued to develop increasing cultural and economic ties with Europe during the early twentieth century, it had remained distant and aloof when it came to the continent's complex politics. America watched with wariness and some trepidation as the major European powers built their network of alliances and engaged in diplomatic battles. Once war broke out, the overwhelming majority of Americans had no desire to take part in the conflict and rightfully so. However, at the same time, they did develop a decidedly pro-Allied bias, primarily because of a highly effective British propaganda campaign that provided lurid descriptions in American newspapers of supposed German atrocities in Belgium and France.

When the war ground down to a stalemate in 1914, and it was clear there would be no quick victory by either side, American resources became a "strategic factor that belligerent planners had to consider." Therefore, the true nature of American neutrality became a critical issue for Germany and its allies, known collectively as the Central Powers.[6] As the war continued, American firms began to provide essential war materials and supplies to Britain and France, and, as a result, the Germans felt they must use their submarines against American commercial shipping traffic in the North Atlantic. While Woodrow Wilson's administration was able to negotiate an end to so-called "unrestricted" German submarine warfare in 1916, the course of the war almost forced the German leadership to resume the practice of sinking civilian American vessels headed for British and French ports. First, the situation along the front with Britain and France had reached a point of total stagnation. Further, the British blockade of the North Sea had led to starvation in several large German cities, while American industry increased its support for the Allied cause, despite Wilson's declarations of neutrality. As a result, the German High Command recommended a resumption of an unrestricted submarine offensive to Kaiser Wilhelm II in early 1917, an act they knew would enrage President Wilson and the American public.

Unrestricted submarine warfare, therefore, became the critical tipping point in determining whether America would enter the war on the Allied side, which the German High Command knew all too well. However, the kaiser's principal commanders, General Paul von Hindenburg, General Eric Ludendorff, and Admiral Rudolf von Holtzendorff, were not concerned. Even if America declared war, they argued, German submarines would stop any significant number of American troops from arriving in Europe, allowing the Germans to go on the offensive and finish off the British and French within six months. Ludendorff even told the kaiser that he did not "care two hoots about America." Holtzendorff then told the kaiser, on his "word of honor," that "not one American will land on the continent."[7] With those assurances from his commanders, Kaiser Wilhelm authorized a renewed campaign of unrestricted submarine warfare to begin on February 1, 1917. Within two weeks, the United States broke diplomatic relations with Germany.

Not long after severing relations with the German government, the British provided the Wilson administration with copies of intercepted communications between the German foreign minister, Arthur Zimmermann, and the German ambassador to Mexico. In a telegram, Zimmermann proposed the creation of an alliance between Germany and Mexico if the United States entered the war. As an incentive to Mexico, Zimmermann said Germany would provide financial aid to Mexico, and, if the Germans were victorious, he suggested that Mexico would be allowed to reclaim its lost territory in Texas, New Mexico, and Arizona.[8]

Newspaper cartoon, left, on unrestricted submarine warfare. (*Library of Congress*) Right, General Paul von Hindenburg, Kaiser Wilhelm II, and General Erich Ludendorff. (*National Archives*)

In late February, the State Department leaked the telegram to the Associated Press, and its contents soon appeared in newspapers across the nation. The information in the Zimmermann Telegram infuriated Americans. As a result, American public opinion began to turn against neutrality. People started to see the war as more than the result of mere European stupidity but, rather, as a war over the dangers of militarism that pitted democracy against authoritarian monarchies. While this viewpoint did not really reflect the realities of the war and was largely the product of Britain's propaganda campaign, by April, the increase in submarine warfare and the change in American public opinion demanded that President Wilson prepare to declare war.

On the evening of April 2, 1917, Wilson made his way through the rain up Pennsylvania Avenue, where a joint session of Congress awaited him in the chambers of the House of Representatives. In his address, he told Congress that the nation must "accept the status of belligerent which has ... been thrust upon it ... [and] to exert all its power and employ all its resources to bring the Government of the German Empire to terms and end the war." Then, he concluded by saying, "To such a task we can dedicate our lives and our fortunes, everything that we are and everything that we have, with the pride of those who know that the day has come when America is privileged to spend her blood and her might for the principles that gave her birth and happiness and the peace which she has treasured.

Introduction: The Great War

God helping her, she can do no other."[9] He received a loud, long, standing ovation, and Congress approved the declaration of war on April 5.

With America now officially in the war, the first question in the minds of both American and Allied officials revolved around how the United States should contribute to the Allied cause. Initially, some British and French leaders merely wanted supplies as well as support from engineering and technical troops, with no commitment of American combat forces. However, when the British and French spring offensive of 1917 failed disastrously, the need for American forces became clear. On April 25, a French delegation led by a former premier, René Viviani, arrived in Washington to discuss America's role in the war. While Viviani was supposed to be the leader of the French team, everyone knew that the man really in charge was another member of the delegation, the hero of the Marne, Marshal Joseph Joffre. When Joffre spoke, everyone knew it was he who had the knowledge and experience to be the voice of French authority, and he told the Americans, "We want men, men, men."[10]

On April 27, Joffre met with Secretary of War Newton D. Baker, Chief of Staff Major General Hugh L. Scott, and Assistant Chief of Staff Major General Tasker H. Bliss in the office of the Army War College's president. Joffre appealed to them to dispatch at least one division to France as soon as possible and to begin organizing and training a large force that would operate as an independent American army. The three American leaders agreed to his request, and President Wilson formally approved their plans on May 2.[11]

WITH THE CONCEPT OF QUICK DEPLOYMENT of one division as the lead element of an independent American army now in the open, a series of complex issues arose that had to be dealt with. Many military leaders in France and, in particular, Britain, believed that American troops should simply be used as a source of replacements within their own national forces. This, they argued, would allow for even faster use of American military resources. Further, they had significant concerns about the quality of American military leadership and whether the American general staff could actually plan and execute complex operations by a large army numbering in the millions of men.

These British and French concerns were not without merit. After all, the US Army had no organized field armies, army corps, combat divisions, or brigades. They also had very few real regiments, and the regiments they did have were small in comparison with those of the French and British units fighting on the Western Front.

As for the question of leadership, the answer was just as bad. Most of the Regular officer corps were relatively young and inexperienced, with 67 percent of Regular Army officers serving in April 1917 having less than one year's service. Further, only Brigadier General John J. Pershing had commanded a force bigger than a brigade (about ten thousand men) in action. Things were also grim when you examined the training and education of American officers. Wielding a large army in combat would require de-

Marshal Joffre, taken while in Washington, D.C., in 1917. (*National Archives*)

tailed, effective planning and staff work. But, in 1917, only 379 officers had completed the command and staff courses at Fort Leavenworth or the Army War College.[12]

There were also questions regarding the army's organization and doctrine. The US Army had no armies, combat divisions, or brigades because their doctrine was based on small units executing fluid tactics in the open without the need for any significant supporting firepower. The infantryman with his rifle still reigned supreme and was the core element of American military doctrine. Therefore, the army had few machine guns, little heavy artillery, and no doctrine for the effective use of either. Despite reports coming from the Western Front since 1914 on the use of artillery and the machine gun, American doctrine did not change, and both weapons continued to be seen as tertiary supporting elements for the infantry rather than as crucial components of an integrated combat force.

In fact, the US Army's 1912 tables of organization, which were in effect when war was declared in 1917, called for only four machine guns per infantry regiment, which was in stark contrast to the German army where there were more than one hundred machine guns in each infantry regiment.[13] Furthermore, the US Army had no automatic rifles, trench mortars, rifle grenades, or hand grenades, all of which were vital weapons in the trenches in France.[14] The situation with artillery was similar in that, while there were batteries of light artillery, there were very few large-caliber guns of the sort being used to blast opposing trenches in France. Colonel Conrad H. Lanza, a career artillery officer who later served in the

American Expeditionary Force's (AEF) First Army, noted that in the official prewar doctrine, "the artillery was considered an auxiliary, sometimes useful, never necessary, and sometimes a nuisance."[15]

Therefore, from the start of the American war effort, it was clear that any American forces sent to France would have to be armed and trained to fight what the British and French saw as a modern, industrialized form of warfare—a war fought in the trenches where massive firepower was a critical element. This added to the perception that no American army would be ready in time to be employed effectively and that the integration or "amalgamation" of American troops into British and French units was the only logical course of action.

At the same time, many leaders recognized that there were disadvantages to amalgamation. First, the idea of using a million American troops in foreign units under foreign command would be an insult to American national pride. Besides, the thousands of Irish Americans who would enlist in the army would never agree to serve in British units. Further, placing Americans in French commands where they did not speak the language made absolutely no sense. Lastly, people close to President Wilson feared that amalgamation would lessen the value of the American contribution to the war effort with an equal decrease in America's role in any post-war peace negotiations.[16]

In the end, it was again Marshal Joffre who had the last word. He knew the American people would never accept amalgamation because the nation would not "allow its citizens to be incorporated like poor relations in the ranks of some other army and fight under a foreign flag."[17] While there would be continued pressure for some form of amalgamation from the British and French until the end of the war, with Joffre's pronouncement, the issue of amalgamation was settled for now—America would mobilize, organize, and train her own independent army.

WHILE THE US ARMY OF 1917 could not compare with either the British or French army, it had made numerous changes to its organization and culture since 1900. Under the leadership of William McKinley and Theodore Roosevelt's secretary of war, Elihu Root, and with mandates from Congress, the army instituted a series of reforms based on the work of the late Emory Upton, a Civil War veteran officer who passionately argued for change until his death in 1881. By 1917, these reforms had begun to lay the foundation of a modern army. The improvements included post-graduate professional education at Fort Leavenworth and the Army War College, the creation of a general staff, regular assignment rotations for officers between line units and staff bureaus, and a formal relationship between the Regular Army and the National Guard.

Post-graduate professional education was a foundational element in Root's reforms. The course of study at Fort Leavenworth's School of the Line and Staff College was particularly important in stimulating a new generation of officers. It allowed young officers to analyze and solve tactical problems with the help of German textbooks and topographical maps, some of which they would later use in combat against the Germans. Even some older officers, such as General Pershing, worked via correspondence to complete this new coursework.[18]

However, the reform that would have the most immediate impact on mobilizing the AEF was the one involving the National Guard. Since the nation's founding, the core of American military manpower had been either state militias or state volunteer regiments. But Emory Upton had seen the results of this system during the Civil War, where it took years to create a capable army from thousands of untrained, inexperienced state troops and where there was a corresponding cost in the form of hundreds of thousands of combat casualties. He had recommended that National Guard units, while remaining under state control until they were mobilized by the federal government, be subject to US Army training standards and regulations, as well as inspection and certification by Regular Army personnel. When Elihu Root included these ideas in his reforms, he added the concept of joint training maneuvers with Regular Army units. The resulting program was of mutual advantage to the National Guard and the army. Officers such as Lieutenant George C. Marshall, who would be a vital member of the AEF staff, were able to observe the capabilities and limitations of the National Guard units. At the same time, the citizen-soldiers learned the art and practice of war from the professionals.[19]

Following the meetings with Joffre, the army decided to organize one division from Regular Army units, which would be designated the 1st Division and sail for France as soon as June 1917.[20] Following that deployment, the Regular Army would be expanded by creating twenty Regular divisions and eighteen National Guard divisions. Any additional units beyond those would be mobilized using draftees in a new category of what was to be called National Army divisions.

The fact that traditional American units were much smaller than those used by the British and French complicated this scheme. Therefore, the army decided to modify its tables of organization and significantly expand the units being formed. Infantry companies would grow from fifty men to two hundred fifty and form battalions of more than one thousand men, which had been the size of a single regiment in the Civil War. Regiments, meanwhile, would have thirty-eight hundred men, and brigades would have a strength of almost eighty-five hundred. A five thousand-man artillery brigade and a host of support troops would supplement these units. With two large infantry brigades, artillery, and the support forces, each new AEF division would number over twenty-eight thousand men, which was twice the size of most Allied or German divisions.[21]

Recruiting and mobilizing to the revised strength numbers would be a challenge. Before the events of 1917, Congress passed the National Defense Act in June 1916. The measure authorized the Regular Army to more than double its current strength during the next five years to over eleven thousand officers and more than two hundred thousand men. The National Guard, meanwhile, was tasked to increase its size to seventeen thousand officers and four hundred forty thousand men. The law also included a requirement that National Guard personnel take both a state and federal oath.[22]

Unfortunately, up until the declaration of war, recruiting efforts had not had enough time to yield any significant increase in troop strength. By April 1917, the Regular Army had about fifty-eight hundred officers and just over one hundred twenty thousand men. At the same time, National Guard totals came to a little over eighty thousand officers and men already called to federal service, plus about one hundred thousand still under state control. Finally, neither Regulars or Guardsmen were properly organized or equipped for the sort of war being fought in France.[23]

While Root's reforms had made progress, the army was, in many ways, still the same one that had difficulty mobilizing to go to war with Spain in 1898. The culture remained one of stagnation and a peaceful, almost sleepy reserve. This was not surprising given that the majority of the officers above the rank of captain had entered the Army before the Spanish-American War, and, before 1900, most US Army units were commanded by officers who had fought in the Civil War. It was not until August 1915 that the last Civil War veteran, Colonel John Clem, the famed drummer boy of Shiloh, retired, which was only a few weeks after Dwight D. Eisenhower and Omar N. Bradley graduated from West Point.[24]

Despite these seemingly insurmountable obstacles, the wheels of mobilization began to slowly turn. The army now decided that, following the deployment of the 1st Division to France, the next two divisions to go overseas would be formed from those National Guard regiments deemed to have the highest state of readiness, as low as that state might actually be given the requirements of warfare on the Western Front. As a result, National Guard units across the country began to recruit new men to increase their regiments to the updated strength levels.

One of these units was the 4th Ohio Infantry Regiment. Ohio would soon be going "over there."

1

Mobilizing the 4th Ohio

"We are young men of promising pasts, but durned uncertain futures."
—*Ohio Rainbow Reveille*, 1918

On the morning of July 30, 1918, the sky above the small French village of Seringes-et-Nesles was clouded with smoke from burning buildings and the regular explosions of incoming German artillery shells. The men of E Company, the Marysville, Ohio, unit from what had once been the National Guard's 4th Ohio Infantry Regiment, looked back down the hill that led up to the village from the Ourcq River about a mile away. In the bright yellow wheat fields that covered the hillside lay almost one thousand of their comrades from the regiment, including their buddies from the company, many of whom were men they had grown up with back home in Marysville. They had all died amid withering machine-gun fire from German emplacements hidden in the wheat fields and a steady rain of enemy artillery fire.

The regiment had crossed the Ourcq under fire three days ago and had been fighting over about a mile and a half of ground since then to secure this village on the slopes above the river. The 1st Battalion made the initial assault and was nearly slaughtered to every man. In C Company alone, there were only fifty men left standing after the first few horrific hours of combat.

Being a hometown Guardsman in Ohio seemed a lifetime ago.

Many of the men who had survived the gauntlet of machine-gun fire through the wheat fields to Seringes-et-Nesles had joined their hometown National Guard company before the war for the fun of it. The companies had actually functioned something like a local social club. The men came to monthly drill sessions where they got to wear a uniform, perform close-order drill, and even fire a rifle on occasion. In the summer, they all went to Camp Perry on the shores of Lake Erie for two weeks of additional drill and unit competitions in marksmanship. For this, the enlisted men, most of whom were farmers or workmen in local factories and shops, got paid $1 per month. For them, this was not an insignificant amount of money in the years before the war. Meanwhile, for the prominent local business-men and attorneys who populated the officer ranks, membership in the National Guard companies provided the ability to foster new business and maintain important political connections.

They all knew that a federal mobilization was possible, but that seemed very unlikely to ever happen, and, even if it did, it almost certainly would not involve any truly dangerous duties. And even after the regiment was actually mobilized and sent to the Mexican border in 1916, no one in their right mind imagined that going to France to fight in this insane European war was even a remote possibility. That certainly would *not* be worth $1 a month in drill pay and the chance to "play soldier" with your buddies every month.

Yet, here they were, in France, praying the next German bullet or artillery shell was not coming for them while contemplating the loss of so many dear friends in the wheat fields on the slopes above the Ourcq River.

THE 4TH OHIO INFANTRY REGIMENT of the Ohio National Guard had a long and proud lineage. Unlike most National Guard regiments, it could trace its ancestry all the way back to the Mexican War of 1846-1848, where the regiment was part of General Winfield Scott's army that landed at Vera Cruz.[1] During the Civil War, the 4th Ohio was part of the Army of the Potomac and took part in the fighting at Antietam, Fredericksburg, Chancellorsville, Gettysburg, Spotsylvania, Cold Harbor, and Petersburg.[2]

The regiment was reformed in April 1898 and called to federal service in May for duty during the Spanish-American War. Arriving in Cuba in late July, the 4th was part of the American force attacking the town of Guayama in the days just before the war quickly ended. The regiment returned to Columbus, Ohio, and mustered out in January 1899. Shortly after that, the regiment was reorganized as part of the Ohio National Guard. During the seventeen years that followed, the companies that made up the regiment took part in the typical National Guard routine, conducting monthly drill sessions at their home armories with an annual summer encampment by the entire regiment at Camp Perry on the banks of Lake Erie.[3]

Except for duty during a few riots and strikes, the 4th Ohio maintained its peaceful routine until June 1916, when it got a dress rehearsal for the big mobilization to come. Raids across the border by the Mexican partisan leader "Pancho" Villa resulted in the mounting of a punitive expedition into Mexico by American forces under General Pershing. In May 1916, President Wilson decided to make a show of strength to the Mexican government. He mobilized National Guard units in Texas, New Mexico, and Arizona and then followed up by ordering units from other states to deploy to the border in June.[4]

Many of the National Guard units that answered Wilson's call were woefully unprepared, and the 4th Ohio was among those with serious shortfalls. Besides delays in their departure for the border that were caused by problems with the construction of its mobilization camp, the regiment had issues related to equipment, training, and strength. The latter was especially troubling. When Regular Army medical officers screened the Ohio Guardsmen, many were found unfit for service. In fact, Ohio actually suffered the highest rate of rejection among the fourteen states providing National Guard forces, at just over 25 percent.[5]

The regiment formed at Camp Willis near Columbus in late June 1916 and began preliminary training. Not surprisingly, Regular Army observers sent to oversee the training were appalled, and they considered the 4th's state of readiness as little more than rudimentary. The same was true for almost all the other National Guard units called to federal service.[6]

The 4th Ohio boarded trains bound for El Paso in late August 1916, arriving at their encampment site near Fort Bliss a few days later. They named their campsite Camp Pershing and began a process of sporadic but mostly ineffective training that seemed to have no clear purpose. This training consisted primarily of close-order drill and occasional field maneuvers. In October 1916, the regiment deployed forward for guard duty with its companies scattered along the border from Fabens, Texas, to Noria, New Mexico. During this deployment, the regiment participated in the one noteworthy event of their time in federal service—the infa-

Top: Camp Pershing, Texas, on the Mexican border. Bottom: The 4th Ohio Infantry's Machine Gun Company at Camp Pershing, Texas. (*Ohio History Connection*)

mous Las Cruces Hike. This so-called hike was actually a grueling march made under a hot, burning sun, covering nearly seventy-five miles through deep, shifting sand, and clouds of alkali dust. No man who made the march would ever forget it. But the 4th performed well, and the Las Cruces Hike became one of the reasons the regiment would later be selected to be among the first to deploy to France.[7]

Despite the many issues encountered, the 4th Ohio's time on the border, sarcastically referred to by most of the men as "our late unpleasantness with Mexico,"[8] was of some value in that it served to familiarize the troops with field service in ways that the normal summer camps in Ohio had not.[9] Also, Raymond Cheseldine, who would later serve as a lieutenant and captain in Company C in France, wrote that "Instructive competition developed, and in drills, maneuvers, athletic contests this competition was the means of building up a morale that was the backbone of the regiment."[10] Cheseldine, who would later write a definitive history of the regiment, was from London, Ohio, and was a 1914 graduate of Ohio Wesleyan University, where he was a member of the Bi Theta Pi fraternity.[11]

As the end of 1916 arrived, the regiment still languished in Texas, and morale sank. The men were tired of the stagnant routine of camp life, and their slogan became "Either go into Mexico or go home!" Finally, on February 16, 1917, the 4th began its return home to Ohio. First, the regiment traveled to Fort Wayne in Detroit, where final paperwork was completed and the formal mustering out of service executed.[12] Also, any equipment that was so worn from service in the desert as to be considered unserviceable was discarded. As companies boarded trains for their home stations around Ohio, the regiment commander, Colonel Byron Bargar, published a notice in the *Ohio State Journal* to let the people of the state know that, as they returned home, the 4th was in less-than-sterling condition.

> In condemning our unserviceable equipment at Fort Wayne, the men's individual kits were largely broken up, and the new articles have not been issued for their use. Some men still carry full equipment, including rifles, blankets, and rolls. Others, whose belts and shelter tents were worn out, carry rifles only. Others appear without rifles, as their arms are undergoing repair and replacement. From a military point of view, we will present a somewhat motley appearance on our return home. But we believe the welcome from our home is extended to the men and not to a military unit clothed in accompanying pomp and panoply, and it is hoped that no hypercriticism will be forthcoming from military experts.[13]

Little did Colonel Bargar or the rest of the regiment know, however, that their time at home would be short.

ONLY A MONTH after starting their journey home from the Mexican border, the leaders of the Ohio National Guard and the 4th Ohio found themselves again preparing for duty. However, this time it was duty of a far more serious and dangerous nature. On April 17, 1917, just fifteen days after President Wilson asked Congress for a declaration of war, Ohio adjutant general George Wood issued a general order for all units to recruit to full authorized strength.[14] Wood had been told by the War Department that the National Guard would be called into federal service as early as July, and his goal was to have the Ohio National Guard mustered in as a complete division rather than be broken up and provided piecemeal to Regular Army regiments.[15]

But recruiting had already begun before Wood issued his order. Charles Gusman, the acting adjutant general, sent General Order 3 on April 4, 1917, to each company in the 4th Ohio. It said, "You will at once recruit your company to War Strength of 152 enlisted men for each letter company, 37 enlisted men for Supply Company, and 74 enlisted men for Machine Gun Company."[16]

At the time Gusman issued this general order, the 4th Ohio's companies were scattered at their home armories across the central part of the state. Columbus was home to the Headquarters Company, Supply Company, and the Machine Gun Company, as well as Companies B, G, and I. Meanwhile, A Company was in Cardington, C Company in London, D Company in Marion, E Company in Marysville, F Company in Circleville, H Company in Chillicothe, K Company in Delaware, L Company in Lancaster, and M Company in Washington Court House.[17]

With General Order 3 made public, the evening edition of the *Marysville Journal-Tribune* for April 4 reported that officers from the local company, Company E, stated they were ready to receive recruits. The paper also noted that the Columbus-area companies, Companies B, G, and I, had started their recruiting the week before and had already added "a number of men to the regiment."[18]

As recruiting began, the 4th Ohio appeared to be in good shape. With fifty-four officers and nine hundred seventy-seven men, the regiment had a considerable gap to close to get to their authorized strength, which was about two-thousand men. However, they were much closer to that total than the other Ohio National Guard units.[19]

Recruiting efforts were stepped up, and the results were, in large part, successful. Only three companies, A, K, and B, were already at full strength, which meant that all the others had to conduct their own recruiting campaigns. In Marion, Ohio, home of D Company, the company commander, Captain George Geran, announced to local newspaper reporters on May 22 that he was opening a recruiting office in the Marion Armory, which would be open until 10:30 p.m. every night to receive new recruits.[20] Geran was a thirty-nine-year-old lawyer who had lived in Marion since 1900 and had run unsuccessfully for local political offices as a Republican.[21] However, his efforts as a recruiter were far more successful because ten days later, on June 1, he reported the recruitment of one hundred twenty-five men, which meant draftees would not be needed to fill out the company.[22] Three days later, it was reported that eight more men had been added to the rolls of D Company[23]

The War Department then ordered all Ohio National Guard units to mobilize at their home armories on Sunday, July 15, 1917. They were told that they could continue to recruit until August 5, when they would be formally mustered into federal service.[24] From July 18 until August 5, the companies of the 4th Ohio recruited, drilled, and gathered equipment. Then, on August 13, only eight days after the regiment joined federal service, all companies received a secret order to assemble at Camp Perry.[25] Once the regiment arrived there, it would no longer be the 4th Ohio Infantry. Instead, it would be designated as the 166th Infantry Regiment of the US Army, and the men would discard the "OH" emblems they wore on their shirt collars that designated them as members of the Ohio National Guard, exchanging them instead for an emblem that said "US."

ONE OF THE MOST IMPORTANT events tied to the regiment's entry into federal service was the assignment of Colonel Benson W. Hough as commander of the new 166th Infantry Regiment. As events in France would later prove, Colonel Hough was a true leader in every sense of that word. Ideally suited to command by both temperament and experience, he was the perfect fit to lead a regiment of citizen-soldiers. Born and raised in Delaware, Ohio, Hough was forty-two years old when he assumed command of the regiment, a graduate of Ohio State University, and a successful attorney.[26]

Since 1892, when he enlisted in Company K of the 4th Ohio as a private, Hough had served on and off in the National Guard, gaining a commission as a first lieutenant in 1902. He became the adjutant general of Ohio in 1915 but resigned in July 1916 so he could go to the Mexican border as a lieutenant colonel in the 4th Ohio. He mustered out of federal service with the rest of the regiment in March 1917 and then was commissioned a colonel on April 9, 1917, following the declaration of war.[27]

Hough was that sort of leader who is quiet, thoughtful, and, as one of his officers put it, "intensely human." He approached his job with great seriousness, and his judgment of men was "uncanny." Alison Reppy, a captain in the regiment, a graduate of the University of Missouri, and a former high school coach from Hillsboro, Missouri, wrote that Hough was a "big man physically and intellectually, who hates formality and shuns publicity; a man who is reserved, yet friendly; a man who is ordinarily quiet and has but little to say, but who, when occasion demands, becomes a veritable volcano of action, sweeping aside all immaterial considerations and speaking directly and briefly on the real point at issue. It is this combination of qualities which binds men to him."[28]

Colonel William "Wild Bill" Donovan, commander of New York's 165th Infantry and later head of the Office of Strategic Services during

World War II, said that Colonel Hough "established a reputation for devotion to the interests of his men" and that he "was beloved by his men not only because of his natural qualities, but because they knew that always he was seeking their interest above his own."[29] Another officer stated the regiment's view of Colonel Hough's leadership succinctly, saying, "We are proud to have been Sons of Our Grand 'Old Man.'"[30]

WHEN THE ORDERS for the regiment to move arrived on August 13, most of the men believed they were headed for Camp Sheridan in Alabama because that was where the other Ohio National Guard regiments had been sent up to this point. The secret nature of the orders, however, prevented them from knowing the real destination until they arrived at Camp Perry, which, of course, was a very familiar place. The reason for their deployment to a different site from the other Ohio units became clearer on August 15, 1917, when the War Department announced the creation of the 42nd Division, which was to be formed from the National Guard units of twenty-six different states, including Ohio's 166th Infantry. This division would be one of the most famous to participate in the war and became known as the Rainbow Division.[31]

The genesis of the Rainbow Division came from discussions at the War Department regarding the problems involved in deploying a National Guard division overseas. Frankly, it was a concept no one had ever considered before. As the secretary of war, Newton Baker, later described the issues, New York and Pennsylvania already had complete divisions of their own while other states, like Ohio, had divisions close to the required strength. Newton's primary concern in the days immediately following the declaration of war was one of public confidence and support. "If I had sent first the New York or Pennsylvania division," he wrote, "the people of those states might well have complained that the peril and burden was not equally distributed throughout the country, while the men comprising all divisions were uniformly anxious to be used, and divisions from other parts of the country would have resented priority given to the soldiers of the larger states."[32]

Newton asked for advice from his assistant, Major Douglas MacArthur, the man destined to be a general of the army and Medal of Honor recipient in World War II. Newton proposed the idea of forming a new division from state units, such as the 166th Infantry, that were surplus to regular National Guard divisions. This, Newton argued, would allow the army to deploy a National Guard division to France that represented as many states as possible. MacArthur thought it was an excellent idea, and he and Secretary Newton next explained the concept to General William Mann, the chief of the Militia Bureau. Mann also supported the idea, so Newton directed that orders be issued to create the new division with Mann as its commander and MacArthur as Mann's chief of staff. Finally, because the division would represent so many different states stretching across the nation "like a rainbow," they decided to call it the Rainbow Division.[33]

Colonel Benson W. Hough, commander, 166th Infantry Regiment (*National Archives*)

But the formation of a new division also meant a complete change in how the 166th and the other National Guard regiments in the 42nd Division were organized. By the time the 166th entered federal service on August 5, they had achieved a strength of 1,925 men, just short of the required 2,020.[34] Now, however, the regiment needed to be equal in size to a French infantry regiment, a total of 3,605 officers and men.[35] To help gain the additional men needed, the War Department issued orders that each company in every other Ohio National Guard infantry regiment was to transfer sixteen men to the equivalent lettered company in the 166th.[36]

ENOCH WILLIAMS, a twenty-two-year-old private from Dennison, Ohio, awoke in the boxcar where he had spent the evening of August 16, 1917. Upon arriving at Camp Perry that night, Enoch and his friends from Dennison discovered there were not enough tents for everyone. So, they were told to sleep in the boxcar. This turn of events should not have surprised Enoch. He and his comrades had come to Camp Perry to be integrated into the rapidly expanding Ohio National Guard's 4th Ohio Infantry Regiment, now designated the US Army's 166th Infantry Regiment. Young Enoch had always been a member of the National Guard's 10th Ohio, but mobilizing to fight in France required that the 166th increase its manpower. So he was one of the sixteen men from each Ohio National Guard company sent to Camp Perry to join the 166th.

One of the companies formed at Camp Perry, E Company from Marysville, Ohio. (*Union County Historical Society*)

Sore from sleeping on the slats on the boxcar floor, he stood up and sleepily went to the door. There, he beheld the sight of a veritable sea of white army tents and dozens of groups of men, marching about in close order drill. There seemed to be thousands of them, and he wrote his mother later that day, telling her it was a "pretty sight" to "see about 2,500 men drilling."[37] But the drilling, of which he would soon be a part, was just the beginning, and much of what was to come would be far from pretty.

By the morning of August 17, trains carrying men had been arriving at Camp Perry for a couple of days. Enoch Williams wrote home that day, saying they had arrived at 7:30 p.m. the previous evening after a tumultuous departure. "The whole Company escorted us to the station," he wrote his mother, "and we got some send-off." As the regiment got settled in and prepared for an unknown length of stay, there were numerous logistical issues to solve. Even after five days of sleeping in boxcars, there still were not enough tents to house the regiment. On August 22, Enoch wrote that, while they had left the boxcars, the regiment had told them to camp out on the porch of the supply building.[38]

The massive increase in unit strength also caused a variety of other problems. The first was the morale and attitude of the men like Enoch Williams, who had been transferred from their old units into the 166th. Initially, many expressed resentments over leaving their comrades, although some were happy about being assigned to a new division that might be headed for France very soon. Meanwhile, in many cases, the men from the old 4th Ohio were just as upset. They saw these intruders as somehow infecting the body and soul of their regiment. Furthermore, merely rearranging companies to accommodate the new soldiers created a problem that "drove company commanders to the verge of insanity."[39] Luckily, however, the strain seemed to resolve itself after a few days, and no further complaints were heard.

At the same time, the increase in unit strength created training issues. Most of the company commanders had spent their National Guard careers drilling perhaps thirty to forty men one weekend per month. Even when they were in Texas, they never had to drill more than one hundred soldiers at a time. Now, however, a company was larger than a peacetime battalion, and a platoon was bigger than a company had been before the war. The challenge was to organize and perform close order drill with 250 men. Initially, all was chaos, but eventually, some semblance of order began to appear. However, despite this progress, the staff in each company soon discovered that drilling so many men was exhausting. This led to the classic military practice of passing the buck. "The captains soon got tired of drilling and found something else to do," wrote Raymond Cheseldine, "leaving the morning grind to the lieutenants." But the young lieutenants soon grew weary of the drilling and "decided that the sergeants needed training." The sergeants, of course, being old hands at passing the buck, "split up the platoons into squads and gave the corporals a chance to learn to command."[40]

Colonel Hough also reorganized the regiment into three battalions and assigned battalion commanders. The 1st Battalion, consisting of companies A, B, and C, would be led by Major Rell G. Allen, a forty-seven-year-old attorney from Washington Court House in Fayette County, Ohio.[41] The 2nd Battalion was composed of companies D, E, and F and was led by Major Louis D. Houser, thirty-eight years old, a grocer from Chillicothe, Ohio.[42] Finally, the 3rd Battalion, made up of companies I, K, L, and M, was led by Major Frank D. Henderson, a thirty-five-year-old farmer and graduate of Ohio State University from Marysville, Ohio.[43]

Once all the companies had been reorganized and noncommissioned officers selected, training in extended order drill began. This involved the basics of combat maneuvering and small unit tactics. Refresher training was conducted on the care and use of the rifle, along with training in the new manual of the bayonet. Also, since the machine gun was to serve in such a prominent role in France, officers from the machine gun school at Fort Sill, Oklahoma, arrived to provide additional instruction in the use of the weapon. More ominous, however, were the new classes in chemical warfare. Attacks using poisonous gas, mostly mustard and tear gas, were almost daily events on the Western Front, so any man who did not learn to properly use his gas mask was risking death or horrible mutilation. With the commencement of all this new training, the men "began to realize that real war was but a step away."[44]

However, despite the seriousness of the training and the information provided about the Rainbow Division's purpose, some of the men doubted they would ever see combat. Not long before the regiment left Camp Perry, Enoch Williams wrote, "The talk is that we go tomorrow, but we are not certain. I never expect to go to France. The odds are four to one that we don't leave the U.S. Hardly anyone thinks we will leave the States."[45]

The days passed with increasing speed as the regiment continued their daily routine of intense training. "Drills, lectures, study, ceremonies," wrote Raymond Cheseldine, "these with passes to Port Clinton and Toledo in the evenings, visits from friends and families, and dancing at the clubhouse made up the schedule." Finally, on September 7, orders came for the regiment to strike tents, and the next day they boarded trains for the long ride from Camp Perry to Camp Mills on Long Island. With much bravado and evident pride, Cheseldine said that, as the regiment left Camp Perry, "It was hardened and bronzed by lake winds and summer sun. It had a morale second to none. It was proud of its choice as a member of the Rainbow Division and resolved to uphold Ohio's pride in whatever test it might have to face."[46]

But the winds from Lake Erie and a hot Ohio summer sun could not possibly prepare these men for the cold, mud, and prevalence of death they would find in the trenches that cut across northern France. Neither Cheseldine nor anyone else in the regiment could truly appreciate just how brutal that test would be. So, the regiment's trains began their journey east, and the men left their beloved Ohio behind. Many of the regiment's men would never see Ohio again because, as fate would have it, "not every man had a round trip ticket."[47]

THE TRAINS CARRYING the 166th left Camp Perry in the dark around 10:00 p.m. on the night of September 8, 1917, amid a steady, drenching rain. The men aboard the train were a miserable lot, "wet to the skin" as they "sat or sprawled three to two seats, trying to get a bit of rest before dawn."[48] The train made its way through Cleveland and then along the shores of Lake Erie to Buffalo, arriving there around 7:00 a.m. The train then paused briefly before moving east to Rochester, Syracuse, and Albany. Finally, it turned down the Mohawk and Hudson Valleys toward New York City.

As the train approached New York City, arriving in Jersey City around 3:00 a.m. on September 9, progress slowed down significantly. Some of the cars had to be removed and replaced with smaller ones because they would not fit through the tunnel under the Hudson River.[49] Then, after passing under the river, the train stopped for two hours in Forest Hills. While the train waited to move again, hundreds of people arrived to cheer on the men of the 166th and provide a variety of food, which greatly pleased Enoch Williams and his comrades. "We layed [*sp*] in Forest Hill about two hours," he wrote his mother, "and you ought to see the eats people gave to us. Apples, peaches, sandwiches, watermelon, and all that kind of stuff."[50] When the train finally arrived at Camp Mills at 3:30 p.m. on the afternoon of September 9, the men were glad to disembark, and, despite the discomfort of the trip, most were in relatively good shape.

Camp Mills was located on a vast expanse of open ground on the Hempstead Plains of Long Island just east of Garden City. The 166th was directed to set up camp in an area immediately to the right of the main entrance and across the road from the tents belonging to the famous "Fightin' 69th" New York Infantry, now designated the 165th Infantry.[51] While the regiment had tents and cots, not everyone was pleased with their accommodations. Enoch Williams complained as soldiers have done throughout the centuries, saying, "This is a bum camp; they haven't got things fixed up at all."[52] Later, he would add that, while things were better, the constant clouds of dust raised by vehicles and men were a great bother. "The only thing that I find wrong with this camp is the dust," he wrote. "This place is the dirtyest camp I ever heard of. If you set anything down for two minutes, it's all dust."[53]

Here, the 42nd Division was being gathered and organized. In addition to the 166th, the division's infantry came from New York's 165th Infantry Regiment, Alabama's 167th, and Iowa's 168th. There were three machine gun battalions, including Pennsylvania's 149th, Wisconsin's 150th, and Georgia's 151st. The division's trench mortar support came from Maryland's 117th Trench Mortar Battery. Its light artillery guns were operated by men from the Illinois 149th Field Artillery and Minnesota 151st Field Artillery, while Indiana's 150th Field Artillery supplied the division's heavier six-inch artillery.[54]

Not surprisingly, there was also a large contingent of support organizations. The 117th Engineering Regiment was made with equal parts from South Carolina and California, while the 117th Engineering Train came from North Carolina. The 117th Field Signal Battalion hailed from Missouri, and there were military police companies from Virginia and a headquarters troop from the Louisiana 2nd Cavalry. There was also the 117th Ammunition Train from Kansas, 117th Supply Train from Texas, 165th Ambulance Company from New Jersey, 166th Ambulance Company from Tennessee, 167th Ambulance Company from Oklahoma, 168th Ambulance Company from Michigan, 165th Field Hospital from the District of Columbia, 166th Field Hospital from Nebraska, 167th Field Hospital from Oregon, and 168th Field Hospital from Colorado.[55]

These units were further divided into two brigades, the 83rd Infantry Brigade, under Brigadier General Michael J. Lenihan, and the 84th Infantry Brigade under Brigadier General R. A. Brown. The 166th Infantry, along with the 165th Infantry, was assigned to the 83rd, while the men from Alabama in the 167th Infantry and the Iowans of the 168th Infantry were in the 84th.[56]

This massive intermingling of organizations from different regions of the country did not occur without some issues. The biggest of these involved the 165th Infantry from New York and the 167th Infantry from Alabama. Their two legacy organizations, the 69th New York and 4th Alabama, had fought one another during the Civil War, most notably at Fredericksburg in 1862, where the New Yorkers of the Irish Brigade were cut to pieces by the Alabamians as they tried to assault Marye's Heights. It seems the twentieth-century members of the two regiments decided to carry on the fight at Camp Mills. The brawls between the regiments were so bad that Raymond Cheseldine would later say that the division's first combat communique ought to have read, "Elements of the Rainbow Division were engaged in hand to hand conflicts in the vicinity of Hempstead this evening."[57] As a result, the military police companies from Virginia were kept busy breaking up fights between the men from New York and those from Alabama. Eventually, however, the brawls ended and gave way to a relative sense of mutual respect between the two regiments.

As the training for the 166th and the rest of the division commenced, the men from Ohio were well served by pre-war officer training initiatives undertaken by the state's adjutant general. In 1913, General Wood had launched a new officer training program that included the creation of the Academic Board of Instruction for Infantry Officers. The board was led

The 42nd "Rainbow" Division marches in review at Camp Mills, New York. (*National Archives*)

by Colonel Bargar, who was then the 4th Ohio's commander, and its primary function was to administer a progressive series of correspondence courses. The first basic course was required for all lieutenants and dealt with "those subjects whose mastery is essential to the proper performance of [a Junior officer's] ordinary duties with troops." These subjects included infantry drill and field service regulations, small unit tactics, militia regulations, map reading, the manual of guard duty, and military correspondence. Once each officer concluded his individual studies, they took a written examination and had to repeat any section they failed. While there was no immediate punishment for failure, General Wood stated that "continued failure or neglect will result in severe measures being taken."[58]

Unfortunately, the confidence the regiment's soldiers had in their officers was undermined somewhat by the inevitable shifting of officers to different assignments. As company officers were moved to new jobs at the battalion, brigade, or even division levels, vacancies were created within the companies that had to be filled immediately. The only practical way to accomplish this task was to bring in outsiders, typically young officers fresh from the Reserve Officer Training Corps or Officer Candidate School.

When rumors began to circulate around the regiment about the impending arrival of these new, inexperienced officers, the grumbling from the enlisted men was very loud. One of the regiment's soldiers was heard to state, "As if it ain't bad enough to be hooked up with that crazy Irish crowd from New York, they're goin' to shove off a bunch of them green trainin' camp birds on us fer [*sp*] officers."[59] Further, these concerns were not merely confined to the enlisted men. When Lieutenant Miesse met the initial contingent of new officers, he was not duly impressed. Miesse, who had recently left Company L for a position at brigade headquarters, wrote his wife saying, "The new Officers came to-day that have been assigned to the Regiment, Co. L got three new ones. One of them is all O.K., but the other two I can't give very much."[60] Later, as the new officers tried to figure out their responsibilities, Miesse told his wife, "The boys in the Company call them the 'Sears and Roebuck Officers.' Most of them are not much good, but you can't say anything except to sit tight with your mouth closed."[61]

With everyone now in place, a relentless training regimen began. The men spent at least eight hours a day on the drill field under the severe and often profane tutelage of tough Regular Army drill sergeants who "hounded and harried" them without mercy. But the men of the 166th were determined to show their worth and took this punishment with no more than the usual soldier's "beefing." The drill field was hot, rough, and overgrown with high weeds and became a "small world unto itself—a drilling, sweating, cursing little world, preparing to fight." [62] Little did the men know it, but this was just the beginning of their training. While the training at Camp Perry and Camp Mills was sound, it was still fundamental—months of more challenging training on new weapons and trench warfare procedures and tactics awaited the regiment in France.

Along with the drilling came the process of equipping and preparing men for life in a combat theater. First, all old ordnance equipment, packs, haversacks, belts, canteens, and mess outfits were turned in and the latest army equipment issued. Each man got a complete set of new clothing, including a trench overcoat.[63] Enoch Williams proudly wrote to his mother about all his new gear, saying, "I have two uniforms, three suits of underwear, five pairs of socks, two pairs of shoes, two hats, an overcoat, and a poncho. We have a bag to carry our extra clothes. On a hike, we have a pack to carry one blanket, poncho, half a shelter tent, underwear, and mess kit."[64]

But, in addition to equipment, the men's health was also a subject of intense interest. Everyone was examined for tuberculosis, and some did not pass muster. Leon Miesse wrote home that "the Captain of A Co. (Capt. Peck) was declared unfit. I fear for the Capt. of Co. L for he hasn't been well since he has been here, and he looks bad."[65] The regiment's soldiers also received thorough physical examinations, as well as inoculations, including one for typhoid, which made many men ill. Enoch Williams reported that he had "a sore arm for we got a shot in the arm this morning. This is the sixth shot we have got."[66] Williams also wrote that he and his tentmates were under medical quarantine for several days, a common event in camp life during the war because many rural soldiers had not been exposed to the same diseases as their urban counterparts. "This life is not so bad," Williams told his mother. "The only thing that bothers me is that we are under quarantine. One of the fellows had spinal menigetis [meningitis]."[67]

Further, the process of making pay allotments for dependents and providing insurance for each soldier was a complex undertaking. Raymond Cheseldine later wrote, "Company clerks and the regimental adjutant's section found enough to do to care for this work, but in a short time every man was cared for as best the government could do it."[68] For his part, Enoch Williams was happy with his financial status, writing, "They pay our little old 30 dollars a month every month."[69] By contrast, however, Lieutenant Miesse found that his transfer to brigade headquarters was proving to be something of a financial burden. "If I land this job," he wrote his wife, "I will have to buy a pair of riding boots, which will cost at least $25.00, and I have a new uniform coming, which will cost me $40.00. I never get thru, [and] I have to get a fur-lined trench coat and hip rubber boots."[70]

Along with all these events, soldiers dealt with issues that any soldier from any era would find familiar. When Private Williams was late getting out of his cot one morning, he was assigned to the infamous duty of kitchen patrol or "KP" as it has been known for generations since. "I had to peel potatoes," he told his mother. "There was three of us peeling, and we peeled about a bushel apiece."[71]

However, just like many other soldiers before and since, young Enoch also learned the fine art of dodging unpleasant duties. One evening, his platoon was assigned to bury a huge pile of garbage that had accumulated behind the company showers. At 7:30 p.m., they were ordered to line up and march to the garbage pile. But as the platoon headed off for this onerous task, Enoch and another soldier veered off to hide at the YMCA and write letters. He wrote his mother, "The Capt. told us that a real soldier got out of everything he could, so we took him at his word."[72]

While the regiment was at Camp Perry and Camp Mills, another important piece of the unit support structure was put in place, one that contributed greatly to morale once the men were in France—the creation of the regimental newspaper, known as *The Ohio Rainbow Reveille*. The regimental chaplain, Chaplain Halliday, and a sergeant from the Sanitary Detachment, Cecil "Scoop" Williamson, who served as its editor, were the driving forces behind the *Rainbow Reveille*. The first issue was published at Camp Perry on August 25, and these two men would manage to turn out a new issue almost every day in France, even when the regiment was in the trenches. The final step that helped the newsletter come to fruition occurred at Camp Mills when the Ohio Society of New York donated a mimeograph machine and a year's supply of paper to the regiment.[73]

The newspaper eventually became quite famous and was quoted in several New York newspapers during the war, and the *Literary Digest* used humorous notes from its articles on several occasions. In fact, as far as anyone knows, it was the only serviceman's newspaper that was published by a combat unit while actually on duty, a unique and honorable distinction. "Scoop" Williamson made sure that, after every important action during the war, the *Ohio Rainbow Reveille* showed up "to bring smiles to worn faces and hope to anxious men in the regiment. As a morale builder, "the Reveille was without equal."[74]

As the weeks of training went by, most of the men began to wonder when they would leave Camp Mills and where they would really be going. "Everyone had a theory," wrote Raymond Cheseldine, "and was only too glad to advance it. The camp was a hive of speculation."[75] Soon, though, men like Enoch Williams, who had believed the regiment would never leave the country, came to realize that France was definitely their destination. In early September, Leon Miesse wrote his wife that "Hearing the talk runs and the way things look, we all expect to be on our way by the latter part of October."[76] Meanwhile, a few weeks later, Enoch Williams told his family that, "I don't think we will stay here all winter, but I think we will be here a month or so."[77] As it turned out, he made a pretty good guess.

In mid-October, the regiment received orders to prepare to break camp. The men packed all the heavy baggage and new equipment for shipment, and everyone knew the time to go was fast approaching. Anticipation built rapidly. On October 17, Enoch Williams wrote his mother that the time to leave was almost here. "I expect to be on the water when you get this," he told her. "We are getting ready to move now. Ammunition was issued to us this morning, and our cots turned in last night."[78] Unknown to the private, orders had been received for the regiment to move out that very night.

The regiment was told they would leave Camp Mills after dark and that their tents were to be left standing so that no word about their departure would get out until they were on their way. After the evening mess

THE OHIO RAINBOW REVEILLE

Send Home An

Easter Letter

Official Organ 166th Infantry

Vol.I, No. 13   Somewhere in France, March 18, 1918   Occasionally

WE WONDER WHO IN THE WORLD THESE OHIO TROOPS COULD BE!

American troops on Saturday evening, March 9, took part for the first time in operations for the destruction of enemy defence works. A destruction raid was carried out on the Franco-American front in Lorraine, east of Reillon, at sunset. The force which carried out this raid was composed of sixty French sappers, carrying explosives and tools, and FIFTY AMER-

BAKER IN FRANCE TO STUDY WAR: OTHER ITEMS FOR BILLET TALK

Mr. Newton D. Baker, American Secretary of War, has come to France to study the war at first-hand. He has started his inspection tour at the several ports of debarkation and will follow out the lines of communication that lead from the ocean to the Front. He plans to visit the Amexforce in the trenches and rest camps. Inasmuch as Mr. Baker is an

March 8, 1918, copy of the *Ohio Rainbow Reveille*. (*Library of Congress*)

was finished, the men waited anxiously for the final order to come, many tired and sleeping on their backpacks. Finally, orders were whispered down the lanes that ran through the regiment's tents. Silently, the men marched through the darkness to the trains that would move them to the docks where their ships awaited them. "Those who were leaving first felt somewhat in luck," wrote Raymond Cheseldine. "Yet the solemnity of that first move in darkness overshadowed any thrill that was felt at the thought of actually 'going somewhere.'"[79]

That somewhere was a place where, as Cheseldine later put it, "hell was manufactured faster than it could be used."[80]

The USS *Pastores*, one of two ships that took the 166th Infantry to France. (*National Archives*)

Over There

"I fear very much that the Kaiser has a surprise coming when this outfit
is turned loose, for I never saw a more determined set of men."
—Lieutenant Leon Miesse, February 2, 1918, in *100 Years On*

As THE USS *Pastores* edged its way up to the pier at Saint Nazaire, Corporal Dana Daniels, a twenty-one-year-old farmer from Marysville in E Company, joined his buddies at the ship's railing to get his first look at France. Saint Nazaire seemed pretty much like one might expect. The harbor was lined with piers, fishing vessels, and warehouses, with a town of mostly stone and brick buildings beyond. The regiment had begun disembarking yesterday, and today would be the 2nd Battalion's turn to go ashore.

It had rained the day before, but now the weather was clearing, and it looked like it would be a lovely fall day. The voyage across the Atlantic had been uneventful with not a single German submarine making an appearance. However, it had also been an extremely uncomfortable passage, as the *Pastores* had been a coastal fruit freighter before the war and not a ship designed to carry thousands of passengers across the open ocean. So, it would feel good to be back on dry land once more.

When the battalion was ashore, they formed up and began their three-mile march to Rest Camp No. 1. The people of the city lined the streets to watch them pass. There was some cheering, but mostly, they all just seemed curious about these new arrivals and wanted to take the measure of these "Yanks." As they hiked inland, Daniels also saw his first Germans. They were prisoners working by the roadside under guard, and they appeared gaunt, dirty, and tired. But this sight gave him no comfort. Daniels was pretty confident that the Germans who waited for them ahead would be tougher than these prisoners. The question, therefore, would be whether he and the others in the 166th would be tough enough to beat them.[1]

MOST OF THE 166TH INFANTRY boarded their trains from Camp Mills in the dead of night on October 17, 1917, and headed for Long Island City where they were loaded onto ferries that took them down the East River, around Manhattan Island, and then up the Hudson to the docks at Hoboken, where their ships, the *Henry S. Mallory* and the *Pastores*, awaited them.[2] Only the 3rd Battalion, Machine Gun Company, and Supply Company remained at Camp Mills, and they would not depart until the morning of October 29.[3]

As the men marched from the ferries onto the pier, they exhibited a "curious sort of breathless confusion" before forming up their companies under the pier's long sheds, marching up the designated gangway to their assigned ship, and crowding onboard.[4] Both vessels had been built for coastal waters, and neither ship was particularly well-suited to the task of transporting several thousand soldiers over nearly 3,500 miles of the open ocean. But they were the best the navy could provide. After all, no one in either the army or the navy had ever even contemplated the idea of moving thousands of soldiers across the Atlantic. So, the navy commandeered what transports were immediately available.

After the war began, the army formed a select committee of shipping executives to study the registries of American shipping and select ships that might meet the army's needs. The committee selected the *Mallory* and *Pastores* along with eleven other American-flagged ships that were sufficiently fast and could carry enough fuel in their bunkers for transatlantic crossings.[5] In the case of the *Mallory*, she had been built in 1916 and operated along the US coast between New York and New Orleans, while the *Pastores* had been built in Belfast in 1913 and operated under the United Fruit Company moving produce between the West Indies and Central America.

As the men reached the tops of their respective gangways, Quartermaster Corps and ships' officers directed them to their quarters. The enlisted men were sent below decks while officers went to staterooms above deck. The differences were yet another clear reflection of rank having its privileges. Leon Miesse later wrote his wife that he and a fellow officer, Lieutenant Wood, had "quite a luxurious place to stay" that included a "suite of two rooms and a bath."

Dana Daniels, a corporal in E Company, from Marysville, Ohio. (*Union County Historical Society*)

Meanwhile, the soldiers of the regiment clambered down metal stairways to a dim interior that created a "terrible, sinking feeling in the stomach region." "Practically the entire interior of each below deck compartment was converted into sleeping quarters," wrote Raymond Cheseldine. "The construction was simple. Hollow pipe fashioned double-deck bed frames over which were fastened canvas strips which sagged like a hammock. In this trough, the soldier spread his blankets, hung his equipment on the frame, and was at home!"[6] Another officer later described the enlisted men's quarters as a "veritable palace for mules, but not so hot for men, and especially for hundreds and hundreds of men, crowded into space much too small for comfort or cleanliness."[7]

By 8:30 a.m. on October 18, all the men were on board, and meetings were called on both ships for discussions on the routine for the journey ahead. The conference included the regiment's officers, navy representatives responsible for the convoy, ships officers, and members of the army's Transport Corps who were charged to transport the troops. The navy's representatives told the group that all men were to remain below decks during the daylight hours until the convoy departed the next morning at 7:00 a.m. After that, the regiment could be on deck during the day for exercise and daily lifeboat drills. While the men could be above decks at night, no light of any kind could be displayed lest it provide targeting for the German U-boats lurking out in the Atlantic.[8]

The group also discussed how responsibilities for command would be allocated during the voyage to France, and it quickly became evident that the divisions of authority would prove to be a significant challenge. The regiment was to assign the senior officer on board each ship as the troop commander. At the same time, a quartermaster captain from the Transport Corps was responsible for the movement and feeding of the soldiers. Finally, navy officers were in charge of ship safety and navigation as part of the convoy, and officers from the *Mallory* and *Pastores* were responsible for ship operations.[9]

Not surprisingly, conflicting sets of instructions were issued to the men almost immediately, and the troop commanders had to take swift action to clear up the resulting confusion. However, despite these challenges, arrangements for meals, exercise, guard duty, lookouts, lifeboat assignments, and bathing were hammered out before the ships pulled away from the pier that afternoon and anchored in the harbor for the night.[10]

On the morning of October 19, at 7:00 a.m., the convoy of seven ships carrying the 42nd Division headed out to sea with the cruiser USS *Seattle* and two destroyers in the lead.[11]

WITH THE CONVOY on its way, the men of the 166th settled down to make the best of life aboard ship. This proved to be problematic. First, there was the matter of cleanliness. When the regiment boarded the *Mallory* and the *Pastores*, both vessels were reasonably clean and had been made as ready as possible to accommodate several thousand men and their equipment. But with men crammed into every available space below decks, "cleanliness was striven for, but not attained to any great degree after the first day."[12]

Without a doubt, however, the biggest problem for the crews of the *Mallory* and *Pastores* was feeding the soldiers, and the biggest challenge for the soldiers was trying to eat what was provided. The atmosphere was far from conducive to anyone who wanted to eat a decent meal. The mess was characterized by the overwhelming presence of "bilge—water— steam—rancid butter—potato peelings—beans floating across the sloppy deck—frozen beef and beef a little spoiled—baking bread and fresh dough—a rotten cigar—sea-sick men." Raymond Cheseldine wrote that "to the landlubber, it was Hell, in capital letters!"[13]

Needless to say, the facilities where the men ate left much to be desired. On the *Pastores*, the mess was set up in an open compartment with two rows of long tables where the men sat for their meals. One end of each table was bolted down to the outside wall of the compartment, and the other was propped up on folding legs. The floor of the room was made of steel plates, which were almost always covered by one to four inches of water. The water consisted of scrub water that could not drain through scupper drains clogged with discarded food, as well as seawater that had flowed into the compartment from the ash and garbage port. Floating in this small lake was a foul-smelling mixture of bread, beans, potatoes, meat, cigarettes, orange peeling, rice, and prunes. Little wonder that anyone who sat down for a meal had not much of an appetite.[14]

Even getting one's food and moving to one of the tables was a challenge most men could not master. If it were a stormy day, the ship would roll from side to side, and water would wash across the deck. Imagine you have gotten into line with your buddies, and now carefully pass down the serving line as the cooks fill your mess pan with today's fare. You soon emerge from the kitchen area out into the open mess compartment, carefully balancing the mess pan and cup filled to the brim with food and topped with three slices of bread as you navigate toward the table. As the ship rolls and water sloshes around your feet, you adopt an odd gait with your legs spread wide and your upper body swaying back and forth with the ship in an attempt to maintain your balance. As you slowly and gingerly make your way toward the table, the ship lurches more violently, and the men ahead of you lose items from their mess pans. A potato rolls toward your feet, followed by a spoon, a fork, and even a full mess pan.

Now, the ship rolls so hard it feels like it has lifted from the sea and become airborne. You spread your legs wider apart, and your hands work to balance your food, but to no avail. The three slices of bread fly away into the water on the deck, and half the coffee in your cup slops over the side as your feet slip underneath you. You quickly regain your balance, but another roll of the ship causes your meat to slide over the edge of the pan, dripping grease on your uniform. One foot now slides forward, and the other slips backward. The beef goes the way of the bread, and the beans soon follow. As the remaining food slides off the pan and down to the soggy deck, all balance begins to depart. You drop the mess pan, trying to clutch to one of your comrades in despair and anger. Both of you go down into the vile mix of seawater and food, and you decide to just go hungry until the next meal.[15]

If the situation for the soldiers trying to eat was not bad enough, the problem of organizing meals for thirteen hundred men was particularly challenging for the Quartermaster Corps on board ship. Trying to serve three full meals a day simply was not possible, given the limited kitchen facilities, so they scheduled two meals a day. This would have worked except for the fact that the amount of food served at each meal was insufficient. Then a rumor spread on the *Mallory* that the quartermaster captain was shortchanging the men to make money off the remaining excess food supplies, and a near-riot ensued.

After several days of short rations of poor quality, the soldiers rebelled when food ran out at the evening meal before even half the men had been fed. The cooks got additional food from the officers' mess and were able to complete serving the meal, but not before tempers were almost brought to a boil. Many men left the mess still hungry, and a meeting was held among the soldiers who decided to make a raid on the ship's storerooms. Guards stopped the raid and called for the troop commander, Major Allen. The leaders of the raiding party explained the situation to the major who requested that the quartermaster captain immediately report to the storeroom. Major Allen insisted that the captain open the storeroom and provide another serving of cold food for each man. The quartermaster captain refused but was soon swayed by the stern nature of the major's request as well as the angry grumbling of the soldiers standing behind him. After that incident, the mess sergeants seemed to miraculously discover more than enough food to feed the men every day.[16]

On October 28, the convoy entered the danger zone for German U-boats, and, two days later, eight torpedo boat destroyers from Admiral Sims's flotilla joined the original escort contingent of the cruiser *Seattle* and its two destroyers.[17] The destroyers darted in and out, circling the convoy "like faithful shepherd dogs,"[18] continually watching for the sight of an enemy periscope. This vigilant visual searching was required because, in 1917, there was no such thing as an operational sonar system. The only way one knew there was a submarine present was to either see its periscope or, in some cases, see the U-boat actually operating on the surface.

Therefore, it was necessary to have as many eyes as possible searching the nearby ocean waters during daylight hours. This, in turn, resulted in the regiment's soldiers performing the unique duty of being lookouts in the ship's "crow's nest." For two-hour periods, two men would climb up an often-slippery ladder to the small metal coop perched on the ship's tallest mast. Once there, they watched the sea for any signs of submarine activity as the vessel rolled from side to side, causing the crow's nest to often be suspended over the ocean waters rather than the deck of the ship. One corporal from C Company would later swear that his fingerprints were permanently embedded in the rounds of the ladder leading up the mast because he was so fearful of falling off into the Atlantic.[19]

LUCKILY, THE CONVOY did not encounter any German submarines. For Enoch Williams, that was perfectly fine. After arriving in France, he wrote his mother saying, "There wasn't a bit of excitement for we never saw a sub. For my part, I didn't want to see any!"[20] With no incidents and good weather, the convoy carrying the 42nd Division slid quietly into the harbor of Saint Nazaire at the mouth of the Loire River in northwestern France at 9:00 p.m. on October 31, 1917, after a voyage of thirteen days.[21]

Once the *Mallory* and *Pastores* had docked, a party of Marine Corps officers boarded with instructions for Colonel Hough and the regiment's officers. They went into a conference with the colonel to let him know how the debarkation would be performed and what was expected of the officers and men once they were onshore. One of the more peculiar requirements involved the officers' uniforms. It seems that Sam Browne belts[22] were required attire, and no officer would be allowed to debark unless he was wearing one. Since not a single officer in the regiment owned one of these belts, this posed a problem. So, Colonel Hough and Lieutenant Cheseldine collected waist measurements for the officers on the *Mallory*, while Lieutenant John Baily did the same aboard the *Pastores*. The three officers then went ashore escorted by the marines and purchased all the belts required so no one would be stranded aboard ship and miss the war due to a lack of the proper uniform accouterments.[23]

The regiment began to disembark from their ships on the morning of November 1, and everyone was onshore by November 2. On November 1, the men marched through what would be the first of many rainy French days ahead to billets designated as Rest Camp No. 1, a collection of wooden barracks just outside Saint Nazaire. The presence of American soldiers in France was still something very new, and crowds of citizens lined the streets curious to see these "Yanks." The arrival of the 42nd Division also presented an opportunity for commerce, and soon, chocolate and cigarette vendors appeared offering their wares to the men of the 166th. Given the inadequate rations available during the voyage, these salesmen were greeted with great enthusiasm. Raymond Cheseldine would later write that "American money was exchanged for francs and these in turn for French pastry and inevitable vin rouge and vin blanc."[24]

Once the regiment was bedded down at Rest Camp No. 1 while they awaited rail transportation inland, many men took the opportunity to write their first letters home since they had left Camp Mills. Enoch Williams told his mother that he was delighted to be off the ship and that

The 42nd Division marches ashore in Saint Nazaire, France. (*National Archives*)

the local population was something of a curiosity. "It certainly looks odd
to see some of the people going around with wooden shoes," he wrote.
"We had a good laugh when [we] first saw them."[25] Private Austin Dewitt
"Dusty" Boyd of D Company also wrote to his family in Marion from
"Somewhere in France." Boyd was from Marion, where he worked buck-
ing rivets inside the boilers made at the Huber Company in Marion. In
his letter, he was clearly trying hard to keep from saying anything that
might catch the eye of the officer censoring his mail while also expressing
some views on the bad weather and the appearance of the French people
he had encountered:

Dear Folks,

I will try to write a short letter. This is the (censored) day we have
been off the boat, and it is dark and foggy. The sun don't ever shine
here very much. I guess it hasn't yet anyway. I am writing this on my
mess pan, and it's not a very good table. There is not much to write
about. They won't let you tell anything that would give any information if a German should happen to get hold of it. We don't have to put
any stamps on our letters now, and it is a good thing for us, too. We
get this paper and envelopes free from the Y.M.C.A. I don't think we
will be here very long but don't know. The climate seems to be about

like ours. There are some of the hardest looking citizens here I ever saw. I am all right. There don't seem to be any sickness among the troops at all. Well, I guess this is about all I can write now.[26]

At this early point in the war, the logistics of providing anything resembling reliable mail service to the troops in France were still impossible for the army to sort out, and, in truth, it would not get much better for the rest of the war. Delivering mail to American soldiers fighting on another continent was yet one more thing no one in the army had thought much about. This was unfortunate since, as anyone who has served in a military outpost overseas knows, mail from home is crucial to morale. Enoch Williams wrote to his mother, complaining that "It seems like a year since I heard from you" and, echoing the feelings of thousands of soldiers before and since, saying, "We have not got any mail yet. . . . I believe it would be more welcome than mess call."[27]

On the morning of November 6, the regiment received orders to march to the rail yards in Saint Nazaire so they could board trains for the area where they would commence training in trench warfare. When they arrived at the railway station, they received an awful shock when they saw for the first time what one soldier referred to sarcastically as "the pride of the French National Railway system."[28] Before them were the boxcars they were to board for the trip. While these men had been transported on boxcars before, the American version was a luxurious palace compared to the French variety. These boxcars were tiny, perhaps only about eight feet wide and ten to sixteen feet long.[29] On the side was a painted label that said, "40 Hommes-8 Chevaux," which meant that the car's capacity was forty men or eight horses. Also, as one soldier pointed out, "the change from men to horses or vice versa, was often only a matter of a few moments."[30]

The soldiers from the 166th were crammed thirty-two at a time into these cars. With all their equipment on their backs, it was so crowded that no one could sit down. Raymond Cheseldine said that the crowding was so bad, it "would make a sardine box green with envy."[31]

The trains began to pull out of Saint Nazaire around 5:00 p.m. on November 6 for a journey that would last three long nights and two days. The weather was frigid and damp and, even though the men were huddled close together, no one could keep warm. But necessity is indeed the mother of invention, and these men had inherited the American soldier's traditional ability to innovate, even if it meant forcibly confiscating the means to do so. First, when the train paused in a rail yard where there

The infamous French "40 Hommes-8 Chevaux" boxcars. (*National Archives*)

were passing trains, the men relieved those trains' boxcars of their load
of straw to provide for bedding, without which, as Raymond Cheseldine
wrote, "no cattle car is complete." Then early one morning, when the train
again stopped in a small French country station, a group of soldiers clambered down from their boxcar, went into the station, and "borrowed" the
heating stove from the waiting room. Once aboard the boxcar, the stove
kept this particular group of men quite warm for the rest of the trip.[32]

Of course, just like the quarters aboard ship, the experience of the regiment's officers on these trains was quite different. In contrast to the freez-
ing cold and damp boxcars where a man could not even sit down, the
officers were treated to relatively luxurious accommodations in passenger
cars where they could also get a nice meal. While he did note the odd signs
about forty men or eight horses on the boxcars, Lieutenant Miesse apparently had too good a time to consider what sort of conditions his men
were enduring:

> I had a delightful trip thru France, we traveled in the daytime and
> laid over at night, so we were able to see all of the territory as we
> passed thru. There was a Diner on the train, and we were able to get
> a very good meal for about 6 francs, which is much cheaper than it is
> at home. The cars are funny-looking and queerly arranged, and the
> freight cars are the size of the streetcars in Lancaster, and they have
> great big wheels under them and printed on the outside it says
> "Hommes 40 Chevedu 8" and they have every car marked that way.

As most of the 166th made its way into France by train, the 3rd Battalion, Machine Gun Company, and Supply Company were making their crossing of the Atlantic. They finally left Camp Mills on October 29, just two days before the rest of the regiment would land at Saint Nazaire. They embarked at Hoboken aboard the USS *Armageddon* and had a much different experience than their comrades who suffered on the *Mallory* and *Pastores*. The *Armageddon* had been confiscated from the North German Lloyd passenger line, where her name, ironically, had been the *Kaiser Wilhelm der Grosse*. Designed for luxurious passenger service, she was ready to take on thousands of passengers and was "spic and span."[33]

The *Armageddon*'s voyage was quiet and uneventful. The convoy took a more southerly route than the previous one, and even the weather seemed to cooperate, providing smooth seas. There was, however, one bit of excitement that was somewhat bizarre.

On the first night in the submarine danger zone, the transport *Von Stuben* collided with the *Armageddon*. Luckily, the blow was a glancing one, tearing away some lifeboats and putting a hole in the *Von Steuben*'s bow. When the collision was felt onboard the *Armageddon*, everyone immediately assumed the ship had been struck by a torpedo and proceeded to their lifeboat stations.

The *Armageddon*'s troop commander, Major Henderson from the 3rd Battalion, immediately ordered a roll call to see if there were any casualties from the collision. There were none, but a machine gun company from Georgia reported one man was missing, and it was assumed he had fallen overboard. Major Henderson appointed a board to investigate so an official report could be submitted to the army. The next morning, a message was sent to the *Von Stuben* requesting any information they might have related to the missing soldier. The *Von Stuben* immediately replied, saying that, yes, they had information—the soldier was aboard the *Von Steuben*!

It was later discovered that the soldier had been standing at the *Armageddon*'s railing, enjoying the fresh night sea air when the two ships collided. The force of the blow threw him over the railing and down onto the *Von Steuben*'s deck. In the general confusion that resulted, all the ships in the convoy thought a submarine attack was underway, sounded their sirens, and scattered, leaving the soldier from Georgia marooned on the wrong ship.

As the convoy approached Saint Nazaire, the navy received an alert telling them that a group of U-boats had moved into position to ambush the convoy as it approached the port. So, they were told to sail instead to

Brest, arriving there on November 16. Unfortunately, the harbor at Brest was too small for the *Armageddon* to enter, so the men had to be taken aboard small lighters for transport to the docks. Since no soldiers had arrived in Brest before, it took some time to get things organized, and so the missing pieces of the 166th did not rejoin the regiment until November 19.[34]

ON THE MORNING of November 10, the trains carrying the 166th Infantry Regiment pulled into the tiny station at Menaucourt, in the province of Lorraine, about 150 miles west of Paris. The men climbed out of the tiny boxcars "half-frozen," formed up in a column, and began a march to the village of Morlaincourt, where regimental headquarters was established in a small chateau on the southern edge of the town.[35] Once there, the companies of the regiment dispersed to villages where they were to take advantage of any available or abandoned buildings to use as billets. The Headquarters Company and A Company remained in Morlaincourt. At the same time, B Company and D Company marched about four miles northeast to Oëy, and C Company moved three miles southeast to Chenneviers. Meanwhile, F Company marched six miles northeast to Vaux-la-Grande, and E Company walked five miles east to Vaux-la-Petite. Once the other units arrived on November 19, the Supply Company remained in Morlaincourt, the Machine Gun Company moved to Chenneviers, and the 3rd Battalion was split between the villages of Meligny-le-Grand and Meligny-le-Petit, about eight and six miles east of Morlaincourt, respectively.[36]

This collection of villages made up what the French designated as the First Training Area. Toul, about eight miles to the northeast, was the nearest city of any size. More significantly, the trenches of the battlefront were only about twelve miles away, and Dana Daniels recorded that they could "hear the big guns very plain."[37] Raymond Cheseldine also noted the close proximity of the war, writing that one could "hear plainly the rumble of the big guns near Toul. Ahead, in that direction, lay 'the front,' that mysterious place toward which many eager feet were being taught to move. The guns of war lay just over the hill."[38]

As they arrived in their respective villages, the soldiers of the 166th found quarters primarily in vacant houses and barns. The Germans had briefly occupied Vaux-la-Petite, where E Company was assigned billeting. The village had been bombarded twice, so it had received considerable damage.[39] But conditions and billets were pretty much the same in all the communities, and, like the innocents abroad that they were, the soldiers took note of what they considered the numerous oddities of French country life.

All the villages were typical of the French countryside at that time, characterized by winding cobblestone streets lined with houses made of stone and plaster and topped with red-tile roofs. There were no gutters on the houses, and every home seemed to have its own pile of manure just outside. The houses themselves usually combined the home and the barn under one roof. Enoch Williams noted in a letter to his mother that he was quartered in "an old barn or house. You can't tell the difference. They all look alike to me."[40]

This design was practical in that the farmer only had to walk out his kitchen door to tend to his livestock. But at the same time, the chickens and pigs could come into the house each time that door was opened. Every house also had a large open hayloft that covered both the home and the barn, which was where most of the men slept. This sort of living arrangement caused Dusty Boyd to tell his family that, as far as he was concerned, France was "about 100 years behind the times in the U.S." He said that he saw six or even eight families living in one house, adding, "They hardly know what stoves is. Use fireplaces, and they burn everything, no waste at all. They have wash houses here just a kind of shed over a concrete pool, and everybody does their washing there in cold water, and it sure is a sight."[41]

Not surprisingly, the barns where the men slept had no heat or even the light from a candle. The war had made coal a scarce commodity, and even using wood required that details make long trips to the woods to cut down trees under the supervision of the local forester.[42]

Food was also in short supply in the villages, which were populated mostly by refugees. The French did what they could to provide food for the regiment, but local sugar beets had to be used to provide the major part of what was a somewhat limited bill of fare. As the regiment began a vigorous training schedule despite the cold and mud, it made for hard days where the men came "in from drill tired, cold and wet, with no fire to sit by, there was nothing to do after supper but climb the ladder to the old haymow and crawl into the blankets to keep warm."[43]

Meanwhile, the officers' billets were, again, quite a different experience. Most of them found a spare bedroom in one of the nicer houses. Leon Miesse, for example, was given a billet with two rooms to himself, one being a bedroom and the other a sitting room with a fireplace "large enough for three men to come down at once with room to spare." Unlike the straw his men were sleeping on, Miesse had a feather bed, which, while it was a little too short for him, seemed otherwise delightful. He wrote to his wife that "if there is anything the French know how to do, it sure is how to sleep."[44]

Miesse also noted the presence of a town crier for the village, something not seen in America at that time for almost a century. This man went about the town on an almost daily basis beating a drum to make himself known. Once a sufficiently large group had gathered around him, he would read a series of announcements, and when he came to the end of a particularly important part of the announcements, he would strike the drum "a good hard lick to make it emphatic." The village also had a shepherd whose job it was to gather all the village's sheep in the morning and take them out to graze. When he came back in the evening with the sheep following, he would whistle to let the villagers know he was back. At that point, the women would all come out onto the street, pick out their sheep, and take them into their barns for the night.[45]

The grandest billet, of course, was the one reserved for regimental headquarters. Located on the southern edge of Morlaincourt, Colonel Hough and his staff occupied a chateau that resembled a small castle with round towers topped with pointed spires at each corner of the house. There was a large courtyard in front of the house with sheds and stables on the opposite side. A woman and her daughter presided over the chateau. The owner had fled to southern France and had hired them to watch over his home.[46]

Hough and his staff converted the large main entrance hall into an office and meeting space. During the winter of 1917, the hallway was usually filled with officers trying to escape the fierce cold and snow. That was because that particular space of the house had a large stove, which Sergeant "Red" Wyatt, the colonel's orderly, kept hot, and he had a wood box always filled with fuel.

Every unit has someone who is the notable odd character, and, in the 166th Infantry, Red Wyatt was that character. To say he was given broad latitude in terms of freedom of speech would be putting it mildly. Red often spoke loudly and on a range of topics. Why he was accorded such freedom to speak was, apparently, a subject of debate. Raymond Cheseldine later wrote, "Perhaps it was because he was never intentionally rude; perhaps it was his unusual line of thought; perhaps he acted as a foil for

Chateau Morlaincourt, home of the 166th Infantry's Regimental Headquarters in the First Training Area. (*Librairie Mlle Laurent*)

the keenly alive mind of the Colonel; perhaps—but who knows or cares? Red was Red—that's all. He worshipped the 'Old Man' and mothered him as if he were a little boy."[47]

Another part of the logistics support that was very slow to catch up with the regiment as it deployed for training was transportation. As the first winter snows arrived, the only transportation available consisted of two trucks borrowed from the division quartermaster. A little later, bicycles were issued for messengers to use for shuttling back and forth between the regimental and division headquarters in Vaucouleurs, as well as amongst the dispersed companies of the regiment. Officers also borrowed these on occasion for official trips between the various villages. However, it must be added that the slick, wet winter roads, steep hills, and, in many cases, a lack of recent experience on a bicycle resulted in several officers tumbling into mud puddles or snowbanks, much to their chagrin and to the amusement of any enlisted men who might be nearby.[48]

Next came the arrival of what was, perhaps, the most essential part of the regiment's transportation support: their first mules. With motor transport in extremely limited supply for much of the war, mules provided the backbone of the army's tactical transportation system. Mules pulled field kitchens, ration carts, and supply wagons and carried heavy weapons and ammunition in the field. As a result, Muleskinners, as they were called, were a vital part of the supply company of the regiment. The first fifteen mules arrived in early December, along with five wagons and French-made breast harnesses. The Muleskinners quickly learned how to use the new harness, which worked well until the American ones finally arrived. Three of the mules were outfitted with saddles for use as officer's mounts. However, the sight of Colonel Hough on his mule was rather comical. At well over six feet in height, the colonel looked like he was mounted "on a mule about the size of a shepherd dog."[49] Soon, however, despite the humorous sight of the colonel mounted on his mule, that mule would provide a life-saving service that no one could have anticipated.

As the newly arrived Americans observed their surroundings, they noted how the French villagers lived and, for their part, the French formed opinions on these new foreign soldiers. Raymond Cheseldine would later write a heartfelt description of the life and people he saw in these country villages:

French village life centers around the public fountain. At the village fountain, clattering groups of women and girls congregate, and over piles of Yank clothing, discuss events of the day. And on Sunday the bells in the village church ring merrily and on the street one sees a strange multitude. Monsieur and Madame Berger, if you please, not "old Jacques," the wood cutter of week days; Annette is the girl in the stiffly starched white dress—the girl you saw kneeling at the public wash house yesterday; His Honor the Mayor, in an antique black suit and hat, scarcely to be recognized as the watchmaker you see every day. They are quaint and interesting, these villages and village folk of rural France.

And the Mothers of France—a little, bent old woman, twisted with age and the unaccustomed toil which the war had brought her in her old age. She had given four sons to France, and all had been killed. They were her only relatives, no others of kith or kin remained to help her bear the burdens of life, yet never did a soldier pass her on the street or on the road far from town where she went to gather fagots for her fire, but she drew herself up proudly, flashed a smile which was at one illuminating and sad, and raised her hand in salute, saying, "May God bless you, my children."

The Mothers of France, how many of them are carrying the burdens of lost loved ones yet smiling at their daily tasks and wishing God's

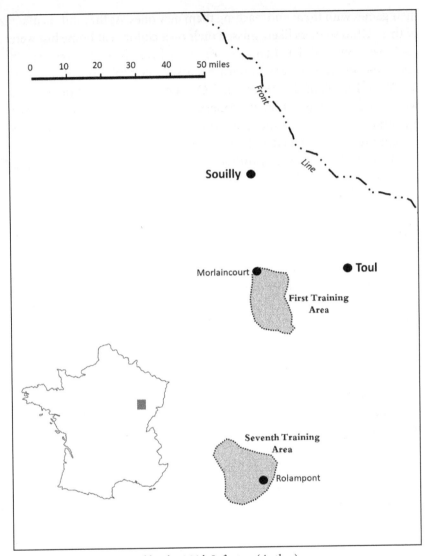

The two training areas used by the 166th Infantry. (*Author*)

blessing on all who pass! The children of France are at work. Children, who in our country, would be going to school or enjoying their play time, over here are busy in the fields beside old and bent women, striving to do their feeble bit to raise a few things necessary to eat.[50]

As has often been the case with American soldiers deployed to other lands, the men of the 166th made friends with the local children, playing their games with them and teaching them new ones. As they did so, many of these Ohio soldiers likely missed their own children at home but were glad their sons and daughters were far away from the horrors of war. In one of the towns, a village schoolteacher asked her pupils to write an essay on "What I think of the Americans." One ten-year-old child in her class wrote the following: "I think the Americans are industrious, polite, clever, and brave. I have noticed they are thrifty men and good soldiers; that they are almost always learned and smart; that they are kind to one another, conducting themselves as brothers because I have seen one who was smoking a cigarette have it snatched by a comrade who smoked it in turn."[51]

Not surprisingly, some of the soldiers also took notice of the women they saw in France, and a few wrote home about them, perhaps to calm any worries their girlfriends and wives might have about the temptation these women might provide. Just a few days after arriving in the village of Oëy, Dusty Boyd wrote home saying, "You can hear a whole lot about the good looking women over here, but I have failed to see any of them yet. The U.S. brand is good enough for me."[52]

Meanwhile, Leon Miesse told his wife that all the women he saw in the villages looked like "the Witch of Endor." "They are all either old or young," he wrote. "There seem to be no young women. It may be that they marry early and therefore get old quicker, for it is no wonder they are born married and live and die in the same villages and hardly ever leave them, they just exist."[53]

Of course, the most crucial part of the regiment's activities in the Morlaincourt area was training, and the training schedule began in earnest almost as soon as the regiment was bedded down. The course of instruction was based on all the Allies had learned during over three years of warfare on the Western Front. Officers and men assigned to use new weapons attended schools and daily drills under the watchful eyes of French instructors. These weapons included the French-made Hotchkiss machine gun and Chauchat automatic rifle, as well as the British three-inch Stokes mortar.[54]

While the 166th had used machine guns, there were not enough American-built guns to send to France. Therefore, the Hotchkiss machine gun was issued to the 166th and the other AEF units in France. During late 1917, the newest version of the Hotchkiss was the Model 1914, which was a refinement of the older Model 1897 gun. When the war began, the French only issued the Hotchkiss to second-line territorial units but, soon,

The model of the Hotchkiss machine gun used by the 166th Infantry. (*National Archives*)

the French army decided to make it the standard machine gun for all front-line units because of its reliability.[55] The Hotchkiss machine gun was gas actuated and air-cooled, which gave it an advantage over water-cooled guns like the German Maxim. Another design advantage of the Hotchkiss was that it could be dismounted from its tripod and reassembled in less than a minute using one tool, and the French manufacturer made the weapon so that it was impossible to assemble it improperly, a critical factor when inexperienced American gun crews were using the weapon.[56]

However, while reliable, the weapon did have its own unique problems. First, it was cumbersome as compared to similar guns, such as the Vickers and Browning, weighing over fifty-three pounds. That meant that the weapon and its ammunition needed to be transported by mule. Second, once the gun got hot, typically after firing around one thousand rounds, it took about four minutes plus sponging with cool water before firing again.[57]

Perhaps the most significant complication of using the Hotchkiss was that employing it in combat required a well-coordinated effort by a three-man team. That was because, while feeding the gun ammunition was relatively simple, each strip of ammunition held only twenty-four rounds

The French-manufactured Chauchat automatic rifle. (*National Archives*)

of 8mm Lebel ammunition. That meant that the crew had to reload the gun several times per minute, requiring a well-choreographed process of reloading during periods when the gun was firing almost continuously.[58] This, in turn, meant that the soldiers in the 166th Regiment's machine gun company had to master this complex process in training if they were to be of any use in the trenches.

When the 166th and the rest of the 42nd Division arrived in France, no unit in the US Army was equipped with an automatic rifle. An American-manufactured Browning Automatic Rifle was being developed, but it would take more than a year to get it ready and produced for field use. The only weapon available was the Chauchat, which was developed in 1915 by a French commission composed of Messrs, Chauchat, Suterre, Rubeyalle, and Gladiator. It fired French 8mm Model 1886 ammunition and was a relatively unsophisticated, crude weapon that could be mass produced very quickly. The Chauchat was light at only nineteen pounds and air-cooled with a magazine that held twenty rounds of ammunition. Its biggest problem was the scarcity of spare parts and poor-quality manufacturing, which often led to misaligned sights and shabby weapons assemblies.[59]

Like the Chauchat automatic rifle, the trench mortar was something entirely new to American soldiers. The British three-inch Stokes mortar that the AEF received in France was a simple but ingenious invention. The Stokes mortar, like all mortars during the war, provided organic support fire for infantrymen by lobbing shells into enemy trenches and shell holes. The Stokes mortar was a simple muzzle-loading weapon. Essen-

The British 3-Inch Stokes mortar used by the 166th Infantry and the AEF. (*National Archives*)

tially, the Stokes was a portable three-inch-diameter steel pipe that fired a high-explosive shell. The propellant charge was, in reality, a shotgun charge (without load) inserted in the base of the projectile. The mortar shell was dropped into the top of the barrel, slid rapidly down the tube, and the charge detonated upon hitting a fixed firing pin in the base of the tube. The resulting explosion forced the shell out of the tube and sent it on its way to the target.

The Stokes mortar was a crew-served weapon, and there were six mortars assigned to each unit within the headquarters company. That unit had thirty-nine men to handle the six mortars, one cart, one wagon, and nine mules. This team's job was to provide close-support mortar fire in a variety of combinations. Squads, or groups of one or two men, could be organized and attached to parts of the regiment for specific fire missions, and they could fire their weapons in pairs or singly.[60]

In addition to weapons training, sixty officers went to specialists' schools for technical training, and a group of sergeants was sent to officers' training, so they were ready to take the place of officers killed or wounded in combat. As to the latter, the rumor was that this training would mean getting "the life of a 2nd Looie in three weeks."[61]

As for the bulk of the regiment, the men were drilled daily on gas attacks, digging trenches, shelters and wire entanglements, the art and science of liaison, grenade throwing, visual and mechanical signaling, tactical maneuvers, and terrain problems. The training was intense, lasting from early morning until dark, no matter how cold or how wet the weather might be.[62] Major Walter Wolf, adjutant of the 84th Brigade, would later write, "Never was training more seriously and feverishly pushed than then on the frozen hillsides and through the snow."[63]

One of the most critical pieces in both the training process and the fighting to come was the French army's interpreters. These men joined the regiment in Saint Nazaire, and one of them, Peter LeGall, remained with the 166th until the end of the war. Known to the men simply as "Pete," this French soldier had learned to speak English during a ten-year tenure as a waiter at Delmonico's Restaurant in New York City. He had returned to France when the war started and had been awarded both the Croix-de-Guerre and Medaille Militaire for bravery. Once during combat, he had been blown twenty feet in the air by an exploding trench mortar but landed back on the ground unhurt. He was a favorite among the officers and men of the regiment, and his services were always in demand.[64]

The first week of December 1917 saw rumors of a move begin to make their way around the regiment. Red Wyatt commented loudly on these rumors, as was his way. "Well, I reckon we have been here long enough now," he stated boldly one day in early December. "Minney the Prophet, over in A Company says we're due to hike, an' bein' soldiers, I suppose we are. They said, 'Join the army an' see the world,' an' you can't do that settin' still."[65] As was so often the case, Red was right.

3

"Valley Forge"

"I recall your courage and your fortitude under all of these trying circumstances, with poor billets and bitter cold nights. But I also felt at the time, and can say now, that the experience prepared you as nothing else could have done perhaps for that trial of courage that came to you on many a battlefield. . . . I felt that nothing could have been more fortunate than that you had that experience."
—General of the Army John J. Pershing, July 14, 1923

LIEUTENANT LEON MIESSE, twenty-eight-year-old Ohio State graduate, engineer,[1] and now deputy commander of L Company, watched his men train diligently every day. The training went on, no matter how much snow was on the ground, how much mud there might be in the practice trenches, or how far below zero the temperatures of early February fell. The training lasted for almost eight hours a day, with two more hours of classroom training on combat problems in the evening. Despite the language barrier, their instructors from the French 32nd Regiment worked hard to convey the serious subject of war in the trenches of France.

A system of trenches had been built for training the men of the company, and they improved upon them every day with pick and shovel. The men from the machine gun battalion practiced firing the new Hotchkiss guns they had received while learning to manage the weapon's peculiarities and even training the mules that carted the heavy machine guns about. The company also had new French Chauchat automatic rifles to master. Miesse wrote his wife that he had "shot one for the first time the other day, they are some weapon for all you do is pull down the trigger, and it will pour a stream of lead and doesn't let up until you release the trigger." Even the French fragmentation grenades were new to Miesse and his men, who he said took to them quickly because "the word fear isn't in their vocabulary."[2]

However, everyone sensed that the time for training to end and the real work of war was coming for the 166th very soon. They had new uniforms, and all the required supplies and weapons had been received. The men were issued new gas masks, and gas attack training occurred almost every day. Finally, the ubiquitous steel helmets arrived, and the men wore them daily, trying to get used to this new but essential piece of headgear. Everything and everyone was as ready as they could be for what was to come. Hopefully, it would be enough.

AS THE REGIMENT worked in the First Training Area, no one in the 166th was aware that the AEF and the French army had never intended them to train there. Rather, the original plan called for them to train in the Seventh Training Area near Rolampont, which was about sixty-five miles south of Morlaincourt. However, the area was not ready for the regiment and the rest of the division when they arrived in France, and since the need to get the men trained was so great, they started their work in the First Training Area.[3]

Now, as December arrived, there were rumors of a German offensive coming near Toul. This meant that seasoned French troops were urgently needed in the area and that the untrained Americans would have to move to Rolampont. The reaction to this news frustrated some of the soldiers in the 166th. One Ohio doughboy was heard to say disgustedly that, "nobody knows nothin' over here. An' the officers is worse than anybody." Upon hearing that the Germans might be on the way, he added that "instead of gettin' ready to fight here, we get the dope that we've got to pull out an' let some Frogs come in to stop the Dutch. I didn't ask for this war, but now that we're here, what's all the training for if we're goin' to run before we've seen a German?"[4]

The problem, of course, was that the 166th Infantry and the rest of the Rainbow Division were simply not ready to fight. More weeks of diligent training were needed to get them prepared to have any chance of standing up to the Germans. So, they would have to move. There was, however, one major complication: there was no transport available. The regiment

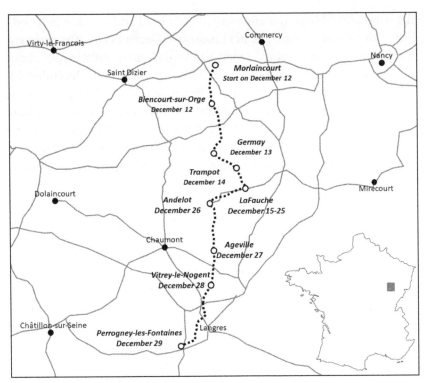

The path of the "Valley Forge Hike." (*Author*)

had only enough trucks to carry rations and forage for the mules plus a few carts and wagons, and the French did not have enough available trains to move the division. That meant the division would have to march there. On December 12, 1917, the 166th formed up in Morlaincourt to begin what came to be known as the "Valley Forge Hike."[5]

To make matters worse, as the men moved out in a column of fours, temperatures were dropping below zero, and the ground was covered in several feet of snow, with more coming down daily. The first day's march was a fifteen-mile trek to Biencourt-sur-Orge. The weather was clear and very cold and, as they started, the men were in good spirits. However, the mood changed as the day wore on. Some men in the column wore shoes so badly worn down that they provided almost no protection from the cold and snow, while others marched without winter overcoats.[6]

When the regiment stopped for the night in Biencourt-sur-Orge, they used any structure they could find as a billet. As the men laid down on the straw and a blanket, many washed their tired and sometimes bloody feet with cold, icy water. The next morning, December 13, the regiment formed up again and began to march toward Germay, a distance of about twelve miles, where they again stopped for the night. On December 14, the march was much shorter, only a five-mile walk to Trampot. Finally, on December 15, they arrived in LaFauche after a six-mile march where the regiment was told they could stop. However, at the time, no one knew whether this stop was to be permanent. But the men had already learned to just make themselves as comfortable as possible wherever they were.[7]

As it turned out, the regiment would remain in LaFauche for eleven days. Despite their sore, swollen feet, the men spent almost all those days outside in the snow, drilling and conducting target practice. But LaFauche would also be where they would spend Christmas, and, for many an Ohio doughboy, this would be their first Christmas away from home, family, and friends. It turned out to be a pretty miserable Christmas. While the mess sergeants did their best to prepare a good facsimile of a Christmas meal, it was hard to enjoy it and feel festive while standing in a bitterly cold French barn, balancing their mess pans. But some made the best of it. Dana Daniels wrote that he received the present of a knife from two of his comrades and that Christmas dinner was good. Others, meanwhile, spent their holiday playing with the local children and doing their utmost to brighten the children's day.[8]

Luckily, an error by the YMCA made it even easier to give those children a happy Christmas. A few days before Christmas, the regiment heard that the YMCA would be distributing gifts to the regiment. "Men, soldiers became just boys again with a child's enthusiasm for a 'surprise,'" wrote Raymond Cheseldine. Most soldiers thought they would be getting chocolates and cigarettes. They were wrong, but they did receive a surprise.[9]

When the truck carrying the gifts arrived with three burlap sacks filled with Christmas presents, the supply sergeant cut open the first bag. The bags turned out to be filled with children's toys, including horns, whistles, drums, and rubber balls. He immediately went to his lieutenant saying with consternation, "If we send this out, we'll be shot!" At first, the lieutenant and the other Supply Company members laughed, but their laughter was soon followed by curses about "that damn Y." However, within minutes, someone came up with an idea. Rather than complaining, why not send a bag of gifts to each village where the regiment's men were billeted and throw a Christmas party for the village children? Everyone thought it a brilliant idea, and they started eagerly planning the parties that, when done, had gladdened "the hearts of the poor, pinched faced" children of the French country villages, "many of whom were already orphans of the war."[10]

As they did their best to celebrate Christmas, most of the men were unaware that orders were received on Christmas Eve to resume the march to Rolampont on December 26. The next morning, an issue of new mules arrived. This would have been a good thing except for the fact that these mules were wild, unshod, and only about the size of a large dog. With orders to move out first thing on the twenty-sixth, the Muleskinners spent their Christmas pressing every French blacksmith shop in the area into service. In a herculean effort, all the mules were ready to go the next morning.[11]

Sadly, the same could not be said for many of the men, who still did not have decent shoes or overcoats. But division headquarters sent word that shoes would be sent to the regiment on Christmas night. About one thousand came in, but the 166th needed thirty-six hundred pairs. Most of the men had one pair of shoes, some of which were pretty worn down, while men in the 1st Battalion, Headquarters Company, and Supply Company had two pairs each. Lieutenants Cheseldine and Morris stood anxiously by at the headquarters late into the night waiting for the shoes to arrive. They ordered the ration carts for the 2nd and 3rd Battalions and Machine Gun Company held back so they would be available to deliver the shoes once they were delivered. But when the clock said it was 10:00 p.m., no shoes had arrived.

So, the two lieutenants decided to go seek out Colonel Hough. Unfortunately, the colonel had already gone to bed, and, while they hated to wake him, they decided this issue was too important not to do so. The two young officers walked down the narrow hallway that led to the colonel's room, and, with great trepidation, they knocked softly on the door. They waited. There was no answer. So, they knocked harder and louder. Finally, they heard the colonel telling them to enter. With "great fear and trembling," Cheseldine and Morris stepped into the darkened room.

"What is it?" asked the colonel. The two officers quickly outlined the situation and finished with, "And, sir, we've come to ask you what to do." The response was silence. After a few minutes, Colonel Hough said, "We move at 7 o'clock in the morning. A great many men are almost barefoot. I don't care where you get them, or how, but every man must have one

Soldiers take a rest break during the Valley Forge Hike. (*National Archives*)

good pair of shoes in the morning." The lieutenants waited for further direction, but none came. The colonel had rolled over and gone back to sleep.

Cheseldine and Morris backed out into the hallway and closed the door. They realized that, as was often his leadership style, Colonel Hough was telling them to figure this problem out on their own. So, they went to the supply room and convened a meeting. Everyone offered ideas, but they finally struck upon the best one possible given the situation: they would call in every extra pair of good shoes from the 1st Battalion, Headquarters Company, and Supply Company, and then distribute them to the other companies. The goal would be to ensure every man in the regiment had at least one pair of good shoes.

Men were dispatched to awaken the company commanders, and the situation was quickly explained. The captains of each company tasked with the job responded, and every company met the emergency. "Men were aroused, and the extra shoes collected," wrote Raymond Cheseldine. "A distribution was made, the shoes placed with the rations, and by midnight the last cart had creaked away over the snow-covered road."[12]

December 26 brought the real "Valley Forge" part of the march to Rolampont. The snow was two feet deep as the men formed up to begin the trek, and the ground was frozen and slippery with ice. Shortly after the regiment started, the winds began to howl, and more heavy snow began to fall. Visibility dropped to almost nil, and huge drifts started to build in the roadway. "The thermometer kept on dropping, and the men proceeded through these conditions in the same uniform in which they passed in review before the Secretary of War on that balmy Sunday afternoon in Indian summer," Major Wolf wrote later. "The same uniform it was, except for the inroads of four months' hard wear." The new shoes helped to be sure. However, many of the men's feet were already so swollen that they could barely get the new shoes on. As a result, as the 166th trudged through the deepening snow, many feet began to bleed, and soon, the regiment's path was marked by a long, red trail in the snow.[13]

While the shoes had been distributed, many men still did not have overcoats or gloves. Not surprisingly, numerous men came down with pneumonia, and there were not enough ambulances to get the men to hospitals as rapidly as they became ill. In one regiment of the 42nd Division, five hundred men were unable to keep on marching.[14]

The first day took the regiment to Andelot, a large town with electric power and decent billets. The men were exhausted, and, once inside their quarters, they immediately removed their heavy, water-soaked hobnailed shoes and tried to bathe their aching feet. If they could find some tallow or French foot grease, they used it to rub the raw places on their feet. When it came time to move again on the morning of December 27, the men groaned in despair but rose to take their places in the column.[15]

That second day of the post-Christmas march proved worse than the first. It continued to snow so heavily that one could often only see a few feet ahead. Perhaps worst of all, the snow came down so thick that it worked its way into every crevice, every part of the equipment the men carried, adding to the crushing weight they had to carry. That night it froze, and the next day it snowed again. The result was a hard, packed, crusted snow that made it almost impossible to walk anywhere but in the broken tracks created by the supply wagons.[16]

The marching process seemed an endless one. They would march for fifty minutes, halt to rest for ten, and then press on. When they stopped to rest, men simply fell into the snow, in agony from their aching muscles and joints. At 11:00 a.m., the regiment would pause for lunch. While the mess sergeants did their best, lunch consisted of nothing more than a frozen sandwich containing two slices of cold bacon layered between two thick slices of bread and a few swallows of cold water. Then the boys from Ohio would move on through the snow "until the shadows of dusk were shattered by the piercing gleam of a cold, winter moon before the next billeting town loomed dark against the snow."[17]

The 166th arrived in Ageville on the night of December 27 after a hike of twelve miles. It had been a hard day. The column seemed at times to only inch forward. Men fell in the snow and could not get up while others dropped out by the roadside, unable to take another step. Within the first few hours, the ambulances were full of exhausted men. However, once that exhaustion was temporarily overcome, the men would climb down and make room for others whose legs refused to work or whose feet were bleeding so badly that they could not go on.[18]

Throughout this ordeal, Colonel Hough displayed the leadership that so endeared him to his men. A tall, lone figure wrapped in an overcoat, Hough walked at the head of the column, never riding his mule, Lucy. Since the regiment had been ordered to keep to the right of the road, only one rank of men could walk in a wheel track, meaning the other three had to trudge through deep, drifting, unbroken snow on the roadside. So, the colonel would walk to the far right of the road with Lucy in the center. As he did so, he purposely dragged his feet in the deep snow, breaking a trail for the weary men of his command.[19]

However, Colonel Hough and Lucy performed an even more valiant service. As soon as a soldier broke down, unable to walk another step, Lucy and the colonel would appear at that man's side, and he would hear a deep, kindly voice saying, "Here, son, ride Lucy awhile. Give me your foot—up you go." The colonel would hoist the exhausted, frozen soldier up onto Lucy's back, and he would soon be leading the column astride the colonel's mule. Then, after a while, once the soldier was rested and his pride would no longer allow him to ride while his buddies walked, he would slip down, take his place in the line of march, and let another weary soul ride on Lucy's back.[20]

As the men approached the village of Vitrey-le-Nogent on the night of December 28, Colonel Hough could have easily gone ahead to his billet and made himself warm and comfortable while the men continued marching into the town. Instead, he remained at the entrance to the village until everyone was safely inside. Major Wolf later wrote, "Those who saw it cannot forget the sight of the Colonel of the 166th Infantry, at the head of the wagon train, indicating the way through the drifts and superintending a long, hard haul outside of Nogent."[21]

Moreover, the local French townspeople were unflinching in their support for the regiment as it made its way to Rolampont. Not only did they open their homes and barns willingly, but as soon as the people of a village heard that these Americans were marching in their direction, they would all gather in the village square and begin the process of breaking trails through the drifts of snow that blocked the roadways through the village. Raymond Cheseldine later recorded, "It was a mark of devotion that did not go unnoticed by the new Yanks."[22]

The final day's march was the longest—almost twenty miles to Noidant-le-Rocheux, followed by ten more miles to Perrogney-les-Fontaines, the regiment's headquarters in the Seventh Training Area. As the 166th approached Rolampont, where Division Headquarters was now housed, the column stopped, and Colonel Hough told the regimental band to take the lead and prepare to play as the men marched through town past the headquarters. Unfortunately, the band reported that their instruments were frozen solid. So, the colonel located a nearby farmhouse that had a fire going in its fireplace and directed the band to go thaw their instruments while the rest of the regiment took a much-needed rest. Then, the regiment marched "swinging stride in spite of aches and pains" despite faltering, tired, and bloody feet, past Division Headquarters with colors unfurled.[23]

The worst of the day, however, was the hike up a long, steep hill that led from the banks of the Marne River past the city walls and into the ancient old Roman town of Langres. The winds roared as the men marched up the hill, sweeping the snow away but blowing icy particles of snow "against raw flesh with a strength that suggested knife thrusts."[24] Little wonder that Dana Daniels's lieutenant in E Company told Daniels that it was the "worst hike he was ever on."[25]

But, after limping across the bridge at Rolampont with his feet wrapped in rags, one soldier of the 166th summed it all up. Struggling to remain upright under the weight of his pack and covered with the snow blown by the gale-force winds, he said with conviction, "Valley Forge—Hell! There ain't no such animal."[26]

As the 166th Infantry arrived in its new training area after the trials of the Valley Forge Hike, they once again divided up to take billets in different villages near Perrogney-les-Fontaines. The Headquarters Company, A Company, and B Company remained in Perrogney-les-Fontaines, while C Company and D Company moved two miles north to the village of Courcelles-en-Montagne. E Company and F Company took billets in Aprey, four miles to the south, and all of the 3rd Battalion was assigned to Noidant-le-Rocheux, some three miles northeast of Regimental Headquarters. Meanwhile, the Machine Gun Company marched about five miles to the southeast, and the Supply Company moved on to Pierre-fontaine, about a mile south of the headquarters.[27]

The regiment rested until New Year's Day 1918. On New Year's Eve, the men put together whatever celebration they could organize given their tired, aching bodies and meager resources. In E Company, Dana Daniels recorded that his comrades managed to cook "a fine potato stew," as well as some cakes, bread, butter, and coffee.[28] After enduring such a brutal march, it must have seemed like quite a feast.

While the initial training of the regiment was intense, the seriousness of the training now increased dramatically. No one had any doubts concerning what it was all about. As Raymond Cheseldine wrote grimly, "Training of the infantry was merely that of initiation into the secrets of new war material and its application to the business of human extermination."[29]

The training did not merely go from dawn to dusk. Training and drills took place in the practice trenches and on the firing ranges for almost eight hours every day, with up to two hours of classroom sessions on tactical problems every night. The men's proficiency in both their weapons and tactics showed noticeable improvement.

At times, they seemed almost like veterans of the Regular Army and not untried amateurs from the National Guard. For example, one night in February, Captain Breed led C Company into the practice trenches near Courcelles. He and his officers developed a plan of attack, employed rockets and flares as signals, simulated going over the top, and charged across a pretend no man's land to attack a dummy German trench just like a veteran unit. Raymond Cheseldine said, "It was a great game for American youth."[30] However, very soon, the real thing would prove to be anything but a "game."

This new training area had numerous practice trench complexes and grenade pits, as well as target ranges for rifles, machine guns, and mortars. In mid-January, Dana Daniels recorded that they received both French and British gas masks, and by early February they were participating in live gas drills, which were not something for the faint of heart.[31] Their French instructors from the 32nd Regiment were back with them, and everything they imparted emphasized a "combat point of view." They tried to instill in the men the idea of hitting the other fellow first and hitting him harder.[32]

Up to now, the men had been wearing cloth headgear in the form of caps and campaign hats. But in early February the men were issued their

Soldiers from the 166th Infantry conducting bayonet excercises at the Seventh Training Area, top, and firing Hotchkiss machine guns, bottom. (*National Archives*)

first steel helmets. These took some getting used to, but now they indeed looked like combat soldiers.[33]

As January turned to February, rumors of a move to the front became rampant. Everyone received new clothing, and the training-issue machine guns, automatic rifles, and mortars were replaced by a permanent stock of new equipment. Even new mules and carts arrived to carry the heavier weapons, and the Supply Company got their first real rolling kitchens, ration carts, and water carts. In terms of gear and clothing, the regiment was now fully equipped.[34]

However, despite the training and new equipment, they still showed signs of their amateur status. One day, the new 42nd Division commander, General Charles Menoher, visited the regiment along with his staff. Colonel Hough decided to give him a demonstration of how much the men had progressed in their capabilities. Major Henderson and his men from the 3rd Battalion staged several exhibitions of bayonet drill followed by one on the use of the new Chauchat automatic rifles. All went well until one young officer from the battalion became so excited over the work of his automatic rifles that he decided he needed new and more demanding targets for them. So, he decided to turn his field of fire down the valley in the direction of Pierrefontaine, where the Supply Company was based. His men began to fire a series of rapid bursts in that direction, and all their rounds reached the village. Soon, the "whiz and snap" of 8mm Lebel rounds were ripping through the streets of Pierrefontaine. Every Supply Company man in the village began to scramble for cover, probably thinking some surprise German attack was underway. One unfortunate Supply Company officer was in the latrine when the firing started. He was so terrified that he adamantly refused to leave the outhouse until thirty minutes later. Luckily, no one was hurt, and quick use of the telephone stopped the friendly fire barrage before any damage was done.[35] There is no record of the general's reaction, but it is doubtful the men's display of marksmanship impressed him.

In fact, it might be said that visits to the 166th by general officers were somewhat ill advised. In late January, General Lenihan from Division Headquarters decided to visit Aprey and conduct an inspection of the men's quarters. Just before his arrival, there had been a heavy snowfall with a corresponding increase in the need for fuel to stay warm. Unfortunately, there was a shortage of axes in the village, and the results from the wood details sent into the nearby forest were less than satisfactory. So, Major Houser, the 2nd Battalion commander, gathered up Captains Baily, Caldwell, and Newlove from his staff and began to canvas the village in search of axes.[36]

While they were away, General Lenihan arrived, and an orderly was sent to find Major Houser. When he found him, Major Houser and the others hurried back to meet with the general, who was waiting impatiently in his car. When Houser reached the vehicle, General Lenihan decided to make a dramatic exit from the car and vent his anger at being delayed. Unfortunately, Aprey sat on a hillside, which means the cobblestone streets were a little steep, and in this case, those streets were covered in ice and very slippery. As the general stepped down from his car, he was wearing riding boots, which do not work very well on icy streets. In the words of one witness, as soon as General Lenihan stepped onto the road, "he turned a back tailspin and crashed in the center of the street." With his sense of dignity severely damaged, the general got back in the car and drove away as fast as possible.[37]

While the men toiled away in the cold, wet, and muddy practice trenches, they became acquainted with a vicious nemesis that plagued the soldiers of both sides: body lice. For the doughboys of the AEF, they came to be known as "cooties" or, on occasion, "crumbs." Before long, every man, officer or enlisted, would be infested with them. As one division commander would say, there were "too few baths and too many cooties." Cooties would be an unforgettable experience for the frontline doughboy.[38] At one point in the war, the chief medical officer of another National Guard unit, the 26th Division, reported that the "command is 99% infested with lice; is filthy, bodily; needing bathing and delousing."[39] When the men searched for lice, they called the process "reading your shirt." One soldier wrote that every morning, officers and men, whether "refined or roughneck," would meticulously strip to the waist for the process of "reading his shirt." Leon Miesse wrote his wife, "They call it the crumb number as crumb is another name for 'cooties' or body lice. . . . I certainly long for a good American bathtub."[40]

By mid-February, in Raymond Cheseldine's words, "the regiment felt itself a working unit now, green because untried, but well-grounded in practice and with morale that had been built on the pride of past achievement at home and during the winter's hike." But he may have gone too far when he compared the regiment to a football team: "A college football coach would have recognized the outfit as 'on edge' but likely to 'go stale' unless it could get into a game soon."

However, as he and the other men of the 166th would learn far too soon, this war was nothing at all like a football game.

Chaplain J. J. Halliday conducts funeral rites for Private Dyer Bird, March 3, 1918. (*National Archives*)

Into the Trenches—
Lunéville and Baccarat

"Orders are we leave early tomorrow morning for the place where the real war is on."—Private Burt Moffett, 166th Infantry Regiment, diary entry for February 19, 1918

THE MORNING OF MARCH 3, 1918, was gray and somber, befitting the ceremony. They gathered in the remains of the town square of the village of Domjevin—Americans from the 166th and French soldiers from the 60th French Infantry, as well as Major General Charles T. Menoher, commander of the 42nd Division, his chief of staff, Colonel Douglas MacArthur, members of the general staff, and high-ranking officers of the French army. They arranged themselves in a square around a rough casket covered in both French and American flags and propped up on two boxes. As the group watched silently, the 166th's chaplain, J.J. Halliday, rendered last rites over the body of Private Dyer J. Bird of D Company from Broadway, Ohio, the first man from the 166th and the 42nd Division to be killed in action.

When Chaplain Halliday finished, everyone marched solemnly to a small cemetery on the hill behind the village. There, Private Bird's casket was lowered into his grave as heads were uncovered, and the chaplain spoke his final words of prayer. Then everyone saluted, and a bugler played the soft, mournful tones of "Taps."[1] Once the burial ceremony was concluded, everyone departed, returning to the business of war.

While Private Bird was the first man from the regiment to die in France, his funeral was the last one that was so elaborate. No more generals would come to honor the dead. In the months that followed, death would become a far too common event in the lives of the men of the 166th. So many men would die, often dying so fast that there would be no time for elaborate burial ceremonies. Of course, the regimental band might come to play at a brief graveside ceremony, but there would be nothing like Dyer Bird's funeral again. Moreover, many of the dead would never be found. Their bodies were either left lying in no man's land, where no one could find them, or they were vaporized by an exploding German artillery shell. These men would end up categorized simply as "Missing in Action."

For those listed as missing, all that would remain to record their sacrifice would be a carving of their name on some cold, stone monument in their town square back home in Ohio.

AS THE 166TH'S TRAINING continued in early February 1918, orders came to prepare for another movement. However, this time, it was clear it would not be a march to a rear training area. The initial orders told the regiment to pack up all surplus baggage and equipment for storage at Longeau. Further, the orders directed that the soldiers should retain only a thirty-day supply of field equipment. "Feverish preparation" began, but not surprisingly, no one was quite sure what ought to be included in thirty days' worth of field equipment. To make sure they did not take too much, everyone cut their gear and clothing down to the bone. While this seemed a very sensible approach at the time, no one could have possibly realized that they would not see their surplus baggage again until March 1919.[2]

On February 15, the orders that everyone had anticipated arrived: they were moving to the front. The entire 42nd Division was to board trains on February 16-17 at Langres, but no one was told what the exact destination was. Some of the men managed a last decent meal provided by the grateful residents of the villages. Burt Moffett, a twenty-nine-year-old private in the regimental band from Gahanna, Ohio, was invited along with his buddies to share dinner with the family whose barn they used for a billet. "Supper was at 6:30," he wrote in his diary. "Sergeant Thorpe, Mr. Sands, Harold Sands, Rollin Durant, Hubert Killam, and myself being 'on the job' of eating it. Had fine rabbit stew, fried potatoes, biscuits, cherries in Cognac, Wine, & plum pie."[3] Given the dire lack of food in most of the

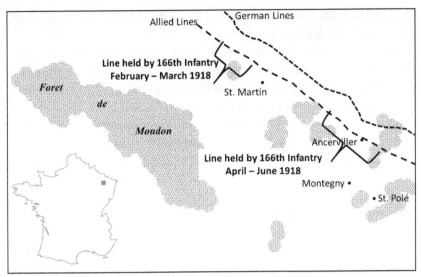

The trenches in the Lunéville and Baccarat sectors. (*Author*)

villages, this particular French family must have made an enormous sacrifice to serve their American guests.

At 3:00 a.m. on February 16, the 166th's Headquarters Company, Machine Gun Company, and 1st Battalion marched from Perrogney-les-Fontaines to Langres and boarded the first train. Luckily, there were no tiny boxcars this time, and the men got to ride in "side-door Pullman" cars.[4] The remainder of the regiment soon followed. In L Company, Leon Miesse spent the morning of February 16 packing his gear and then instructing his men on how to make their packs and clean up the area before departure. At 5:00 p.m., the 3rd Battalion formed for inspection, and, at 11:00 p.m., they began the march to the train station at Langres, arriving there around 2:00 a.m. "The men were tired from the long hike and heavy equipment," he wrote his wife. In a few hours, the last remaining element of the 166th was on its way north. Their destination was a portion of the front in Lorraine, referred to as the Lunéville Sector.[5]

Lunéville was what the French and the AEF called a "quiet sector." When the war began in 1914, the Germans drove deep into the area, reaching Rambervillers and destroying villages along the way. Then they withdrew to a line that ran roughly from Reillon southeast to Domèvre-sur-Vezouze. After that, both sides dug trenches and strung barbed wire and seemed to develop a tacit agreement not to intrude on one another.

Up to now, neither side had used gas along these lines, and "in the day-time, a shot was seldom heard."[6]

The trains carrying the 166th took them through Chamont, Neufchâteau, Toul, and Nancy to Saint Clément, a small village train station twelve kilometers southeast of Lunéville. While the train paused briefly at Lunéville, the men saw their first enemy aircraft when a German plane appeared overhead, and another appeared once the train stopped at Saint Clément. Here, the regiment detrained and marched to their billets in Moyen, Vallois, Bénaménil, and Domjevin. Dana Daniels of E Company recorded that his company arrived on February 19, unloaded from the train, and hiked to Vallois, a distance of about two miles. He wrote that "this village had been captured by the Boche in the early part of the war" and that they "stayed with a kind old lady" whose father had been blinded by gas.[7]

On the morning of February 20, Regimental Headquarters moved out of Saint Clément and headed toward Domjevin, a mere two miles from the trenches near Blémerey. Along the way, the signs of war were every-where. Deep in the woods, the men saw a heavily camouflaged observation tower, a French heavy artillery battery concealed by wire mesh and grass, and a large ammunition dump. Perhaps more ominously, however, were the deep shell holes that pockmarked the landscape.[8]

But the village of Domjevin itself offered the most telling evidence of war. It was a "mere shell of a town." Years of artillery fire had destroyed virtually every house, and the only structures in the town were dugouts and stone shelters built with the remains of what had once been homes and shops. Not surprisingly, the villagers had all left long ago, and the only current residents were the French and Italian soldiers who manned this section of the front.[9]

As for the front, the complex of trenches was not quite what the men of the 166th had imagined. Rather than a long, continuous line of works, the Allied lines consisted of a series of small defensive positions separated from the enemy by as little as four hundred to five hundred yards.[10] The lines ran parallel to the original Lorraine frontier about seven miles northeast of Domjevin. The trenches assigned to the 166th were part of the Saint Clément subsector of the Lunéville Sector and were known as Center of Resistance (or CR, for short) Rognelle. The system of trenches included what was called "boyaus," a series of smaller trenches built in a zigzag pattern that served to connect forward and rear positions. CR Rognelle ran for about two miles and was located about five hundred yards northeast of the ruins of the small village of Blémerey.[11]

Dana Daniels in Domjevin, March 1918. (*Union County Historical Society*)

Division Headquarters attached the 166th to the French 60th Infantry Regiment, forming part of the VII Corps of the 8th French Army. The 60th Infantry was to act as overseers of the 166th during the time the Americans received their first test in the trenches under fire. The French infantrymen made for "most capable instructors" and a strong relationship developed between them and the Ohioans, who came to greatly admire these veteran soldiers who wore "horizon blue."[12]

On February 21, the orders came, the ones that made the final, fateful changes in the lives of every member of the 166th Infantry Regiment—on the night of February 22, they were to take positions in the trenches

Lieutenant Colonel George Florence, 166th Infantry deputy commander, left, and Major Rell Allen, 1st Battalion commander, second from left, in the trenches at Lunéville, February 1918. (*National Archives*)

along the front. Upon receiving those orders from Division Headquarters, Colonel Hough selected the 1st Battalion along with elements of the Machine Gun Company and Stokes mortarmen from the Headquarters Company to take the first turn, or "trick" as it was called, in the trenches. The 3rd Battalion would move to Bénaménil in support while the 2nd Battalion would be held in reserve at Moyen and Vallois. The Supply Company, meanwhile, was positioned in Laronxe, where there was a narrow-gauge rail line connecting it to the main rail line at Saint Clément. A couple of weeks later, in anticipation of action that might come, Enoch Williams ended a letter to his mother with a postscript that read, "P.S. Am going to get a Dutchman sometime in the near future."[13]

In fact, the entire 42nd Division was moving up, and the Rainbow Division was finally going to war. Along with the 166th, the 165th from New York, as well as two companies of the 150th Machine Gun Battalion from Wisconsin, were with the French 164th Division along the front in the

Forêt de Parroy far to the left of the 166th. Meanwhile, the 168th from Iowa, the 167th from Alabama, and the 151st Machine Gun Battalion from Georgia were assigned with the French 128th Division to the Baccarat Sector, which was located to the right of the Lunéville Sector.[14]

In the deep, inky darkness of the night of February 22, the 1st Battalion relieved a French unit in the line. When the 1st Division was the first American unit to take up positions at the front in a nearby sector, they had done so in daylight with a great show, which aroused the German's suspicions. In response, the Germans poured artillery fire down on their heads and conducted a raid on the first night in which they took several Americans prisoner. So, learning from that unpleasant experience, A, C, and D Companies of the 1st Battalion pushed their way through the mud from Domjevin to the trenches and took their place in the line with as much stealth and quiet as humanly possible.[15]

Once deployed, it did not take long for the Ohioans to realize that the difference between their trench warfare training and actual life in the trenches was beyond anything they could have imagined. First, there was the discomfort of the cold and the mud, along with the presence of innumerable rats who scampered about up and down the trenches. But the sights and sounds were far more disquieting. Flashes of gunfire would suddenly light the night, punctuated by the distant rattle of machine gun fire. Occasionally, a signal rocket or flare would erupt from the German trenches, portending what exactly they did not know. All of this served as a reminder that this was no game, that thousands of men who wanted to kill you were only a few hundred yards away.

When they peered through the darkness across no man's land, their imaginations took hold. "Wire posts," wrote Raymond Cheseldine, "looked like Germans and many an unoffending stick of wood was made the target of a shower of rifle bullets and hand grenades." Uncertain about what they saw and heard, many a nervous man sent up a warning flare. But after a while the nervousness turned into a more balanced sense of vigilance, and war in the trenches became a phenomenon characterized mostly by tedium. Still, as the British would say, trench warfare was "damned dull, damned damp, and damned dangerous."[16]

The "damned dangerous" part of that statement was tragically demonstrated on the evening of March 1-2, 1918. That night, the men of the 1st Battalion remained at their positions, anxiously awaiting the arrival of the 3rd Battalion, which was scheduled to relieve them. One of the men from D Company, Private Dyer Bird of Broadway, Ohio, in Union County,

Men from D Company in the trenches at Lunéville, February 1918. (*National Archives*)

stood vigil at one of the forward listening posts. Young Private Bird had just turned eighteen on January 5. His mother had died when he was only three months old, and he had been raised by his grandparents in Broadway. He lived most of his life in Broadway but was working in Marion when war was declared, and he enlisted in the Ohio National Guard a few weeks later.[17] His job on this night, like all those assigned to these posts, was to watch for any signs of German activity that might portend a raid or even a general attack. Staring out into the black night, he saw movement in no man's land. Probably concerned that his eyes might be playing tricks on him, he looked again and saw a German raiding party emerging from a nearby trench. He immediately hurled two grenades in their direction, and, as they exploded among the Germans, he turned to run back to the main line and warn his comrades. As he leaped from the trench, the Germans cut him down with gunfire. He fell forward into the mud, shouting out before he died, "The Germans are coming in the form of a wedge. Boys, I'm dying."[18] The 166th and the people of Union County had lost their first man in combat. He would not be the last.

Private Bird's death was part of the elaborate but deadly game the two sides played in this "quiet" sector. Every night, both sides would send out patrols into no man's land. For the 166th's part, this usually meant detailing three to ten men and one officer to slip out of the trenches in the darkness and find their way through the tangles of barbed wire toward the German lines. For an hour or two, these patrols would roam about no man's land. Sometimes, they were assigned to capture German prisoners, while, at other times, the mission was to counter and block a German patrol believed to be headed for the American side of the barbed wire jungle that stretched between the trenches.[19] In any case, it could be a very treacherous and dangerous exercise that, in hindsight, seems to not have had sufficient potential for gain to offset what were very real losses in terms of life and limb.

When the 1st Battalion first moved into the trenches, they found them in appalling repair and spent many hours making them more habitable. When the 3rd Battalion arrived, Leon Miesse noted that the trenches were wet and muddy,[20] but they actually were an improvement on what the 1st Battalion had encountered on their arrival. The dugouts were almost livable, but there was still a need for pumps to keep the water from becoming knee-deep in places, and, as Raymond Cheseldine said, "one battalion never could exterminate all the rats in a week."[21]

After completing his first trick in the trenches, Miesse wrote his wife describing his experiences:

> Imagine a ditch, such as they lay sewers in, 6 to 8 feet deep, water in the bottom, and then still more water and mud. Put a bunch of wire out in front of it and then on the darkest night imaginable, stand looking over the top, with an occasional zing of a sniper bullet and at frequent intervals light up the heavens with a star shell rocket which turns everything into day, and you have had near as I can tell you the experiences of the men of the Company. With us, we got very little sleep, never had my clothes off for the whole time, and sometimes not even my shoes. During that time, I washed my hands three times and shaved twice, scraped the dirt off my hair, and lived in a dugout with the Captain.... We have heard the scream of the shrapnel and H.E. [high explosive] shells and heard the spat of the M.G. [machine gun] bullet, and believe me, it is no pleasant sound.[22]

On the night of March 9, D Company made the 166th's first offensive action of the war. A team of forty-five men, including eight from the regimental band,[23] would be led by Lieutenant Caleb Lear from D Company, a twenty-three-year-old from Chester, Pennsylvania, who had originally been a member of the Pennsylvania National Guard's 6th Infantry Regiment.[24] They would make what was called a "come and go" raid, performed in coordination with a similar French attack on their left. There was to be an hour-long artillery barrage on the enemy trenches plus supporting fire from the Stokes mortars and machine guns. The idea was to soften up the German position and keep their heads down so the raiders could achieve some surprise that would allow them to return with prisoners.[25]

At the appointed time, American artillery opened fire and "all Hell broke loose." One observer who stood behind the lines watching the barrage erupt said, "There were guns everywhere it seemed. Places on hillsides that in daytime resembled only green spots, clumps of trees or haystacks, became furnaces pouring forth tons of white-hot metal—great steel monsters belched forth from innocent valleys and sent shrieking through the air to the Boche lines over the hill, shell after shell so accurately timed that with four guns to a battery firing it was impossible to tell when the last one fired and the first one began."[26]

As the barrage commenced, Lieutenant Caleb and his men rose from the trenches and made their way carefully across no man's land, picking their way through the tangled barbed wire and shell holes. When the friendly barrage lifted, they rushed the German trenches only to find that the intense artillery fire had caused the enemy to abandon the position. So, the patrol returned with no prisoners and, luckily, no casualties. Afterward, Caleb and twenty-three members of the patrol received the French Croix de Guerre despite the fact they achieved little if anything on the raid.[27]

As activity in the sector picked up, so did German artillery fire. Between March 9 and March 11, three men from L Company were killed by the shells exploding around the trenches, and another was killed by accidental friendly rifle fire. Burt Moffett and the regimental band played at their funeral, and he commented in his diary that, "Deaths are so numerous, also other casualties, that it is a hard matter for me to get the facts in each case."[28]

Two days later and four days after the raid the Germans retaliated for "what they considered undue activity and inexcusable curiosity" on the part of the Americans. They shelled Domjevin heavily for more than thirty minutes, killing two French soldiers and wounding four others, while the 166th suffered two men slightly wounded. French officers believed the shelling was "unintentional." However, Red Wyatt, the colonel's orderly, was of another opinion entirely. As the shells arrived one after another, Red nervously commented that the "gunner over there is either drunk or a new beginner."[29]

The process of each battalion taking its trick in the trenches continued, and, on the night of March 11-12, the 2nd Battalion made its way quietly into the line. Dana Daniels of E Company recorded that his initial night in the trenches was March 12 and that the first heavy artillery barrage came from American guns. While he thought the guns were holding off a German attack, that turned out to not be the case.[30] Chalk it up to the nervousness everyone felt during their first few nights in the trenches, but the artillery barrage was caused by members of Daniels's own battalion in F Company.

F Company was assigned to hold one side of a U-shaped trench, while G Company occupied the other side of the "U." However, in the darkness, neither company realized that was how they were deployed—they could not see the "U" shape of the trench. Around 2:45 a.m., one of the soldiers from F Company was staring into the blackness of no man's land, where his mind was sure that seemingly invisible Germans were everywhere. He suddenly saw what he was sure was an enemy soldier but was actually a fence post across the "U" from his position. He called out the alarm and began blasting away at the imagined German soldier as his comrades joined him in opening fire. Across the way, the men in G Company saw this sudden eruption of gunfire, ducked for cover, and then returned fire.[31]

Hearing the rifle fire, the artillerymen were certain an attack was underway and began to fire shells into both no man's land and the friendly trenches. This inter-American warfare continued with the crack of rifle fire and roar of exploding artillery shells until someone in the battalion realized what was happening and restored order. Amazingly, no one was hurt.[32] However, one has to wonder what the Germans across the way thought as they watched two groups of Americans firing at one another as their own artillery shelled them. No doubt they found it very amusing.

A week later, on March 19, 1918, Secretary of War Newton Baker made a rather hasty visit to the regiment as part of an inspection tour of American units in France. Being from Cleveland, Secretary Baker wanted to see a regiment from his home state in action. The first stop for Baker was the village of Moyen, where he talked with doughboys from the 166th just before daylight. The secretary's party next traveled to Montigny from where they would go forward to the trenches. But about the time Baker was to make his visit, German artillery opened fire on the road leading to CR Ancerviller, and Colonel Hough recommended canceling the tour of the trenches. To his credit, Secretary Baker was adamant about going to the front, so an alternative route to the trenches was used. He agreed to carry a gas mask and wear the standard-issue steel helmet for the occasion.

The party made its way forward, slipping and sliding through the mud that seemed a constant feature of the trenches. Secretary Baker entered a communications boyaus and moved toward the main line. Once there, he inspected the dugouts and talked to some of the men. Then, over the protests of members of his party, he insisted on going farther forward to a listening post, where he conversed with the soldier on guard and peeped over the parapet into no man's land. As he did so, being the politician that he was, he made a statement clearly intended for the reporters that accompanied him, saying, "Now I am on the frontier of freedom."[33]

However, as he began to leave, things got a little more perilous for the secretary of war. German artillery spotters had apparently noted the arrival of his car and the activity surrounding it. So, they opened fire once more, and a 105mm shell exploded less than fifty yards from the secretary's vehicle. Another round then hit a nearby dugout, and Baker's staff had to stop him from going to check on any men that might have been in it. About that time, his driver, realizing the danger, hustled Baker into the car and sped off as fast as the car would go.[34] As a clearly unimpressed Burt Moffett wrote in his diary that day, the secretary arrived, and then he "beat it."[35]

On March 21, the 2nd Battalion completed its ten-day trick and handed over the trenches to the French during a massive bombardment from German artillery. This severely complicated the withdrawal process, but the battalion managed to complete their assignment without incident. With this, the 166th had finished thirty days in the trenches with a loss of six killed and fourteen wounded.[36] Although there had been little real fighting, this initial combat assignment gave the regiment invaluable experience. The officers and men now understood what real life under fire was like, and men had the experience of firing their first shots in anger. For his part, Dana Daniels diligently recorded that he fired his first shot at the German trenches on March 19, 1918.[37]

On the night of March 21, as the regiment prepared to move to a rear area, Colonel Hough remained in Domjevin to confer with his French counterpart and formally turn over command of the sector to the French. The two men were standing next to Colonel Hough's car discussing activities along the front when the Germans began a fierce artillery barrage

Secretary of War Newton Baker, right, visits the 166th Infantry in the trenches at Lunéville, March 19, 1918. (*Ohio History Connection*)

of Domjevin, spraying shrapnel everywhere. Red Wyatt stood anxiously by as the colonel talked to the French officer, but Red wanted to get on their way. Finally, as a shell exploded over the roof of a nearby church, Red could contain himself no longer. He grabbed Colonel Hough by the arm and pushed him into the car, saying, "Hell, Colonel, let's get a move on. You've been here for a month an' you've been pretty reasonable. Don't make a damn fool of yourself the last day and get us both killed. Get a move on and do your visiting some other time!"[38]

These first thirty days at the front were also key for the support organizations in the regiment such as the Supply Company, who learned how to do a job "about which no textbooks were written"[39] C.C. Lyon, a reporter for the new *Stars and Stripes* newspaper, paid a visit to the Muleskinners and came away with a profound sense of admiration. One staff officer told Lyon, "You've got to take off your hats to the boys who drive the mule teams up to the front. . . . They travel these roads night after night regardless of how many shells the Germans throw over at them. I've seen the shrapnel and the high explosives breaking all around them, but they merely stop occasionally to inspect the holes in the road and then drive on with their loads of food and ammunition for the men in the trenches."[40]

The Supply Company developed a system of organization in these early days of combat that "was the pride of the regiment." Under the leadership of Captain O.O. Koeppel, the company established a system in

Looking into no man's land from the 166th's trenches at Lunéville, March 1918. (*National Archives*)

which each battalion had a wagon train assigned to it under the command of an assistant wagon master, and each battalion also had a dedicated supply officer responsible for their logistical needs. This serves as an example of a situation where a National Guard unit had an advantage over a Regular Army unit. The Guardsmen did not feel constrained by years of using an established traditional system that might not fit the tactical situation. Therefore, when needed, they found ways to implement innovative and effective solutions that Regular Army units might not even consider.

"Every night the ration train came up to Blémerey under its corporal," wrote Raymond Cheseldine, describing the actions of the Muleskinners. "Every night, the Boche shelled the hilly road from Domjevin to Blémerey. With mathematical precision, he put his shells, so many minutes apart on that road. Between shells, with the skill of a train dispatcher, the corporals sent out one wagon. A shell—a wagon—a shell—a wagon—and so on until all had cleared. Never was a wagon struck on that road, and supplies were regularly received at company kitchens."[41]

THE REGIMENT WAS TOLD they would be returning to Rolampont and began their hike to the rear by going through Hallainville, Damas-aux-Bois, and Clezentine, where they were told to halt on March 22 for a few days of much-needed rest and resupply.[42] The next morning, Burt Moffett wrote that he slept until 10:30 a.m., an incredible luxury. The weather was warm, as were the nights, which Moffett said was a good thing except for the fact that warm weather meant "the 'cooties' will soon be on the job." He also indicated that the band was to play a concert that afternoon and that, after thirty days on the front, everyone was enjoying being in a town that was so quiet.[43]

However, after just a few days of rest, rumors began to fly once more. On March 21, the Germans had launched their great offensive of spring 1918 at Cambrai. The British were not faring well, and French reinforcements were being hurried to that part of the front. The rumors were that the 166th's rest would be short-lived, and on March 27, the rumors proved to be true once more. New orders arrived on that day, telling the 42nd Division to move to the Baccarat Sector, which was just southeast of the Lunéville Sector, and relieve the French VII Corps.[44] With this move, for the first time, an American division would be entrusted with an entire divisional, two-brigade-in-the-lines sector with no French support or supervision.[45]

These orders dictated that the regiment be ready to assume its new position on the Baccarat front by the morning of March 31. To cover the distance of twenty-five miles meant that the regiment would have to move out by midnight on March 29. A mad scramble ensued to replace worn-out equipment and unpack all the gear that had been prepared for shipment to Rolampont. Once that was done, the first elements stepped off for Montigny, where the regiment would set up its headquarters, late on the night of March 29. The first day's march brought them to Roville-aux-Chênes on March 30 with a hike of seventeen more miles through Baccarat to Montigny the next day, Easter Sunday, March 31. It rained all day that Easter, and everyone was in place by the end of the day after a wet, miserable march.[46]

Late that afternoon, the 1st Battalion under Major Rell Allen took over CR Ancerviller, which was part of the Merviller subsector of the Baccarat Sector. As he and his men moved into place, the regiment's headquarters set up shop in Montingy, while the remaining battalions spread out to billets in Reherrey, Vaxainville, Brouville, Gelacourt, and Merviller, which Dana Daniels wrote was "a pretty village about 5 miles from the trenches. You can see the Alp's Mountains in the distance."[47] The 3rd Battalion arrived around 2:00 p.m. and tried to find billets in Reherrey, but there were none left. So, they were told to go to Mignéville, where they would be in support of the 1st Battalion. When they reached Mignéville, Leon Miesse reported that there were only ten civilians in town and that they were "badly shot up."[48]

As the division deployed, the 84th Brigade was on the right of the division's front. They held the Neufmaisons subsector, which connected with the VII French Army under General Gerard to the south in the Vosges region. Gerard had overall army command for the entire area, including the 42nd Division. On the 84th Brigade's left was the 83rd Brigade, which included the 166th Infantry, and to their left was a French division. To the south, the division's boundary ran across dense forest all the way to the foothills of the Vosges Mountains. On the north side, the boundary followed good roads through a pastoral region blossoming with spring, while the Meurthe River formed the rear line of the division. The entire division front ran for a little over eight miles.[49]

While this sector had also been quiet, it had strategic importance. The regiment's CR and the entire division front was only about eight miles from the German border of 1914. When the German lines reached the Baccarat Sector, they veered to the south, creating a large hinge in the entire Alsatian front. If the Germans could break through and cut the major road that ran from Baccarat to Ramberviller and Epinal, they could block the Allied lines of communication to Alsace. Worse, the Germans might be able to cut off the Vosges from the rest of the Western Front and allow them to sweep across the Meurthe River past Lunéville and threaten the line near Nancy and Pont-a-Mousson.[50]

CR Ancerviller took its name from the village of Ancerviller, which was on the extreme right of the line. The 166th's positions consisted of a series of six strong points running from the edge of the Bois-de-Comte forest on the far left, across a small hill, to Ancerviller. The entire area formed a rough triangle, with Montigny as the apex. From there, a road led to the far left of CR Ancerviller in the woods of the Bois-de-Comte and a narrow-gauge railroad and trail ran from Montigny to Ancerviller. The trenches made up the base of the triangle with a front of about one and a quarter miles. Battalion Headquarters was established in Ancerviller, and the Regimental Post of Command, or "PC," was at Montigny. However, on April 6, it was decided it would be wiser to relocate the Regimental PC to Reherrey and the Battalion Headquarters to Montigny. The 166th now held the far left of the 42nd Division's line, with the 167th and 168th on its right, and the 165th in reserve near Deneuvre.[51]

As the battalions of the regiment took up what would now be eight-day tricks in the trenches, the same pattern of nightly patrols that characterized their time in the Lunéville Sector resumed. However, in Baccarat, there was a new sense of urgency. The major German offensive to the north caused concern that the enemy might undertake a similar action in this heretofore quiet sector of the Western Front. Therefore, the regiment's nightly patrols sought to identify any signs of an impending attack by the Germans. However, the Germans were just as active at night, and a series of clashes ensued with artillery barrages and counter barrages punctuating the action.

On the night of April 7, one of the German patrols made it through the wire all the way to the main street of Ancerviller. Private Pearl Smith of B Company was standing guard in the village that night, and the first he knew of the Germans being there was when he heard a heavily accented voice say in English, "You're my prisoner." That statement came with the unwanted feeling of a gun being pressed into Private Smith's back. But the private did not plan to become a prisoner, so he whirled about, shouted, "You're a damned fool," and delivered a hard punch to the German's face. The German fired his weapon, hitting Private Smith in the stomach. But as Smith went down to the cobblestone street, he returned fire and, upon hearing the shots, other guards came running to his assistance. A firefight began that drove the Germans from the town at the cost of one German sergeant killed and Smith and one other Ohioan wounded.[52]

The next night, 3rd Battalion relieved 1st Battalion in the trenches. Around 9:30 p.m., just before moving his company into position, Leon Miesse was notified to go to the rear to meet twenty-five replacements being assigned to his unit. As it turned out, they were all new draftees, the first the regiment had seen so far. This would become increasingly common as the regiment's casualties mounted, and the draft became the primary source of new manpower. But as time went on and the pipeline to France needed to be filled more quickly, many of these new men would arrive after having received only minimal training. Miesse wisely chose not to put these new soldiers into the trenches and sent them back to the company billets to be fed and bedded down.[53]

A few nights after 3rd Battalion assumed their places in the trenches, Lieutenant Milton Monnett of M Company saw something moving in no man's land. When it came closer, he opened fire, killing a black dog. The dog was wearing a collar with a dispatch case containing German messages attached. Apparently, the Germans were using the dog to carry orders and information to an unknown spy behind the American lines.

From then on, the 166th and the rest of the division began using code for all telephone calls and messages, as well as employing nightly passwords.[54]

Each evening, 42nd Division Headquarters would issue a password that was only to be distributed to guards by Regimental Headquarters. Anyone who would need to be out at night and might pass a guard had to get the password before venturing out. For their part, the sentries were given strict orders to shoot anyone who failed to provide the correct password.[55]

However, the system was not without its complications. For example, every night, the Supply Company sent Muleskinners out with their carts to carry rations to the men in the trenches. As they made their way forward, the Muleskinners had to stop every time they encountered a sentry, climb down from their seat on the cart, and provide the correct password. For the most part, this system worked fine. One night, when the password was "Garibaldi," the Germans began to shell the road leading to the front. As a result, no Muleskinner wanted to stay in one place along the way for very long as the barrage exploded around them. One of the drivers, a private named Sam Shaw, was particularly nervous that night. The first sentry Shaw encountered challenged him, and the Muleskinner quickly dismounted, gave the password, and then hurried on his way amidst the exploding shells. A few yards later, he was stopped again and repeated the procedure. But now the German rounds were raining down with even greater force as he was halted for the third time. Shaw again got past the sentry with the password, but a shell exploded dangerously close by as a sentry attempted to stop Shaw for the fourth time. The sentry called out, "Halt! Who goes there?" The now frightened and exasperated Muleskinner refused to rein in his mules as they dashed by the astonished sentry, replying to the challenge by shouting, "Garibaldi, two mules, and a ration cart! Get out of the way, you damn fool, and let me go!"[56]

As April passed, the pattern of nightly patrols continued. On April 20, an unusual four-man patrol was put together to reach a point closer to the German trenches than had previously been accomplished. The four men were to attempt to reach an intermediate position and then press on to the final position before turning back. Lieutenant Thomas J. Koger of H Company, a twenty-two-year-old salesman from Memphis, Tennessee, was to lead the patrol. However, as he had recently left the hospital and was not completely fit, Sergeant Orville G. Fuller, a twenty-six-year-old farmer from Circleville, Ohio, was listed as second-in-command. Also, out of concern for his friend, Lieutenant Koger, Lieutenant B. Carroll

Reece from the Headquarters Company, a former teacher and twenty-eight-year old native of Butler, Tennessee, volunteered to be part of the patrol along with a French officer.

The patrol moved out, got past the German wire, and made it to their initial point without incident. Then suddenly, machine gun fire erupted from the German trenches ahead. All four men dropped to the ground as a stream of bullets zipped through the darkness around them. As they fell to the ground, Lieutenant Koger heard the all too familiar sound of a gasping cough that meant one of the patrol members had been hit in the chest and was choking on his own blood. He quickly checked and found that, indeed, Sergeant Fuller had been hit. However, no one could move to his aid because of the deadly fire from the enemy. Finally, the firing stopped, and the three officers made their way to where Fuller lay bleeding. They would not leave him there, so, despite the danger of exposing themselves, they picked Fuller up and carried him back through no man's land to their own trenches. Sadly, when they got to safety, they found that Fuller was dead.[57]

On April 23, each battalion had completed its trick in the line, and the New Yorkers of the 165th relieved the regiment. The Ohioans dropped back to Deneuvre, about nine miles from the front, where they became part of the Army Corps Reserve for the Baccarat Sector. The Regimental Headquarters, Headquarters Company, Supply Company, and 3rd Battalion, less L Company, were assigned to Deneuvre, while L Company was in Neufmaisons; A Company and the Machine Gun Company were billeted in Veney; and B, C, and D Companies went to the Haxo Barracks in Baccarat. Meanwhile, the 2nd Battalion was assigned to quarters in Brouville and Camp Grande Voivre, a barracks set on very low ground which, in the heavy spring rains, became known as "Camp de Mud."[58]

Dusty Boyd wrote home that rumors said they would get twenty days of rest. In fact, he related that the men did not think the war would last much longer and that they would "Parade in Washington on the 4th of July."[59] However, Boyd and his comrades would soon be returning to the trenches at CR Ancerviller instead of packing for a trip home.

In the meantime, while the regiment was supposed to be resting, that did not mean an end to either training or actual operations. Shortly after arriving in Deneuvre, the regiment was tasked to plan and prepare for a large-scale raid deep into the German lines. The target would be a well-fortified German position in the Bois de Chien forest near Ancerviller. The enemy had filled those woods with a complex network of barbed wire and concrete trenches and blockhouses, all defended by hundreds of troops armed with mortars, machine guns, and 77mm artillery. The entire area was covered by dense forest, and it had a commanding view and field of fire over the open ground of no man's land on three sides.[60]

It was decided that Major Henderson would lead L Company and M Company on the raid. They would be accompanied by a Machine Gun Company from the 150th Machine Gun Battalion as well as a platoon from the regiment's own Machine Gun Company. The raiding force would also include a demolition team from the 117th Engineers who were assigned to destroy the concrete blockhouses and a small detachment from the Supply Company with hand grenades and flares. They trained under the watchful eyes of French instructors in an area near Baccarat designed to replicate the Bois de Chien down to the foot. Once the instructors were satisfied that Henderson's men were ready, the raid was scheduled for the night of May 2-3.[61]

For several days leading up to the attack, American artillery had steadily increased their fire on the German positions in the woods. On May 2, they prepared to send every round they could fire into the Bois de Chien. The raiders rode trucks on an hour-long trip to Sainte-Pôle, where they dismounted and marched through Saint-Maurice-aux-Forges to their jumping-off point for the attack. As they arrived at the trenches opposite the forest, they suffered their first casualty even before they began the assault when Corporal Dan Stout of Lancaster, Ohio, was hit by machine gun fire and fell wounded. Zero Hour was scheduled for 4:00 a.m. on May 3.[62]

At the appointed time, American artillery opened fire with a massive barrage that Leon Miesse described as being "like hell had broken loose."[63] With Major Henderson leading the way, the Ohio doughboys went over the top. The American guns maintained a rolling barrage as the raiders crossed no man's land that penetrated the Bois de Chien and then boxed it in on all sides. By 1918, these types of barrages had become a standard part of any offensive operation. As the name implies, rolling barrages preceded the attacking infantry in a carefully choreographed process that provided supporting fire while on the move. Each barrage might be different, but they all moved forward in measured steps, focusing artillery fire on one line before moving forward to the next set of targets at a designated time. If successful, this allowed the infantry to move forward through areas cleared of enemy defenses. The exact speed and timing of rolling barrages varied based on the nature of the terrain and the strength of the enemy's position, but a typical rate for advancing infantry was about eight hundred feet in ten minutes.[64]

In response, the "Boche rained shells and M.G. [machine gun] bullets on us," wrote Leon Miesse. The ground they covered as they attacked was described by Miesse, who said, "I never saw such a shell-torn area, shell holes, trees uprooted." As they approached their objective, a German shell exploded in front of L Company's commander, Captain William Belhorn of Lancaster, Ohio, and he went down severely wounded by shrapnel. Lieutenant Miesse now took command, and L Company pressed on with the other attackers as they reached the objective.[65]

Amid the dense smoke, Henderson and his men found that the artillery fire had been too much for the Germans, who had abandoned their trenches and blockhouses. Many of the concrete trenches had collapsed under the force of the exploding American shells, most of the above-ground works had been leveled, and "the forest itself turned into almost a bare field."[66] So, the raiders set about blowing up the remaining blockhouses and departed for friendly lines after about forty-five minutes. They made their way back across no man's land, carrying both their nineteen wounded and two dead.[67] While the attack was executed with near perfection, and the Germans never tried to occupy the Bois de Chien again, it seems doubtful that the results were worth twenty-one casualties.

One of those killed in the attack was Davis Bryant, a twenty-two-year-old private in M Company from Hopewell, Virginia. Bryant was one of the new draftee replacements the company had received, and when he heard about the upcoming raid, he begged his platoon commander, First Lieutenant Paul Jarrett, to allow him to be part of the attack. Jarrett, a twenty-three-year-old former cattle rancher from Polk, Nebraska, hesitated to agree to Bryant's request. Jarrett had been trained by the British as a hand-to-hand combat specialist and had been on several night raids into the German trenches. He knew just how brutal this raid might be and was not keen on the idea of allowing an inexperienced, untrained draftee to be part of the raid. However, the private's earnest pleas wore Jarrett down, and he finally agreed to Bryant's request.[68]

When Jarrett's platoon reached the first line of German trenches, he ordered Private Bryant to remain there and guard the flank as the rest of the platoon advanced. Jarrett figured this might be the safest place for the young draftee. Later, when the platoon was almost back to friendly lines, Jarrett stopped and asked each of his corporals to account for their men. Everyone was still with the platoon except for Bryant, whose corporal said that, as they withdrew, he found the private dead in the first line of trenches. Jarrett refused to leave Bryant's body behind, so he ordered three men to accompany him back across no man's land to retrieve Private Bryant's body while his sergeant took the rest of the platoon back to the regiment's trenches. They made their way through the barbed wire and shells holes to the first line of German trenches in the Bois de Chien, where they picked up Bryant and started to carry him to American lines. In the process, they were pinned down for several hours by German machine gun and artillery fire, but they eventually made it back with the private's body.[69]

In addition to operational maneuvers like that conducted against the Bois de Chien, the rest of the regiment conducted training maneuvers. However, upon hearing that they would be "going to maneuver," one of the new draftees became confused and asked, "Where the hell is Maneuver? Is it far from here?"[70]

During this lull and rest period, there were, however, opportunities to enjoy a spring that seemed absolutely delightful after a hard, cold winter. There was rain, to be sure, and the cooties did, in fact, seem to "frisk about a bit livelier." But there was also enough sunshine to help restore a soldier's sanity, and there were also opportunities to explore the nearby villages and towns, play baseball, and even dance. Raymond Cheseldine would write about that spring in the Vosges:

> Don't you remember the real green of the trees and grass and the myriads of wildflowers on the hillsides? And the cool, still depths in the forests atop the hills near Baccarat? Didn't you ever stand on the terrace in Deneuvre and look down into the valley at the town of Baccarat bathed in the glow of fading day, the river cutting the spotted pattern of red-tiled roofs and gray stone walls with a curving ribbon of sparkling silver flecked with tiny spangles of gold? Beyond the town, an orchard abloom with white and pink petals, clinging to a hillside of vivid green, which served as an anchorage for a chateau surrounded by the inevitable wall of stone and plaster. Along the land far below came the sheep and cattle, back to their barns after a day of grazing in the pastures near town. A peasant's low wheeled, high-sided cart drawn by an ancient ox seemed scarcely to move as it brought its burden of women and children home from a day in the fields.... And the nurses from the hospital "over the hill" came down and danced to the music of "the best band in the army." "Le Grand Colonel," as the delighted villagers called the Old Man [Colonel Hough], led the dancing and

caused gales of laughter when he bent his towering height to dance with one little nurse who, on tiptoe scarcely reached beneath his arm.[71]

But despite the beauty of spring in the Vosges, there were also grim reminders of war. Every evening, the regimental band traveled to Baccarat to perform a concert for the men in the hospital. Here, one could find men from the regiment whose bodies had been damaged by machine gun fire and shrapnel. Sadly, one could also see men whose minds had been broken by war, and some, like Raymond Cheseldine, came face-to-face for the first time with what was then called "shell shock." He described it as "raw, jagged nerves in healthy bodies, strong men broken by the strain of a Hell-born war."[72]

Cheseldine's description was an accurate one. The term shell shock was coined in 1915 only six months after the start of the war by Captain Charles Myers of the Royal Army Medical Corps. At first, doctors believed that shell shock was the result of a physical injury caused by the concussive effects of high-explosive artillery shells. But soon they discovered that many soldiers who exhibited the characteristic symptoms such as trembling "rather like a jelly shaking"; headache; tinnitus, or ringing in the ear; dizziness; poor concentration; confusion; loss of memory; and sleep disorders had been nowhere near exploding shells. This, in turn, led them to realize that these men's condition was one of what they referred to as "neurasthenia," or weakness of the nerves, a nervous breakdown precipitated by the severe stress of combat. Unfortunately for the thousands afflicted by this horrible emotional collapse, the Allied armies decided that, since this was just an emotional problem, they would not officially classify them as wounded and, once they gave these soldiers a little rest, they would return them to the front.[73]

Spring also brought an opportunity to do good works for others. In May 1918, a campaign was started by *The Stars and Stripes* to support the thousands of homeless war orphans of France. The paper asked for American units to contribute whatever money they could to the effort and made it a competition to see which outfit could give the most. *The Ohio Rainbow Reveille* took up the cause for the 166th, urging the men to contribute. Scoop Wilkinson wrote in the regimental newspaper, "Back home they may have their Liberty Loan whirlwinds and their Thrift Stamp campaigns, but those little financial undertakings are mere carbon-copies of a regular knock-'em-down-and-take-it-from-'em drives for francage [*sp*] that is hereby launched in the 166th by THE REVEILLE!" Scoop went on to say, "We've been in France for months. We know the condition of poor waifs, whose fathers have made the supreme sacrifice. There is no need pleading their cases."[74]

Scoop's words clearly struck a responsive chord among the doughboys of the 166th, who contributed over twenty-seven thousand francs, which set the record for the entire AEF. More importantly, the money was enough to support fifty-four children for a year. The American Red Cross sent a list of the fifty-four children "adopted" by the 166th along with a photograph of each child. *The Stars and Stripes* wrote a first page, first column story about the regiment's remarkable support, saying that it was the "ace of aces" outfit in the AEF, and the AEF praised Scoop Wilkinson for his work in the campaign.[75]

Edmond Esposito, one of the children adopted by 166th Infantry. (*Library of Congress*)

Unfortunately, the report of a brief twenty-day rest proved all too true, and on May 13, the 166th returned to CR Ancerviller to relieve the men of the 165th Infantry. Within a few days, the regular routine of nightly patrols and raids had resumed, and the men of the 166th found themselves once again risking their lives for what was usually minimal gain. On the night of May 18-19, a patrol was dispatched from B Company to gather intelligence on enemy positions and movements near the village of Hameau d' Ancervillers. The patrol included three sergeants and was led by Lieutenant John H. Leslie. Leslie, or "Les" as everyone called him, was twenty-four years old and had been a worker at a plow manufacturer in Minot, North Dakota, before the war. He had enlisted in what became the North Dakota National Guard's 164th Infantry Regiment in 1916 and was one of the new officers assigned to the 166th at Camp Mills.[76]

The patrol left CR Ancerviller around 11:00 p.m. with each man carrying a .45-caliber pistol, a gas mask, two hand grenades, two sandwiches, and a canteen of water. They crept down the road that led from Ancerviller to Hameau d' Ancervillers, dropped down to crawl under the German barbed wire, and proceeded to the edge of the village. At 2:50 a.m., they took a position in a small clump of willow trees about seventy-five yards from the German trenches. Here, they would hide the entire day, "daring not to move except when the breeze moved the willows." They took careful notes on everything they saw and heard. Around 7:00 a.m., they observed a German soldier with a dog outside the wire, heard machine gun fire from two different directions, and heard occasional firing by a battery of German 77mm guns starting around 3:00 p.m. They also noted the sounds of trucks, a train, and a band playing. That night, the patrol began its return and, for the first time, drew fire from the enemy. Luckily, no one was hit, and they returned to friendly lines about 3:00 a.m. on May 20.[77]

While Lieutenant Leslie's patrol did gather some valuable intelligence on enemy machine gun emplacements, it was decided to try something more ambitious and dangerous the next night. Rather than only five men, this patrol would be more like the one conducted at the Bois de Chien, using a team of twenty-four men led by Lieutenants Monnett and Packard from M Company. Unlike simple intelligence gathering, the mission would be to explore an area called Ouv de la Group, actually enter the German trenches, engage the enemy, and take prisoners. Monnett and Packard's team included two sergeants, four corporals, and sixteen enlisted men armed with rifles as well as two Chauchat automatic rifles.[78]

At 11:00 p.m., the two lieutenants led their men out through a chicane, a serpentine trench that led into no man's land. Lieutenant Monnett assigned two men to remain behind at the exit point from the chicane to provide a rear guard. The patrol moved forward through the darkness until a group of three Germans jumped up from a nearby shell hole and ran for their own trenches. The patrol pursued them but lost contact near the road to Hameau d' Ancervillers. Monnett's men continued forward toward their objective until they saw a five-man German patrol moving toward them. The Americans crouched down, shifted to their right, and laid in wait for the Germans, looking to take them prisoner. But before they could do so, another German patrol of thirty men started moving out of the trenches toward them.[79]

Monnett decided to fall back to prevent this new threat from getting behind them. As the patrol moved, they saw a new German patrol of sixteen men emerge from the German lines. Badly outnumbered, Monnett realized they were about to be flanked and possibly cut off from their line of retreat. So, he ordered his men to fall back even farther. Now, yet another German patrol appeared, but this one had managed to work its way to a position blocking the route back to the chicane. Monnett and his men had no choice but to open fire on these Germans and rush their position, tossing grenades at them as they attacked. The grenades went off, wounding several Germans as the enemy returned fire with rifles and pistols. The Germans decided to retreat, and the Americans captured one wounded and one unwounded prisoner. The patrol returned to American lines about 3:50 a.m. without any losses but also without reaching their objective.[80]

On May 20, E Company moved from Vaxainville to a reserve position in Sainte-Pôle, which Dana Daniels described as a "ruined town." But Daniels also reported the men had good billets and a "splendid view" of the Vosges Mountains.[81] While in Sainte-Pôle, one of Daniels's men, Private Robert L. Thorn, took the time to write a letter. Robert Thorn was a twenty-three-year-old hotel clerk from Marysville who had enlisted with E Company in May 1917. Thorn's father had been killed in an accident when Robert was only five years old, and his mother was a useless alcoholic. So, when he was in his teens, Robert became the family breadwinner, working with his grandmother to raise his two younger brothers and a little sister. The letter Robert Thorn wrote was going to his brother Hillis, the youngest of the family, who was just turning nineteen and who worshipped his older brother.

> May 26, 1918
> Dear Brother,
>   I rec'd your letter today, and it sure was good to get a letter from you as it has been a long time since I heard from you. I am still in good health and looking as good as ever. This is the last day we can write while located in this town. . . . Well, kid, I have seen quite a lot of France, but I didn't see it in the right way. A lot of hiking, and you know we wouldn't take much interest in the country then. I am glad you are taking care of Grandmother and hope she is in good health. . . . I am sending Reveilles and show it to Johnny Scholl. Well kid, this is all at present. Give my love to Grandma.
> With love to all and yourself,
> Robert Thorn
> Co. E. 166 Inf A.E.F
> via New York[82]

It would be the last letter Robert Thorn would write to his little brother.

The day after Robert Thorn wrote his letter, Burt Moffett reported that the front was getting very active. He and his comrades in the band were told to start wearing British gas masks, as the Germans had carried out a gas attack on CR Ancerviller, the first gas attack the 166th had experienced. Moffett was unsure of the number of men injured by the gas, but

Private Robert Thorn (far right), a young hotel clerk from Marysville and a member of E Company. (*Author's Collection*)

he estimated about 150 men were affected. Also, he heard that two YMCA workers who were trying to assist those wounded by the gas were killed in the attack. Moffett also wrote that two German planes were downed nearby, one at Reherrey and the other at Montigny. "One plane was ablaze as it came down," he wrote in his diary, "and one of the Germans was burned to a crisp. The other fellow leaped from the burning machine to his death, a distance of about 500 ft. One of the occupants of the other machine was still alive when their plane was brought down and had been a resident at one time in the U.S. He asked for a chew of tobacco. He was badly hurt, though."[83]

On the night of June 2, E Company and the 2nd Battalion were back in the trenches, and another large patrol was sent into no man's land. This patrol consisted of thirty privates, six corporals, and three sergeants led by Lieutenant Fred Flick. Once again, the objective was to penetrate

Hameau d' Ancervillers and take prisoners. However, this patrol would go badly, and E Company would suffer its first losses in combat. About an hour after the patrol moved out of the trenches, they ran into a German patrol numbering over eighty men. Both sides immediately sighted one another and opened fire. Flick attempted to flank the enemy, but their superiority in numbers prevented him and his men from doing so, and he was forced to fall back to friendly lines. Eight of Flick's men were seriously wounded, and one, Corporal Ralph Berger, twenty-one years old from Marysville, had to be left behind in no man's land. He was initially listed as missing, but he was never heard from again and was officially listed as killed in action on June 2, 1918. Another man, Private Mack Winget, eighteen years old from Marysville, was hit in the chest, with the bullet going through his lungs. He died the next day in the hospital at Baccarat.[84]

On June 3, Private Winget was buried at Baccarat, and Dana Daniels was one of his pallbearers. He later wrote, ". . . all of our boys died men, and they died for the right of all humanity which we stand for. . . . It was a hard thing for us to do because it was just like losing a brother, but I guess we will all have to be prepared for still more sacrifices, I know all the boys are ready for what is next, no matter what it may be."[85]

A few nights later, on June 5, the Germans attempted the first direct assault the 166th had experienced. It began with an enemy artillery barrage along the entire 42nd Division's front but soon concentrated on the 166th at CR Ancerviller. The 1st Battalion was in the line that night and had sent two patrols out into no man's land before the German barrage began. One of the patrols was from A Company under Lieutenant Aubrey DeLacy, twenty-six years old from New York City, and Lieutenant Charles Baskerville, thirty-one years old and also from New York City.[86] Both of these men were from the "Sears and Roebuck Officers" group the men had complained about at Camp Mills but seemed to have overcome that stigma.

As American artillery began to respond to the German fire, DeLacy noticed a large group of German infantrymen moving out from their trenches in what was undoubtedly a significant attack on the regiment's lines. He immediately sent a runner back to CR Ancerviller with a message to lay down artillery fire forward of his position to counter the enemy assault. DeLacy and Baskerville had their men take cover and remain in place while the American artillery fire blasted the German infantry, preventing them from making their attack. However, other German units

Men from the 166th Infantry on the streets of Bénaménil, a village in the Lunéville Sector, March 1918. (*National Archives*)

also made attempts to reach the trenches at CR Ancerviller but were cut down by the regiment's rifle and machine gun fire.[87]

Finally, on the night of June 18-19, the French 61st Division and the American 77th Division relieved the regiment and the entire 42nd Division. But the relief took place amid a heavy German artillery barrage and gas attack that lasted for much of the following day. L Company alone had forty-one casualties with thirty-seven injured by gas, three wounded by shrapnel, and one killed, the first combat death in the company. As the shelling spilled over into the village of Ancerviller, the few remaining civilians tried to take cover. In one house where an elderly couple lived with their granddaughter, a German shell came through the roof, setting the house on fire and causing the old woman of the house to die "of shell shock and fright." Men from the 166th put the fire out and managed to save what was left of the family's furniture.[88]

The entire regiment would move to Moriville, Rehaincourt, and Menil for what was supposed to be a rest after 120 days at the front. However, once again, the rest was not to be. In less than forty-eight hours after pulling out of the Baccarat Sector, the 166th received orders to march to Chatel-sur-Moselle on June 23, where they would board trains for an unknown destination.[89]

What the men of the 166th Infantry did not know was that, with this move to a new location, the nature of their part in the war would change forever. They had proven themselves in Lunéville and Baccarat, but now much more would be asked of them. The trench warfare routine of those two quiet sectors where they conducted nighttime patrols, dodged artillery shells, and fought the rats and mud was ending. Now, the regiment was moving 130 miles to the west across France to become part of what the men called the "Big Show."

Guardians of the Pass— The Champagne Defensive

"Your men are like steel, God bless them!"—Lieutenant Colonel Pean, commander, French 17th Infantry Regiment, speaking of the 3rd Battalion, 166th Infantry Regiment, July 19, 1918

On the afternoon of July 14, Lieutenant Clyde Vaughn arrived with his men from I Company at their assigned position in a small trench on the plains north of Ain Creek in the Champagne sector of the Marne. The ground in the trench had a chalk-like color and consistency, and, within minutes of beginning their work to prepare their position, everyone was covered in fine, white dust. Their trench was about a mile forward of the main defensive line, what was being called the intermediate line, where the rest of the 3rd Battalion was dug in.

Vaughn was a twenty-three-year-old schoolteacher from Liberty Hill, Texas, who had joined the regiment at Camp Mills. He and the small detachment of twenty-five men he commanded this day had all volunteered because their assignment demanded that only volunteers be used. His company commander, Captain Henry Grave, had told him he and his men were to fight a "delaying action until either annihilated or captured."[1] The upper command echelons were calling these positions "sacrifice posts," which seemed terribly appropriate.

They would be the first line in what General Gouraud, commander of the French 4th Army, referred to as a defense in depth. Gouraud had or-

dered the main line of trenches two miles north of Vaughn's position to
be abandoned so that the expected enemy artillery barrage would fall on
empty positions. Once the German infantry discovered there was no one
there to oppose them, they would move on, and the sacrifice posts would
be the first real opposition they would encounter. Vaughn was to send up
red flares when he saw the Germans coming and then open fire with his
detachment's rifles, machine guns, automatic rifles, and a single anti-tank
gun. The idea was for him and his men to break up and slow the German
advance, even though they would almost certainly be overwhelmed and
"submerged by it—just as the rocks break up the advancing wave."[2] If
they could do enough damage, perhaps the Germans would be unable to
strike a fatal blow against the primary defense in the intermediate positions.

As night fell, Vaughn's team had dug in and was as ready as they could
be. Later that night, he received word that the German infantry attack
would start around 4:00 a.m. the next morning and that American and
French artillery would open fire on the German lines at 11:45 p.m. So,
the young lieutenant and his men settled down for the night, waited anxiously for their part in the "Big Show" to begin, and wondered if this
evening's sunset would be the last one that they would see.

THE 166TH INFANTRY boarded their trains at Chatel-sur-Moselle on the
afternoon of June 23. Once again traveling by side-door Pullmans rather
than the hated small French boxcars, the train passed through Lunéville,
Nancy, Toul, Bar-le-Duc, and Neufchâteau before the regiment arrived at
Vitry-le-Francois in the Marne River Valley the next day. The troops disembarked and began marching toward the villages of Pogney,
Francheville, and Vesigneul near the critical French city of Châlons.
Colonel Hough set up his headquarters in Pogney, and the battalions
spread out to the other villages. Unlike the small villages near Morlaincourt, Rolampont, Lunéville, and Baccarat, these were described as "clean
and comfortable."[3]

The weather was warm and sunny—so pleasant one would not have
thought there was a war raging just a few miles away. Leon Miesse even
found time for a swim in the Marne Canal.[4] Despite years of war, the
Marne River Valley remained relatively unscarred. It was here that Marshal Joffre turned back the first great German offensive of the war in September 1914. However, since then, it had been relatively quiet. One British

soldier wrote that the area presented "a pleasant well cultivated scene, unmarred by the shell holes, trenches, and barbed wire to which we had become so accustomed on the static front."[5]

The region was characterized by five rivers: the Aisne, the Vesle, the Ardre, the Ourcq, and the Marne. All these rivers flowed east to west except for the Ardre, which ran northwest into the Vesle. However, most Americans would not have considered these to actually be rivers but, rather, just large creeks. Still, the rivers presented advantages to any defender in that their banks often rose as high as two hundred feet, with those along the Aisne even higher. Further, these rivers produced marshy flats that would slow the movement of vehicles and artillery.[6]

The Marne also was home to dense forests, as well as large grain fields, filled mostly with tall corn and wheat. The latter provided what General John Pershing later called "excellent cover" for infantry and machine gunners.[7] In the coming months, all these geographic factors would lead to warfare in the open, unconstrained by trenches and no man's land.

The regiment was able to enjoy its new billets for only four days because, at 6:00 p.m. on June 28, orders were received to leave that night on a march through Châlons to the French training area at Camp de Châlons. Colonel Hough called out the regiment, and by 7:30 p.m., the men were on the road. The hike proved to be a daunting one. The march was slow due to frequent stops caused by trains and trucks, making the hike more exhausting than otherwise might have been the case. Dana Daniels remarked that it "was the worst hike on the men up to this time."[8]

The regiment passed through Châlons about 2:00 a.m. after a hike of seventeen miles as men began to drop out of the line of march. They finally arrived at the villages of St. Hilaire-au-Temple, St. Étienne, and Dompierre around 6:30 p.m., where they camped for the night.[9] Here, they awaited orders, which were not long in coming, because the Germans were planning a major attack.

Starting on March 21, 1918, the Germans had conducted a series of four major offensives. The first had been named Operation Michael. It lasted fifteen days and was the most successful of the four. In it, the Germans attacked a thinly held area in the Somme using seventy-two divisions, driving the British back more than twenty-five miles across a fifty-mile-wide front. The British and the Germans each suffered more than two hundred thousand casualties.[10]

Next came Operation Georgette on April 9. This attack sought to weaken the British before a third attack was launched on the channel ports. In this offensive, the Germans advanced only five miles in the area around Armentières, while both sides each lost approximately one hundred ten thousand men. The third offensive, Operation Blücher-Yorck, came in late May and was mounted against both the British and French lines on the Chemin des Dames. It penetrated deep into the Marne Valley, causing panic in Paris and creating a large salient that penetrated twenty-five miles into the Allied lines. This time, each side lost about one hundred thirty thousand men.[11]

The fourth offensive, dubbed Operation Gneisenau, came in early June. The Germans attempted to enlarge the Marne salient but had minimal success due to a lack of German reserves and a stubborn defense by the French.[12]

That lack of progress in June's offensive led to General Ludendorff planning a fifth offensive, which he called Operation Friedensturm or the "Peace Offensive." Ludendorff gave it that name because the objective was to envelop and capture the ancient French city of Reims, threaten Paris, and inflict such severe losses on French forces that they would be forced to propose peace negotiations. The target would be French forces in Champagne, and this time, German planning and preparation would be meticulous. Three German armies totaling fifty-two divisions spent more than five weeks getting ready for what would be an attack across a thirty-five-mile front.[13]

Ludendorff's plan was to assemble five hundred thousand men backed by thousands of artillery pieces. He expected the forces of the French 4th Army under General Henri Gouraud, which numbered less that one hundred thousand men, to be swept away. This was probably sound thinking by Ludendorff since, along the front lines east of Reims, Gouraud had only forty thousand men to face Ludendorff's three hundred thousand.[14]

On July 3, the 166th received orders to take positions along the line in an area called Sector Esperance, about twenty-two miles northeast of Châlons. On July 4, the men marched forward to the Bois des Echelons and the Bois de Lyre just to the rear of the defensive positions. That night, they moved again into three defensive subsectors named Alger, Nancy, and Niger.[15] From here, the regiment would redeploy over the next eight days to form part of General Gouraud's concept for a defense in depth.

The main French defenses had been in a line of trenches near the Py River about four miles forward of Sector Nancy. Clearly, any German of-

Dugout used by the 166th Infantry at Champagne. (*National Archives*)

fensive would focus on these trenches, likely subjecting them to a massive artillery barrage using both high explosive and gas shells, followed by an assault using thousands of German infantrymen. Therefore, Gouraud proposed to let this massive German blow fall on empty trenches. He planned to order his men to quietly withdraw at the last moment to a second line, called the intermediate line, and a third defensive line, which included the positions now occupied by the 166th. Once the Germans found the first line of trenches empty and pressed their attack across the two miles of open ground toward the intermediate line, Gouraud would strike them with massive barrages of Allied artillery.[16]

The final element of the French general's defense in depth would be the establishment of signal posts about a mile forward of the intermediate line. The men stationed at these positions would signal when the Germans began to move forward and then hold their positions until killed or captured, inflicting whatever damage they could on the advancing hordes of German infantry.[17]

On the night of July 7-8, the 166th began to deploy its battalions as part of Gouraud's plan, a deployment which they completed by July 12.[18] The 3rd Battalion under Captain Robert Haubrich was sent forward to dig in along the intermediate line. Haubrich, a married forty-year-old machinist and father of four from Columbus, was born in Biersdorf, Prussia, and immigrated to the United States in 1881. As a result, he spoke fluent German. He had joined the regiment in 1899 as a private and had steadily risen in rank to captain and command of the 3rd Battalion.[19]

View of the terrain defended by the 166th Infantry at Champagne. (*National Archives*)

Meanwhile, the 1st Battalion remained at subsectors Nancy and Alger. The 2nd Battalion was sent to the third line of trenches in the rear where their job would be to carry ammunition and supplies to the forward positions and act as a reserve.[20]

Along the crucial intermediate defensive line, Gouraud deployed the 2nd and 3rd Battalions of New York's 165th Infantry on the far left and the 2nd Battalions of both Alabama's 167th Infantry and Iowa's 168th Infantry on the extreme right.[21] In the middle was the 3rd Battalion of the 166th. Captain Haubrich sent K Company to the extreme left of his line with I Company and M Company to their right. For the sacrifice post, Haubrich selected I Company, and he told the company commander, Captain Henry Grave, to ask for twenty-five volunteers as well as an officer to command. Lieutenant Clyde Vaughn stepped forward to lead the detachment, as did the twenty-five soldiers needed to cover the position and its supporting anti-tank gun.[22] Vaughn and his men were to await orders to move out, which were expected to come as soon as Gouraud was sure the enemy attack was imminent. As the men of the 3rd Battalion took their places along the intermediate line, they did not know that not only was that attack coming very soon but that they would receive what Colonel Hough later called "the full shock of the attack."[23] As it happened, the intermediate defensive line ran along the ancient Roman road to Chalons-sur-Marne, which inspired Major Tompkins to later write that the men deployed there were "the guardians of the pass."[24]

As the battalions took their positions and awaited the coming assault, they repaired trenches, laid down sandbags, and stocked large supplies of ammunition. Every night the ration carts would make their way forward, ensuring the men had food and water. About midnight each night the regiment would receive an "alerte" or "stand to" order that directed them to their stations where they would watch for any enemy activity. When the sun came up, they would stand down and try to sleep in the blazing heat. Raymond Cheseldine described the scene: "The chalk plains glared white in the blazing sun, their baldness relieved here and there by the red of the poppy and the blue of the corn flowers."[25]

When the 3rd Battalion first moved to its place on the intermediate line, Captain Haubrich met with Lieutenant Colonel Pean and Major Goune from the French 17th Infantry, who had overall command. Neither Haubrich nor his officers could speak any French, and neither of the French officers spoke English. Luckily, both Major Goune and Captain Haubrich spoke German, so, ironically, the meeting was conducted using the enemy's language to translate the proceedings.[26]

Haubrich later said that the two Frenchmen were tough, "hard-boiled" regulars. Their uniforms were covered with ribbons and were immaculate down to the shine on their boots. Haubrich and his officers, meanwhile, were unshaven and wore uniforms still dirty and muddy from more than one hundred days in the trenches at Lunéville and Baccarat. Not surprisingly, Lieutenant Colonel Pean seemed to take notice of this, and he looked at the Ohioans with obvious disgust. Pean then turned to Major Goune and said, "Major Goune, ask Captain Haubrich if his men are good fighting soldiers." Goune translated Pean's question for Haubrich who, at first, was more than a little insulted. But before replying, he allowed his sense of humor to frame his response. Realizing that Pean likely was asking this question based on he and his men's disheveled appearance, Haubrich told Goune in German, "Tell the Colonel, that my battalion is one of the best battalions in the best damned regiment in Europe, bar none!" As Goune quickly translated the remark, Pean's face broke out in a broad smile, and he replied, "Ah, is it so? C'est tres bien, tres bien."[27]

Meanwhile, Private Enoch Williams had his own opinion about the regiment's fighting abilities. "Our division was praised by a French general for their coolness and fighting spirit," he wrote his mother on July 9. "It isn't fighting spirit, it's just 'I don't give a damn' spirit. For we were in the lines for a couple of months and, then when we moved, we just moved to another front."[28]

Unknown to Captain Haubrich or anyone else in the 166th, neither Lieutenant Colonel Pean or even General Gouraud expected these untried Americans to actually hold the intermediate line. That was one reason why they prepared a second line where the 1st Battalion was stationed, a line that some referred to as "the real line of defense." Behind the third and final defensive line were hundreds of shelters containing animals and wagons with huge stockpiles of ammunition and other supplies nearby. There were also hundreds of American and French artillery batteries, all camouflaged in groves of trees where the crews slept next to their guns at night. Farther back of the line was a third line where reserves, such as the regiment's 2nd Battalion, awaited any German breakthrough. In total, it was an impressive defensive position. Colonel Hough noted that there were really "seven distinct lines of resistance (infantry) in the formation," while another officer stated his opinion on the German prospects for success by saying, "Even had each man been mounted on a motorcycle, not one could have passed through our line." [29]

As the men of the 166th waited for the coming attack, Captain Haubrich issued a bulletin to the soldiers of the 3rd Battalion communicating how critical the coming battle would be and the importance of their role along the intermediate line:

> The Third Battalion, 166th Infantry, has been put at the disposal of the Commanding Officer, 17th R. I. [Regiment of Infantry] French; and it is needless for us to say that we will do our best to defend the ground assigned to us; and that we will fight shoulder to shoulder with our French comrades to the last. We wish to impress on all that this may be the most serious part of this war for us, and our sacrifices may be great, but God grant we will be the victors.
>
> Let us keep up the reputation of the Rainbow Division, the 166th Infantry, and especially the Third Battalion, 166th Infantry. We are sure our French comrades are with us, and we are sure we will stick with them; there is no backing, it's stand-fast, and kill the Boche as they may come.
>
> We are fortunate to be assigned to the 17th R. I. as all indications point to the fact that they are an excellent regiment, and although we are comparatively new at this game, let us try to be as good as they.
>
> Our sacrifices will help win the war.[30]

IT HAD BEEN DECIDED that, once the Allies had indisputable evidence that the German offensive was imminent, an alert would be issued to all commands by transmitting the code phrase "Francois 570." While American and French aerial reconnaissance revealed the massive buildup of German forces that portended the coming attack, there still was no definitive intelligence as to its timing. Then, on the night of July 13-14, that all changed.

First, in the evening hours of July 13, a solitary German officer crossed the Py River to scout the French positions he and his men would soon be assaulting. He found them quickly, but unfortunately for this German officer, the skeleton crew of French soldiers still guarding the lines also found him. They took him prisoner before he could cross the river back to German lines and discovered that the officer had foolishly carried a complete copy of the German attack orders with him.

Then, while the French were interpreting and breaking down the information in the orders, five French soldiers led by a daring young lieutenant staged their own raid across the Py. They managed to capture twenty-seven German soldiers, including an officer who told his interrogators the exact time for the German artillery barrage and subsequent infantry attack down to the minute. As a result, the Allies now knew that the enemy artillery would open fire at 12:10 a.m. on July 15 and that their infantry would cross the Py at 4:00 a.m.[31]

The information these German prisoners had provided was sent up the chain of command to be analyzed and evaluated. While that was happening, on the afternoon of July 14, General Gouraud held a Bastille Day dinner at Colonel Hough's dugout. The champagne flowed, and the conversation was free and easy. Suddenly, the telephone rang. As Colonel Hough's operator took the call and copied down a coded message from Division Headquarters, the room became silent. The operator verified the message, and the caller at the far end said, "Good luck." Then, turning to the rest of the men in the room, the operator repeated the message: "Francois 570." With that, the men in the dugout scrambled out the door to get back to their units.[32]

After the message was sent down to the Regimental Headquarters, the word began to filter to the men in the forward positions. Leon Miesse was having a relatively quiet day at L Company's position on the intermediate line. His biggest concern was the health of the company commander, Captain Otto Kindler. Kindler was not well, and despite Miesse's plea that the

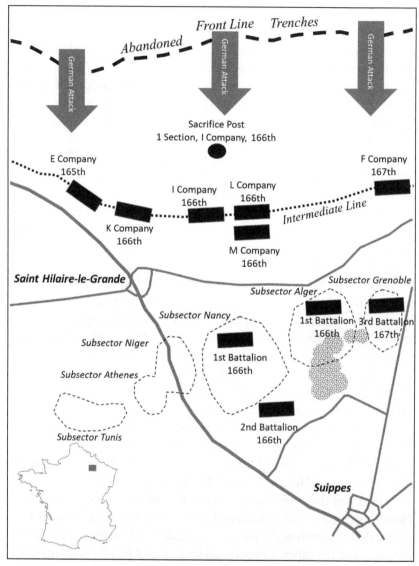

Positions manned by the 166th Infantry at Champagne. (*Author*)

captain report to the hospital, Kindler would not go. Finally, Kindler agreed to go to a dugout just at the rear of the line. Then, at 11:00 p.m., Miesse and the other officers in the company learned of the imminent attack and its timing.[33]

In response to the new intelligence, General Gouraud not only alerted his command but also ordered American and French artillery to open a massive barrage on the German positions starting at 11:45 p.m., twenty-five minutes before the planned German bombardment.[34] Gouraud hoped this barrage would not only do damage to the assembling German infantry but also sow confusion among both the German soldiers and their commanders.

As the clock ticked toward midnight, the men of the regiment waited in anticipation for the Allied artillery barrage to begin. At precisely 11:45 p.m., the guns opened fire. The Ohioans had heard their own artillery fire many times since they entered the trenches in February, but nothing prepared them for this barrage. The crash of the massed guns "fairly lifted men from their feet."[35] Thousands of guns that had been silent and hidden now roared to life, belching flame. The dark night was suddenly illuminated as the guns "fired with an intensity that caused the atmosphere to shake with a constant rolling, unbroken sound."[36]

The roaring symphony the artillery produced was a mix of the deep blasts from the heavy guns, sharper detonations from the middle calibers, and a constant bark from the 75mm cannon. The symphony was endless, shaking the air with the swishing sound of the departing shells. Major Wolf remembered it as "a hellish music."[37] The light from the gun flashes caused the stars to disappear from sight as the deadly projectiles arced through the night sky toward the men and artillery of the kaiser's army.

Across the Py, a German infantry regiment commander named Kurt Hesse was napping in a shell hole behind the German lines after completing his unit's final preparations for the coming advance. Suddenly, he awakened to the sound of heavy artillery fire. He quickly glanced at his watch and saw that it was not yet time for the German barrage to begin. He thought perhaps they had made a mistake. But when he jumped out of the shell hole and looked around, he saw that shells were falling everywhere around him—the French and the Americans had opened fire first. He ran to his dugout to contact his battalion commanders but discovered the Allied artillery fire had cut his telephone lines. He darted out to check on his men and found that the incoming artillery was focusing on railroad crossings and crucial road junctures, anywhere the Germans might assemble their infantry. The intense and accurate concentration of the Allied shells caused mass confusion on the roads where German infantry were trying to move forward to their jumping-off points. When Hesse got to his battalions along the first line, he found his positions littered with hundreds of dead and wounded and discovered that two of his battalions had been severely mauled by the shelling.[38] The initial phase of General Gouraud's defensive plan was working to perfection.

A few minutes later, the German guns opened fire as scheduled at 12:10 a.m. Their barrage was even more hellish than the one unleashed by the French and Americans. The Germans had almost seven hundred more field artillery pieces than the Allies and two hundred more heavy guns with a total of more than two thousand guns covering the Marne salient.[39] As their shells began to rain destruction down on the Allied lines, rockets and flares of all colors rose into the skies from the German lines, seemingly turning darkness into day with "blinding and wavering plans of light" so bright one could read as though it were noon and not a little after midnight.[40]

The sound of shells shrieking both ways in the sky filled the night, and the German superiority in guns was soon horribly apparent to everyone in the 166th. The men could see flashes of light and geysers of smoke that indicated every shell's impact with the earth, and soon the air was filled with smoke and clouds of the powdery chalk from the soil in the Champagne plains. Some of the regiment's ammunition dumps exploded with ferocity while supplies caught fire and burned in great flaming pyres. Barracks and huts also burned brightly. As ration carts and wagons were destroyed by the exploding shells, their mules ran in every direction seeking safety from this man-made hell, but many ended up screaming in agony as they fell from horrific wounds.

When the initial warning of the attack arrived, Colonel Hough immediately ordered the Supply Company to swing into action. The company responded as they always seemed to do, sending ration carts forward to supply the kitchens at the trenches. Also, extra wagons carrying ammunition quickly started toward the lines, and a continuous process of shuttling critical supplies began. Throughout the German bombardment that night, the carts and wagons continued to move up and down the roads leading to the front despite the intense enemy shelling. One man was killed when he was hit by shrapnel while driving his wagon, and seven others were wounded. When one of the Muleskinners was hit, Wilbur Jones, a seventeen-year-old private from Cincinnati, leaped down from his cart, lifted the wounded man into his cart, and took him back to the field hospital before turning about and heading back to the lines with the rations in his cart.[41]

The regiment's men from the sacrifice post to the third line of defense also felt the onslaught of the German guns. H Company, which waited in the last line, was hit particularly hard. The men lay down as flat as they could in the shallow ditches they had managed to dig as the "deadly H.E.'s" crashed all around them. The shells were set with instantaneous fuses that exploded on contact, and Lieutenant Everett Brown said they swept "everything above ground with a veritable hail of jagged fragments."[42]

In a letter written a few days later, Raymond Cheseldine wrote, "A perfect night, and then the sky lighted by countless flares, the air full of shrieking shells and bursting shrapnel, the atmosphere choked with powder smoke and gas, the earth torn into bits by great explosives—the calls of men, the rattle of wagons, the shrieks and cries of horses and mules, the whirr and thrum of airplanes—never can I forget it if I live forever."[43]

The shelling continued nonstop for four hours. Major Wolf recalled the "transformation that these minutes worked is beyond the conception of the single mind. Along the roads, ammunition boxes were tumbled in irregular piles, men lay dismembered. Animals lay across the trails, and most important roads passed over and plowed through by the hard-ribbon caisson and ammunition columns."[44] When the guns finally paused, on came the first waves of gray-clad German infantry.

Despite the Allied shelling, the German infantry had eventually made it to their jumping-off points. The first wave included six first-class divisions, a Guard Cavalry Division along with the 2nd, 88th, 1st, 5th, and the 7th Bavarian Divisions. They had only recently returned to the front after two weeks of rest in the rear. Three divisions made the attack on the French in the center, and two assaulted the positions manned by Alabama's 167th and Iowa's 168th, while one full division made its way against the 166th and New York's 165th.[45]

The Germans quickly crossed the Py River and charged what they thought was the first line of defense, only to find the trenches that had been battered by their artillery to be empty. Despite their surprise, they overcame their initial confusion and reorganized to press on with the attack. As they climbed out of the old French trenches and began to advance through the tangles of wire blocking the open ground to the rear, Lieutenant Vaughn and the men in the sacrifice post saw them coming and fired red flares into the air, signaling the other men from 3rd Battalion in the intermediate line of defense that the Germans were on their way.

Almost immediately, the line of 75mm guns stationed directly behind the intermediate line opened a brisk, practically continuous fire at what was a virtually point-blank range for the artillery.[46] As the first of the American and French shells arrived amidst the surging German infantry, they were hit by a withering blast of small arms fire from the sacrifice post and the intermediate line behind it.

Of course, Lieutenant Vaughn and his men were the first defense the Germans had to overcome. This small detachment fought furiously, sweeping the enemy infantry with automatic rifle and machine gun fire while blasting their advancing lines with their anti-tank gun. The firing from these twenty-six men was so intense that it staggered the first wave of German shock troops, forcing them to stop, reorganize, and lay down covering fire for their own men who now advanced only a few yards at a time. Eventually, numbers and superior firepower would prove too much for Vaughn and his men. Every man in the sacrifice post was either killed or wounded before the survivors ran out of ammunition. Vaughn himself was hit in the face by a German bullet that tore away part of his jaw and chin. The Germans took the survivors prisoner, but Vaughn and his detachment had managed to hold up the German assault on the intermediate line until almost 8:00 a.m. while killing hundreds of the enemy whose bodies were stacked in piles in front of the sacrifice post.[47] More importantly, the time Vaughn and his men bought the 166th meant that the enemy would have to continue their attack against the intermediate line in broad daylight.

Despite the terrible beating they took from the combined artillery and small arms fire, the German infantry pressed the attack forward toward the intermediate line. Raymond Cheseldine would later describe the attack by saying, "Doggedly, and bravely, he came on! Behind him, thousands pushing forward. No man could turn back. On they came, and in spite of all that were killed, their bodies piled before the American wire, thousands more were there to take the places of the dead. It was impossible to kill them all, and some gained a foothold in the trenches."[48]

The Germans had begun a rolling barrage at 4:15 a.m. that focused its shells on an area less than two miles in depth around the 166th's intermediate positions and the second defensive line at Subsector Nancy and Alger. The intense artillery fire was "designed to obliterate the garrison and, so far as the few survivors were concerned, to shake their nerves asunder."[49]

The fighting at the intermediate line was bitter and violent, as the four companies of the 3rd Battalion tried desperately to hold their ground against the overwhelming waves of German infantry. On the far left of the regiment's intermediate line positions, K Company occupied a post with good trenches and well-placed machine gun and automatic rifle emplacements. The company was now commanded by Captain Orestes Hardway, a forty-one-year-old farmer and father of two from Union, Ohio. Hardway had enlisted in the regiment in 1898, served in Cuba during the Spanish-American War, and risen steadily in rank to be a company commander.[50] One of Hardway's problems was the twenty-two replacements he received just one night before the German offensive began. All of them were recent draftees, most had been in the army less than thirty days, in France less than nine, and three of them had never fired their Springfield rifles.[51]

Hardway's men crouched low in their trenches as the initial artillery barrage pounded their position. Hardway later said, "All we could do was watch and wait—wait for daybreak when we knew the enemy infantry would appear." His men gripped their rifles a little tighter "as they hugged the forward side of the trench and peered over the parapet." The men assigned to throw grenades made sure their small bombs were placed conveniently nearby, and those with automatic rifles "looked their weapons over and made sure that sufficient loaded clips were at hand." Some of the men tried humor with a little bravado thrown in, attempting to calm their buddy's nerves. One man said, "Come on, Jerry and let's get it over with; I'm sleepy!" Another chimed in, "If you won't believe our artillery, try us, we'll convince you!"[52]

As the men of K Company waited for the German infantry to make their approach, Hardway saw a party of men approaching the trenches from the rear. It turned out to be Supply Sergeant George Havens and Mess Sergeant William Keefe, who was leading a small band of mechanics, cooks, and kitchen police. When someone asked them what "in the hell" they were doing there, Havens told them there was a standing order for all mechanics, cooks, and kitchen police to move forward in case of attack and take their places on the defensive line. Havens looked at Hardway and asked him where he wanted them to go, and the captain assigned them their positions as riflemen.[53]

When daybreak came, and the Germans had subdued Vaughn and his men at the sacrifice post, small groups of enemy infantry appeared through the dust and smoke on the skyline of the small ridge to the company's front. They saw one of their officers give a signal, and the groups began to tactically deploy. Unfortunately for the Germans, machine gun fire had disrupted their advance, leaving them at least a half-mile behind their rolling barrage. This, in turn, allowed K Company to mount a defense without having to deal with enemy artillery fire. A few of the German tactical groups advanced through boyaus that led from the forward observation line to the main trenches of K Company's position. One of these groups had donned French overcoats and helmets. Sergeant Evans noticed them coming, and, at first, he thought they were French soldiers. Then he recalled that all the French troops to their front had been assigned to the sacrifice posts from which they were ordered not to retreat. Therefore, they had no business being in the boyaus. He ordered his men to open fire with everything they had, and only a few of the disguised Germans escaped.[54]

The rest of the German infantry advanced carefully toward the tangles of barbed wire in front of K Company's trenches. Still, the doughboys proceeded to shoot slowly and calmly, picking off one German after another. As the enemy came closer, the pace of the American firing increased, decimating the enemy ranks as they neared the wire. Not a single German managed to cross the wire, and the waves of enemy infantry "again and again broke and retreated in disorder, and the ground before the wire changed from the white of chalk dust to the gray of dead German soldiers."[55]

After the Germans fell back, Hayward took stock of his losses. His company had suffered thirty-three casualties. Tragically, over half of those killed were the new, untrained replacements who had just arrived. Raymond Cheseldine would write that their deaths were "little short of murder."[56]

Meanwhile, on the far right of the regiment's line, L Company awaited their turn after the rolling barrage began around 8:00 a.m. Captain Kindler, who Leon Miesse had earlier convinced to remain in a dugout because of his poor health, had returned to his PC when the first artillery fire began. In L Company's sector of the line, the Germans added gas shells to the high explosives, and Kindler was almost overcome by the gas. Miesse could see that the captain's condition was rapidly deteriorating, and he urged him to go to the hospital in the rear. Kindler stubbornly refused, not wanting to leave his men. Miesse asked Lieutenant Harry Christopher to order Kindler to evacuate to the rear. Christopher, a twenty-seven-year-old Medical Corps officer from London, Ohio, was operating the first-aid station for K and I Companies. He came forward, examined Kindler, and immediately ordered him to the hospital, while Miesse assumed command of the company.[57]

When the German infantry attacked, the brunt of their assault came against L Company's left flank, where it connected with I Company. The platoon assigned there was composed of men from Lancaster, Ohio, commanded by Lieutenant John Early, known to everyone as "Jack." The dapper Early was a twenty-three-year-old from Wellesley, Massachusetts, and another of the "Sears and Roebuck officers" who joined the regiment at Camp Mills. Before the war he had risen from grocery clerk to be a buyer at a brokerage house where he "made much money, but lost more." He joined the Reserve Officer Training Corps and went to Plattsburgh, New York, for training in 1916. Alison Reppy would later write, "Jack's greatest quality is his ability to make any action he may want to take seem plausible. When occasion arises, he will argue that black is white, and if you do not watch your step, he will convince you that it is."[58] Clearly, however, Colonel Hough saw enough leadership qualities in Early to assign him to command a platoon.

Like K Company, L Company had also received a new supply of replacements and, again, just like K Company, very few of the new arrivals had received adequate training before being assigned to a front-line unit. In fact, of the thirty-three draftees who arrived right at L Company before the offensive, only ten even knew how to load their rifles. With these men in the line, L Company withstood seven German attacks between 8:00 a.m. and noon. At one point, a group of Germans approached Lieutenant Early's platoon wearing French Red Cross uniforms. Early called out to them in French, and one of them answered. However, the reply sounded very guttural, much more like German than French. Early ordered his men to open fire with rifles and machine guns, cutting the Germans down and leaving their bodies draped across the barbed wire.[59]

As the rest of the enemy infantry attacked in squad-size columns, Miesse's men picked them off by the dozens, firing so many rounds that their rifle barrels soon became extremely hot. Steadily the German ranks thinned as their dead piled higher and higher just beyond the wire. Then, suddenly, French artillery began to drop short, hitting L Company's positions. Miesse sent runners back to the artillery batteries in an attempt to get them to change the ranging on their guns. To their shock, they learned that the French were firing on them on purpose. Apparently the French were so sure that the 166th's positions would fall to the Germans, their artillery had been ordered to start shelling the intermediate line at a designated time. Luckily, when they learned that L Company had sent the Germans fleeing to the rear in disorder, they stopped firing at the American position.[60]

Leon Miesse recorded in his journal that night that he "had 7 killed and 21 wounded besides the ones which were gassed. The Boche were driven off in the first attack they made, a second attack which also failed. The first real war experience. . . . Captain was sent to hospital in afternoon. Boche made 7 attacks in 80 kilometers, 7 out of 7 which failed."[61]

However, as K and L Companies battled the Germans, the real brunt of the enemy attack hit I Company. The company was led by Captain Henry Grave, known throughout the regiment as "Hell Roarin' Henry." Grave was born in Germany in 1881 and lived in Columbus before the war. He was a big, powerfully built man with gray hair and a deep voice "like a foghorn." Raymond Cheseldine wrote that Grave was "feared, hated, and loved by every man in his company." [62]

With Lieutenant Vaughn and his detachment from I Company operating the sacrifice post, Grave had carefully deployed the remainder of his company. He placed 2nd Platoon under Lieutenant Christenson in the front trench with 4th Platoon under Lieutenant Joseph Smith in the support trench along with half of 3rd Platoon under Sergeant Gibson. Finally, 1st Platoon under Lieutenant Lippett manned the reserve trench. Grave placed his company headquarters with 4th Platoon in the support trench and deployed the company kitchen to the rear where M Company was positioned as a reserve. With Grave at the I Company PC was a French lieutenant who commanded a battery of three 75mm guns placed just behind the company's position.[63]

When the waves of German infantry descended on I Company, the men in the front trench took the full weight of the enemy assault. Grave reported that "Lt. Christenson handled his men in the same cool manner for which he was noted on the drill grounds," but the process of pushing the Germans back was "a close shave." At one point, Christenson had to leap up on a parapet and throw hand grenades at the Germans at point-blank range. His platoon "used every weapon issued to a platoon to perfection, rifle and hand grenades, automatic rifles, trench knives and on several occasions, the bayonet and pistol." Christenson was wounded twice, refusing to go to the rear until Grave ordered him to do so.[64]

As the Germans pressed their attack harder, things became so desperate that Grave pulled up all his reserves, and he feared they would not be enough. He requested reinforcements from Captain Haubrich at battalion headquarters. Haubrich sent a message via runner to Colonel Hough a little after 8:00 a.m. saying, "We are doing our best to hold out. I Co. is appealing for help, but we have none to give them."[65]

Throughout the attack on I Company, there were numerous examples of individual heroism. As the Germans appeared to be closing in and forcing their way into the front trench, seeing their approach and realizing his rifle was damaged, Fred Grumley, a twenty-three-year-old corporal from Columbus,[66] grabbed hand grenades, jumped up on the parapet, and hurled them "with deadly accuracy into the advancing ranks."[67]

Meanwhile Corporal Fred Umbaugh was employing his Chauchat automatic rifle to stop the enemy advance. Umbaugh was twenty-three years old and, like Captain Grave, was the son of German immigrants who lived in Columbus. He was assigned to cover a road and communication trench with his weapon and did so to great effect, forcing the Germans to retreat in disorder, "leaving their dead in piles and carrying away several wounded."[68]

Jollie Messer, a seventeen-year-old private from Ironton, Ohio, was assigned as a runner by Lieutenant Christenson. At the height of the fighting, Messer dashed into Captain Grave's PC with a message from Christenson requesting immediate reinforcements. As the captain read the lieutenant's urgent appeal, Messer staggered a bit, complaining about a "funny feeling like bees buzzing around" his head. He removed his helmet and found that a German bullet had gone completely through it, leaving a shallow furrow at the top of his skull.[69]

As the fight at the intermediate line continued, the 1st Battalion was subjected to tremendous artillery fire, even though they were in a reserve position. The men huddled in their trenches trying to get cover from the waves of shrapnel around them, and many were wounded. When one of the men in C Company was gravely wounded, stretcher-bearers went out amid the shelling to retrieve him, but both of the medical team were killed. On hearing this, Lieutenant James Moseley left his shelter to search for the wounded soldier. He found him almost four hundred yards away, and despite the intense shelling, Mosely carried him back to safety. Sadly, an explosion had severed the young man's leg, and he died a few moments after Mosely got him back to the field hospital.[70]

As the battle for I Company's position slackened around noon, Captain Grave assessed his company's situation. Their line's trenches and dugouts were "shot to pieces," and the position was in bad shape. Since he anticipated another attack, he had his men start repairs as best they could. In total, he found he had lost seventy-four men, including the twenty-six assigned to the sacrifice post.[71]

With a deep and justified sense of irritation, Grave later noted that the official records said I Company occupied a "supporting position." Grave stated that, while that might be true up to midnight on July 14, he desired to "state emphatically that we were very much the front line at daybreak, July 15th." Furthermore, Grave added with appropriate sarcasm that "the official reporter at my front was conspicuous by his absence, as we were left to shift for ourselves from midnight July 14th to 8 a.m., July 16th, when a French adjutant paid us a visit and insisted on our immediate repair work on trenches and dugouts, which resembled a plowed field about that time."[72]

After ten hours of battle, the German infantry attacks died out. Every assault on the 166th's positions had been repulsed with great loss by the Germans. Leon Miesse wrote his wife later, "From prisoners afterward, it was learned that they lost from 50 to 60 percent of their men and that one Division of the Boche, which was to make the attack was so cut up by our artillery that they had to be taken back and replaced by another Division before the attack started. . . . One of our men counted 150 [dead] in just a small place."[73] The enemy continued to fire artillery shells into the regiment's position, but what would be their last great offensive of the war had ended in disaster. However, the regiment's victory had come at a cost. The 166th reported suffering 326 men as killed, wounded, or captured in a single day of fighting, a total much larger than the 202 casualties they suffered during four months spent in the trenches at Lunéville and Baccarat.[74]

On the night of July 18-19, French troops advanced and relieved the 166th Infantry. Only the 3rd Battalion was delayed in departing their positions, but that came with a cost. The French were late arriving at the 3rd Battalion's line, and the men were forced to leave the trenches in daylight. German observation planes saw them marching in the open and called in artillery fire, which killed three men and wounded another eleven. A tired, dirty, hungry regiment went into camp near Cuperly that night.

Earlier that day, Captain Haubrich went to say goodbye to Lieutenant Colonel Pean, the French officer who had expressed his doubts about whether Haubrich and his men were up to the task of holding back the Germans. He found the colonel's opinion of his men had changed significantly. When Haubrich arrived, Pean took the captain's hand, while placing his left hand around Haubrich's neck. With tears running down his cheeks, the Frenchman said in a voice choked with emotion, "Your men are like steel, God bless them. Goodbye, my captain, and good luck." Later, Pean issued an Order of the Day that read:

Our brave friends of the 3rd Battalion of the 166th Regt. of the U. S. have received the order to leave us. They will go to do near others what they have done near us. With all our heart having admired them in battle and loved them as comrades and as true friends for all their good qualities, with all our heart we thank them. Our heart will be with them when they fight elsewhere; they take our regrets with them. We wish them good luck. Long live the battalion of Captain Haubrich.[75]

As events would later prove, the fight on the plains of Champagne marked a turning point in the war. The Germans had suffered tremendous losses while utterly failing to achieve their objectives. Reims remained in Allied hands, and Paris was safe from any German attack. The next step in the war would bring an end to fighting in the trenches and initiate something new in the war: offensive operations fought in the open. On July 22, the 166th entrained at St. Hilaire-au-Temple and headed for a new position north of Château-Thierry, where they would join the forces gathering for a great Allied offensive.[76]

As they would soon discover, however, this new phase of the war would come at an even higher cost.

Photo of Robert Thorn's post-war grave marker in the Oise-Aisne American Cemetery sent to his family by the American Red Cross (*Author's collection*)

6

The Ourcq—River of Death

"... on July 28th, they paid the price. Then gallant charges to come to grips had turned the wheat from yellow to red."
—Raymond Cheseldine, *Ohio in the Rainbow*

IT WAS ABOUT 4:00 p.m. when E Company began its advance. Their objective was the village of Seringes-et-Nesles, which sat on high ground just under two miles away. The first problem for Corporal Dana Daniels and the men in his squad was the Ourcq River, which stood between them and the town. American artillery began a brief barrage on Seringes-et-Nesles to cover the advance of E and F Companies of the 2nd Battalion down the gentle slopes south of the river. Once at the river's edge, they splashed into the hip-high water and made their way across, even though they were carrying full packs on their backs. After they waded across the Ourcq, they climbed up the steep bank on the far side and into open, flat ground. Daniels signaled to his men to advance to the position held at great cost by 1st Battalion for the last twenty-four hours. As the men moved across the little road that paralleled the river about three hundred yards away, the battered remnants of the 1st Battalion fell back and crossed the river. A few moments later, Daniels's squad and the rest of E and F Companies reached the 1st Battalion's old position, stopping in an orchard behind an old stone wall to rest for a few minutes, drop their packs, and prepare to advance with just their rations, ammunition, and weapons.

Daniels could see that F Company was ready on his left and that their commander, Captain Stevenson, was having a brief meeting with the E Company commander, Lieutenant Doellinger. The meeting ended and Doellinger returned, telling his platoon officers and sergeants to form a skirmish line with the 1st and 4th Platoons as the initial wave. The question was how this wave could best make the advance across open ground and a gradual hillside covered by wheat fields that stood between them and the village. The Germans had carefully placed hidden machine gun nests all across the ground to their front, and the chattering fire of their Maxim guns could already be heard along with the deadly "whiz, whiz, whiz" sound their rounds made as they swept through the air.

Doellinger and Captain Stevenson had recently learned from the experience of the 167th Infantry two days before at the Croix Rouge Farm. That fight had shown that a full, frontal assault against these German machine guns would lead to disaster. So, Daniels and the others were ordered to have their men advance by squads a few yards at a time. This meant that one squad would rush forward a short distance in one direction and then drop to take cover as the enemy machine guns opened fire on them. They would be followed by another squad that would make a quick dash forward in another direction before the enemy guns could shift and fire on them.

Daniels went to his squad and quickly explained the plan of attack. When the first men rose up to move out, they were met with more machine gun fire, and now German artillery fire was added to the mix. Everyone dropped to the ground as Daniels tried to determine the position of the nearest enemy machine gun emplacement, a real challenge given that they were hidden in waist-high wheat. While they were lying there, one of his men, a newly arrived draftee named Harry Bell from Brownsboro, Alabama, was hit in the leg, and Daniels sent him to the rear. About that time, Daniels was hit in the helmet by a round from an enemy machine gun, making a quarter-inch dent in the steel headgear. He decided to change tactics and only send one or two men forward at a time.

As the first couple of men began their rush forward, an unseen machine gun position opened fire at almost point-blank range from a position on the squad's right flank. Robert Thorn, the young hotel clerk from Marysville, was hit immediately and fell dead amid the stalks of wheat. He would be the first man in E Company killed in the attack[1] but, sadly, not the last.

Thorn was buried a few days later on a hillside about a mile to the northeast along with thousands of other members of the 42nd Division in a place that would eventually become the Oise-Aisne American Cemetery.

With the German defeat at Champagne, Marshal Foch began a general offensive designed to drive the Germans from the Marne salient with the hope of possibly cutting them off and destroying them. General Ludendorff could see what Foch was doing, and he was determined to conduct an orderly evacuation from the salient to save his armies. That meant falling back to a series of defensible positions and using terrain, artillery, and well-emplaced machine guns to slow the Allied advance.

The first Allied units to advance into the salient were the 1st and 2nd American Divisions and the French Moroccan Division south of Soissons and New England's 26th and Pennsylvania's 28th Divisions from the Marne at Château-Thierry. As these units pressed Ludendorff's armies, he did everything he could to shorten the line of retreat while maintaining an orderly process that would allow him to escape the salient with as many supplies as he could salvage. Therefore, he decided to employ every piece of artillery at his command, plus thousands of Maxim machine guns to fight a bloody delaying action.[2]

The 166th Infantry's train ride from Saint Hilaire-au-Temple lasted forty-eight hours. However, in normal circumstances, it should have only taken three hours to make the trip to their destination at La Ferté-sous-Jouarre near Château-Thierry. But the line had been cut in several places, so the trains were routed through Neufchâteau, Saint Dizier, to Meaux, and the outskirts of Paris. The regiment detrained at La Ferté-sous-Jouarre mid-morning on July 24 and began a seven-mile hike through Méry-sur-Marne and Nauteuil-sur-Marne to Crouttes-sur-Marne. This line of march took them along the Marne River, which they crossed twice on the way to Crouttes-sur-Marne. The summer weather was lovely, as was the scenery. This part of the Marne Valley was filled with lush green meadows and wheat fields, and one would not have known there was a war raging a short distance away. When the regiment arrived at their destination and was billeted, the men unslung their packs, stripped down, and dived into the waters of the Marne for the first real bath they had taken since arriving in France over eight months before.[3]

While this luxury likely buoyed many spirits, the fun and relaxation did not last long. That afternoon, Colonel Hough received orders from 83rd Brigade Headquarters to form the regiment at 7:30 a.m. the next morning and proceed through Château-Thierry and then move out onto the Soissons-Château-Thierry road where the regiment would receive further orders. The colonel apparently decided to wait as long as possible to interrupt the men's reverie because Leon Miesse recorded that he was not told about the orders until he was awakened at 4:00 a.m. on July 25 and told to get his company ready to move.[4] When the regiment arrived in the early afternoon, Hough was told that trucks would arrive shortly to take them to a point just south of Épieds, some five miles to the northeast of Château-Thierry. However, the trucks did not arrive until 4:00 p.m., and the congestion caused by men and vehicles made for a slow trip.[5]

Dana Daniels described the trip to Épieds in his diary, writing, ". . . we passed thru a country here that was badly torn up and had been hard fought for. Here is where we began to see the real horrors of war, dead horses, cattle, & dogs and a number of dead Germans lying on the battlefield." He recorded that the regiment passed through Château-Thierry about 7:00 p.m. where "barricades were still in the streets," and German weapons were scattered everywhere.[6]

Another soldier wrote about passing through Château-Thierry, saying the traffic was heavier than any he had seen, including New York City. "I never saw such traffic in any city," he wrote. "New York at its busiest corner could never produce the traffic that one corner of Château-Thierry had that day! Lines of motor trucks miles long, filled with men—miles and miles of big tractors pulling the big guns up—miles of wagon trains—miles of ammunition trains." At one point, all the roads into the town converged, and it took three military policemen to keep things moving. But, like Dana Daniels, he also noted the signs of destruction, which he called "ghastly." There were "ruined homes and "ruthless destruction" that left the town "a scene of desolation." "Household goods all over the streets," he wrote, "trees down, buildings torn to pieces, marks of rifle and machine gun bullets on everything, old barricades built in every alley and narrow street—everything pointing to a terrible struggle that ended with the hurried departure of the German army."[7]

The regiment was finally offloaded just outside Bézu-Saint-Germain, about two miles west of Épieds, and, as the rain began to fall, they marched through the forest of Bois de l'Hermitage where the men camped for the night.[8]

The move forward through Château-Thierry was not, however, without incident. Colonel Hough had ordered the Supply Company to take their wagons directly to the camping place in the Bois de l'Hermitage. Once there, they could set up their kitchens and prepare meals for the men who would be arriving that evening. But, when the wagon train reached La Gouttiere Ferme, which was selected as Supply Company Headquarters, several marauding German fighter aircraft saw the wagons on the road and swept down to strafe them with machine gun fire. The Muleskinners dove off their wagons and into the ditches by the road, where they stayed until French aircraft appeared and drove off the Germans. Luckily, no one was wounded, and no damage was done to the supply wagons.[9]

Following their performance at Champagne, the regiment and the entire division were starting to be seen as some of the best in the AEF. Besides the 1st Division, which was composed of Regular Army troops, the combat abilities of the first two National Guard Divisions, the 42nd and 26th, had improved to rival those of the professionals. Moreover, the divisions comprised mostly of draftees, what was called the National Army, were simply not ready to fight, and those that had been sent into combat had performed miserably. Therefore, the 166th and the other National Guard units would now get the tough assignments.

On July 26, the regiment was ordered to move up and relieve the French 170th Regimental Infantry, who were in reserve positions in the Bois de Beuvardelle Moucheton woods, and Bois de l'Hermitage. The next day at 3:15 p.m., the regiment advanced into the line as part of the 42nd Division's relief of the French 164th Division. The regiment's 1st Battalion marched along the Beauvardes-Preaux Farm road until it reached the northern edge of the Forêt-de-Fére around 10:00 p.m., with 2nd Battalion and 3rd Battalion forming lines behind them.[10] About three miles ahead at the foot of some gently sloping hills lay the Ourcq River, where Ludendorff's men had set up their next line of defense.

The area immediately around the Ourcq made for a natural defensive position, and the Germans, being the well-trained soldiers that they were, could see the value of the terrain to their delaying action. A high ridge extended from the Forêt-de-Ris onto high ground north of the Ourcq, and the headwaters of the Ourcq began at that point. The river runs north from there until it begins a gentle curve to the east until reaching the town of Fère-en-Tardenois, where it begins its course straight to the southeast. On July 27, when the 167th Infantry drove the Germans back from La

Croix Rouge Farm, located just under two miles southeast of Beuvardes, the Germans abandoned their line on the Forêt-de-Ris ridge and fell back to the high ground north of the Ourcq. From here, German observers could gain a clear view of any approaching attackers, rain down artillery fire on them, and position hundreds of machine guns in the wheat fields north of the river.[11]

From the south, what would be the 166th's side of the river, the ground sloped gently down to the river's edge. In the last two miles before reaching the river, there were no hollows, no natural features of any kind to provide cover against observation by the enemy, much less protection from artillery and machine gun fire. Therefore, when the regiment's men would be asked to attack across the river, the Germans would see them coming immediately and could begin mounting a defense long before they reached the riverbanks.[12]

RAYMOND CHESELDINE later wrote about the Ourcq River saying that, if you asked any man in the 1st or 2nd Battalion about crossing the river, they would probably say, "The river Ourcq? Oh, yes, that little creek, you mean? Say boy! That was Hell, gettin' across the place. There wasn't any river, just a little 'run,' but, brother, get me straight, Heinie sure made it hot there. He had everything on us. There wasn't a bridge in sight. All you could do was crawl along to the bank, jump up, into the mud and water and fall flat on the other side and dig in, boy, dig in!"[13]

Once the regiment's men reached the banks, the river itself was small by American standards and could be easily forded. The real problem was the terrain on the far side. From the river, the ground sloped upward and was covered by vast fields of wheat. To the right was the Meurcy Farm along a small creek called the Ru du Pont Brûle, while just over a mile to the northwest was the village of Seringes-et-Nesles, which sat atop the ridge and commanded the view over the Ourcq. To secure the area both Seringes-et-Nesles and the larger town of Fère-en-Tardenois to the west would have to be taken and held.

On the night of July 27-28, Colonel Hough received orders that were very disquieting at best. Brigade Headquarters wanted the regiment to begin an advance the next morning to the north. But, while the orders provided the locations of any Allied troops to be relieved, they gave only a very general idea of German positions, included almost no useful maps, and came with instructions to "leap-frog the French and take up the ad-

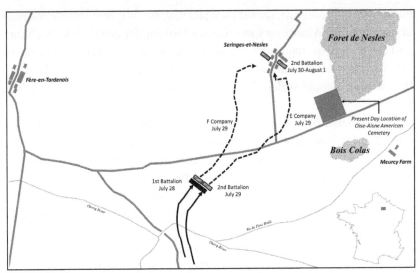

The attack across the Ourcq River to Seringes-et-Nesles. (*Author*)

vance."[14] Apparently, the idea was for the regiment to develop information about the enemy's positions by actually establishing and maintaining contact with them. Once the fighting started, the regiment was essentially on its own. Hough's officers and men would have to develop attack plans and tactics on the spot to press the Germans and hurry their continued retreat. It was a lot to ask of citizen-soldiers who had never been trained to undertake this sort of operation.

The move toward this uncertainty began in the dead of night on July 27 in a driving rainstorm. Company B of the 1st Battalion led the way and had halted at the edge of the Forêt-de-Fére. Unknown to them, the Germans had left a few soldiers behind to act as observers. Hidden in the dense woods, when they saw B Company moving forward, they called in artillery fire. Suddenly, the men of B Company heard the frightening shriek of enemy shells streaming toward them. Explosions happened everywhere because the Germans had used the forest to store their own supplies and ammunition a few days before, and every inch of the woods was carefully registered—they knew exactly where to place their shots.[15]

One of the first incoming shells exploded amid a group of soldiers, knocking one of them unconscious. When that soldier managed to shake off the buzzing in his skull, he stood up and found that he was uninjured. However, the other twenty-one men in his group had been killed by the blast. Another soldier, Sergeant Paul Jackson, showed remarkable courage and leadership. While everyone else was looking for cover, he took charge and led efforts to make sure the wounded were attended to and sent to the rear. His coolness under fire led to a battlefield commission. In total, the company would suffer 125 casualties and was unable to move an inch forward.[16]

Before dawn on July 28, the battle for the Ourcq River began. At 1:00 a.m., the 1st Battalion was ordered to advance down the slopes to the riverbank at 3:45 a.m., cross the river, and take the village of Seringes-et-Nesles on the heights above the river. The goal was to take and hold the town as well as the Forêt-de-Nesles just beyond it, allowing the New Yorkers of the 165th to take and hold the Meurcy Farm on the 166th's immediate right. Curiously, the orders said there would be no Allied artillery support. This proved to be costly because, as one soldier from the regiment said bitterly, "Only God can tell where those machine guns are located—and there isn't any artillery to drive them out!"[17]

One historian described the problem of countering the German machine guns along the Ourcq this way:

> The biggest tactical problem for the Allies involved locating and eliminating the deadly German machine gun nests. The Germans made excellent use of the rugged terrain to conceal their guns. They then waited until the Allies, often unaware of their presence, came into point-blank range. One British company lost all of its officers in less than thirty minutes when it walked into such an ambush. By the time small units recovered, found leadership from their NCOs, and called for support, the German gunners had often moved to another location in preparation for repeating the ambush somewhere else along the line. The Germans also used concealed machine guns in ways designed to exploit American inexperience. In their rush to move forward, the Americans often failed to "mop up" all positions before going on to the next line of enemy defenses. The Germans learned to hide machine guns in woods, in champagne cellars, and even in hastily dug underground bunkers, then wait for the American line to advance past their positions.[18]

The 1st Battalion was able to move down the slopes to the river without incident, but things changed as soon as they waded across the Ourcq. When the men emerged from the river and crawled up its banks, they were hit with withering machine gun fire from numerous hidden emplacements, as well as carefully placed German artillery fire. As the sun came up and the morning wore on, forward progress was measured in feet or even inches.

The C Company commander, Captain Oscar Koeppel, was hit in the back by a jagged piece of shrapnel from a shell that exploded just above him as he crawled across the open ground. The shrapnel almost severed his spinal cord, but Koeppel refused to leave his command until the new line was established. Finally, Private Harry Leonard was able to drag him back across the river to safety amid a rain of enemy artillery shells. Lieutenant Milton Latta from Goshen, Indiana, took command of C Company and tried to keep the men moving. But he soon discovered that one of the other platoon commanders, Lieutenant James Moseley, had been hit in the head by a machine gun bullet and killed, leaving only Latta and Lieutenant Sinclair Wilson plus Sergeant William Farrar in command. Between the three of them, they found there were only about fifty men alive and able to continue. With those fifty, they moved to their final position three hundred yards north of the river where they dug in. Meanwhile, two platoons from D Company made it as far as La Fontaine-sous-Pierre, about five hundred yards north of the river. But murderous machine gun and artillery fire forced them back to where the tattered remnants of C Company had finally dug in for the night.[19]

Their Machine Gun Company support was in similarly bad straits. They had lost three lieutenants and six sergeants in the fighting and continued to fight with one officer, Lieutenant Frank Radcliffe, who had just joined the company a week before and had no previous experience employing machine guns. But faithful to their task, his remaining sergeants came forward, took command of the company's three platoons, and continued the fight.[20]

As 1st Battalion held on for dear life, a French infantry unit managed to advance through the wheat fields toward the village of Fére-en-Tardenois, about a half-mile to the west of 1st Battalion's position. They were able to force the Germans out of the village, clearing the battalion's left flank. The Germans fell back to the crest of the ridge above the town and dug in. The French moved cautiously up the slopes of the ridge until they too were struck with heavy machine gun fire that drove them back to the east-west road leading from the village.[21]

The lack of Allied artillery support on July 28 allowed German artillery to operate without fear of counter-battery fire, and they made the most of it. Just like the positions in the Forêt-de-Fére, the Germans had care-

fully registered every road leading to the Ourcq River, making movement
by the regiment's Supply Company impossible during daylight. The only
option was to take food and water forward at night, an operation that
could be quite hazardous on unfamiliar roads using unreliable maps. But
the Supply Company did its best, as always. They sent ration carts carrying cooked food and water carts filled with hot coffee as far forward as
possible under cover of darkness. From there, groups of men from the
Pioneer and Stokes mortar sections of Headquarters Company and members of the regimental band carried the meals and water forward under
cover of darkness.[22]

As the 1st Battalion held its perilous position during the afternoon
and night of July 28, the 2nd Battalion entrenched in positions south of
the Ourcq. 3rd Battalion, meanwhile, spent most of the day in the Forêt-
de-Fére. Then, at 6:00 p.m., they were ordered to move forward to a new
position just west of the chateau in the Bois de Villemoyenne and about
two miles south of the Ourcq.[23]

On the night of July 28-29, the regiment made plans for 1st Battalion
to attempt another assault on Seringes-et-Nesles. Despite their heavy
losses the previous day, 1st Battalion began to move forward under intense machine gun fire around 8:00 a.m. However, they could get no further than D Company had the day before and finally dug in at
La-Fontaine-sous-Pierre, an advance of only two hundred yards. When
they were in position, one of C Company's platoon leaders, Eddie Coyle,
noticed that one of his men had been severely wounded and was lying
out in the open. Coyle, a young lieutenant from Pittsburgh, climbed from
his shallow trench and started to crawl through the wheat field toward
the wounded soldier as German shells continued to fall around him.
When he reached the wounded man, Coyle grabbed him by the shirt collar and dragged him back to safety.[24]

COLONEL HOUGH DECIDED to have 2nd Battalion relieve the 1st Battalion
that afternoon before they renewed the attack, and this time the assault
would have some artillery preparation. The barrage would start just before 4:00 p.m., and while it would be relatively brief, it might be enough
to make a difference in the outcome. As the artillery barrage began, E and
F Companies from the 2nd Battalion made their way down the slopes to
wade across the Ourcq and relieve the battered men of the 1st Battalion.
Captain John Stevenson from Columbus led F Company and was in over-

all command of the attacking force, with Lieutenant Herman Doellinger of Marysville in command of E Company.[25]

As the men rested in an orchard behind the cover of a stone wall, Stevenson quickly moved to the right, searching for Lieutenant Doellinger. In a matter of minutes, he found Doellinger, who was on his way to find Stevenson. The two officers crouched down and discussed how they should execute the attack. They knew from what they had heard about the 167th's attack at Croix Rouge Farm as well as their observation of 1st Battalion's attack the day before that a frontal assault by the entire force was doomed to failure. As one veteran later recalled, "rushing through the open up to the concealed German machine guns in the hope of frightening the gunners into surrender, or of catching them off guard, was sheer suicide."[26] So, rather than attack in a rush, they would make the assault at a pace characterized by one 42nd Division officer as a "crawl."[27]

The idea behind this "crawling" pace tactic was to minimize exposure, complicate the enemy machine gunners' task, and allow each machine gun emplacement to be neutralized in turn. The advance would be made by short burst squad rushes and even rushes by individual soldiers when necessary. From the machine gunner's perspective, they would suddenly see a few men in olive drab jump up from the wheat to their right, run ahead for a few yards, and then disappear from view just as the gunner shifted his weapon and opened fire. For a moment, the field would be still and quiet. Then, off to the left, another small group would rush forward before taking cover, again just as the gunner was able to shift his fire to the left. Next, there would be a group rush into the center, then another to the right, and one to the left, advancing in a continuing process and taking quick dives for cover whenever the German machine gun would turn to them.[28]

Soon, a half-dozen Americans would be converging on the machine gun emplacement, and now their attack had supporting cover fire from their comrades' rifles. The process might take thirty minutes, or it might take an hour, but eventually the Americans would close in. Once within range, they would toss hand grenades into the emplacement and charge forward to kill any surviving Germans with rifles and bayonets.[29]

Stevenson and Doellinger decided that E Company would swing to the right and attack the left flank of the Germans in Seringes-et-Nesles while F Company made an assault directly ahead toward the road leading into the village. Once the American artillery lifted their barrage, the two companies began their approach. As soon as the Americans emerged from cover, the German machine guns opened fire from positions to their front and from their right flank.[30]

Corporal Dana Daniels sent the men from his squad forward in small rushes, as ordered. Despite the machine gun fire and enemy artillery that now resumed its firing, "the boys in khaki never stopped a second." One of Daniels's soldiers, George Leffler, a twenty-four-year-old private from Marysville, was lying to the right of Daniels. When Leffler started his rush forward, he only got a few steps before machine gun fire cut him down. The bullets hit him on the right side and came out the left. Daniels could see Leffler was badly wounded, and he assigned another soldier to take him to the rear, where Leffler died in a field hospital the next day. Now it was Daniels's turn to advance, and, having seen Leffler get hit, he was "pretty doubtful" of his chances. But he got up anyway, knowing any delay on his part would hold up the entire platoon's progress. He ran forward as "Boche bullets went whiz whiz whiz [underlined in original] around" him. All of the bullets missed, and he made it up the hill.[31]

As F Company made slow progress up the hill, E Company reached its position on the village's left flank. By this point, they had lost several men, with most of them wounded. Corporal Daniels now received orders to shift their position to the road leading into the village, and he sent his men running in that direction, where they took cover in a shallow ditch about eighteen inches deep. The enemy turned their fire on Daniels's new position, which, since it provided minimal cover, he described as a tight place. In fact, while he was lying flat on his stomach in the ditch, a machine gun bullet skidded across the top of his helmet.[32]

The German artillery fire now increased its pace, and shells began to drop all around E Company's position. Daniels's platoon commander, Lieutenant Joseph McMinimy, jumped up and began running up the road with a few of his men when a German artillery shell landed right next to him. The blast shredded McMinimy and one other soldier, killing them instantly while wounding three others including Daniels's friend, Sergeant Neal Davis. Davis was badly hit and died on the way to a field hospital. A few seconds later, Daniels's automatic rifle gunner, Private William Elliot, was hit and sent to the rear. Another soldier took Elliot's Chauchat forward on the advance into Seringes-et-Nesles.[33]

Daniels formed his squad just inside the village along a hedge fence, quickly deploying machine guns to cover the town. The rest of E and F Companies continued their advance up the road and into the village but

Men from the 166th Infantry engage the Germans near Seringes-et-Nesles. (*National Archives*)

at a great cost. The well-concealed German machine guns continued to fire right up to the moment the Americans entered the village. F Company lost Lieutenant John Hanford from St. Paul, Minnesota, during their attack as well as Lieutenant William Hyman of Iowa Falls, Iowa, who was killed as he tried to take out an enemy machine gun that had his men pinned down. Both were "Sears and Roebuck" officers who proved their worth.[34]

The men of the 2nd Battalion now deployed into the village and mopped up the enemy in a house-to-house search. They only found a couple of Germans because the rest had fallen back to the crest of the hill overlooking Seringes-et-Nesles. With the Germans gone, Stevenson now positioned the platoons of both companies at strategic points around the village.[35]

Captain Stevenson could see that his men were in a badly exposed position. The Germans were on three sides of the town with machine guns placed on the left and center at distances from seventy-five to three hundred yards. On the right, the enemy had withdrawn about a half-mile away across the valley, but from there the Germans had an excellent view of Seringes-et-Nesles and could observe all of the American defensive positions. Luckily, Stevenson's men soon discovered that the attics of a few houses provided a view directly down into the German trenches and gun pits. So, Stevenson placed men in each attic to watch for signs of enemy

Soldiers from the 166th Infantry engage in house-to-house fighting at Villers-sur-Fére. (*National Archives*)

movement and gave them strict orders not to fire at the Germans so the enemy remained unaware that they were being observed.[36]

While the 2nd Battalion was attacking Seringes-et-Nesles, the 3rd Battalion was ordered to move up to the Ourcq in support. At the time the orders were issued, 3rd Battalion was deployed in Villers-sur-Fére, about three-fourths of a mile southeast of the Ourcq, where they had been sent to support possible operations by the 167th on the regiment's right. That attack had been canceled, so Captain Haubrich was told to cross the Ourcq and be prepared to help the 2nd Battalion repulse a potential German counterattack.[37]

However, what should have been a simple maneuver became very complicated due to a bungling staff officer who mistakenly sent two of Haubrich's companies back to the Forêt-de-Fére as well as intense German artillery fire on Villers-sur-Fére. The two missing companies were retrieved, but Haubrich wisely decided to get the other two companies moving forward in case the 2nd Battalion needed them. As enemy shells came crashing down on the town, Haubrich had the two companies advance on opposite sides of the street, with each man separated in the column by about fifteen feet. With "fragments of shells, pieces of brick, stone, and tile roofs" raining down on them, the men slowly made their way to the northern side of town, where the artillery shelling finally stopped. From there, they moved up the road leading to Fére-en-Tardenois, crossed the Ourcq, and dug in. The other two companies crossed the Ourcq and joined the battalion late on the night of July 29.[38]

All during the night of July 29 and into the next day, the Germans subjected Seringes-et-Nesles and the 2nd Battalion to continuous artillery fire. Because of this, no attempt was made to advance and clear the crest of the ridge of Germans, most of whom had retired to positions on the edge of the Forêt-de-Nesles. On July 29, the 165th Infantry had difficulty moving up the Ru du Pont Brûle toward Meurcy Farm to the right of Seringes-et-Nesles while the French on the left at Fére-en-Tardenois were pinned down by strong German resistance. As a result, the 166th position north of the Ourcq and at Seringes-et-Nesles created a vulnerable salient. As Raymond Cheseldine would later say, "Ohio stuck out in front of the sector like a sore thumb."[39]

On July 30, the leading battalions of the 165th Infantry used enfilading support fire from the 166th to take Meurcy Farm and advance into the Bois Brûle to the east of Seringes-et-Nesles. The French were also able to make a small move forward, but, while these operations were ongoing, the 166th had to wait to make any advance of their own.[40]

Meanwhile, the heavy shelling of the 2nd Battalion in Seringes-et-Nesles continued unabated. Dana Daniels wrote that the "big shells were falling like hail all around us, and our faces were black with powder and smoke." When the position he and two other men were occupying seemed to be attracting attention from the German gunners, they decided to move to the other end of the village. After a mad dash through the shellfire, they dropped down behind a stone wall to catch their breath. As they crouched there, a German shell came roaring in, exploding just beyond the wall while a second shell blasted a building only fifty feet away. So, deciding the wall was also not a good place to be either, they got up and ran through a garden toward an old building.[41]

As they dashed across the garden, more shells fell close by, and one of Daniels's buddies, James Odensoff, was hit in the leg by shrapnel. Odensoff, a twenty-four-year-old private from Toledo, had been born in Shela, Russia, before immigrating with his parents to Toledo, Ohio. He enlisted in the 6th Ohio Infantry in June 1917 and was one of the men transferred to the 166th to fill out its ranks at Camp Perry.[42] Odensoff shouted over the shellfire that he could keep going. So, the men went into the old building, where they found a cellar in which to take refuge. Once below ground level, Daniels tended to Odensoff with his first aid kit, and soon another man entered to take refuge in the cellar. He had been wounded in the hip, so Daniels did his best to bandage the wound. The artillery barrage slackened a little, and Daniels went back upstairs and outside, where he learned that another of his men had been hit by shrapnel in the head and throat and died instantly.[43]

That night around 8:00 p.m., the Germans increased the intensity of their artillery fire on Seringes-et-Nesles, and Colonel Hough believed a German counterattack might be about to occur. He ordered 2nd Battalion to withdraw to prepared positions about three hundred yards southwest of the village and wait for the German barrage to lift. At the same time, American artillery was able to fire on the German batteries and the open ground between the crest of the ridge and the village. As it turned out, the Germans were attempting an infantry assault on the village. However, the American artillery fire was so effective that only a few of the Germans managed to reach the village.[44]

At 9:30 p.m., A Company and B Company of the 1st Battalion advanced from their positions near La Fontaine Sous Pierre to attack the Germans who had made it to Seringes-et-Nesles and drive them out. They swept into the village with fury, killing most of the Germans there and forcing the rest to retreat back to the Forêt-de-Nesles, while losing one officer, Lieutenant Lee Kortz of Fort Dodge, Iowa. By 10:30 p.m., the village was secured, and E and F Companies returned to their positions in Seringes-et-Nesles.[45]

As the shelling of Seringes-et-Nesles continued on July 31, Captain Geran, the 2nd Battalion commander, called for some organic artillery support. During the previous weeks, the regiment had received some new ordinance, the 37mm one-pounder. This French-manufactured gun was intended to provide fire support at ranges from 1,300 to 4,900 feet, and it was the smallest field gun used by the US Army.[46] It was designed for mobility and could fire up to thirty-five rounds per minute. Lieutenant Theodore Bundy of Delta, Ohio, had been given command of this small battery, and he had been rigorously training his men and the mule teams used to move the guns. Now, he had his first opportunity to take his battery into action.

Geran sent word back to the Regimental PC asking for Bundy's help using what everyone called his "Pound-Wonders" to subdue a concealed German gun position located in some woods northwest of Seringes-et-

Soldiers using the 37mm gun in action. (*National Archives*)

Nesles. Bundy hurried forward, set up his battery near La Fontaine-sous-Pierre, and quickly opened fire. Within minutes, his battery's fire had put the German gun out of action. However, this apparently angered the Germans who replied by shelling Bundy's position. In the process of trying to find his battery, the enemy began dropping shells much too close to Captain Geran's position for his comfort. He sent word for Bundy to get out and to do so quickly. Apparently the captain's desire for Bundy to leave was now much stronger than his desire for him to stay. While Bundy was happy that his battery had done its job, he was "disconsolate at the apparent ingratitude of the Captain."[47]

Around 1:00 p.m. on July 31, Dana Daniels was taking cover in a shell hole in the village with two of his buddies, Corporal Richard Thrall of Marysville and Private Millard Heiberger of Mason, Ohio. Daniels could see that Heiberger was in terrible shape. The two days of intense German artillery had been too much for the private, and he was clearly suffering from shell shock. Daniels went to Lieutenant Doellinger, who then came over to the shell hole to talk to Heiberger. The lieutenant agreed with Daniels and told him to take Heiberger back to the field hospital in the rear. Along the way, Daniels picked up two more wounded men from E Company and got them back to the hospital about 6:30 p.m.[48]

Daniels stayed in the rear long enough to have a quick meal and then started back for Seringes-et-Nesles. But when he reached the river, the village was taking another severe shelling, and a guard held him back. The shelling continued until around 3:00 a.m. on the morning of August 1, when the German infantry advanced once more in an attempt to retake the village. However, this assault was quickly turned back by determined resistance from E and F Companies. Daniels arrived to rejoin his squad the next morning, but he learned that he no longer had a squad. During the night, the last two survivors from his small command had also been sent to the rear with shell shock.[49]

Just before midnight on August 1, the enemy began another heavy barrage against the regiment's forward positions in Seringes-et-Nesles, the sort of shelling that usually meant they were about to make some sort of significant move. Soon, the nature of the move became clear when the ground reverberated from massive explosions behind the German lines— the enemy was destroying any ammunition dumps in preparation to hurry their retreat out of the Marne salient. The artillery fire was an attempt to hold back any Allied advance while the Germans evacuated the area.[50]

The 166th was badly in need of relief, with E Company alone having lost over one hundred men. However, it became clear no relief was coming, and the assignment to pursue and make contact with the retreating enemy would fall on the regiment. At 6:00 a.m. on August 2, the orders to do exactly that arrived. Raymond Cheseldine wrote, "Exhausted men, worn from days of toil and nights of tortured nerves and bodies, pushed themselves out of the woods and villages and, led by the 2nd Battalion, moved up the hill beyond Seringes-et-Nesles." To make matters worse, as the men formed up to move out, it began to rain, and it would rain all day.[51]

G Company from 2nd Battalion took the lead, as they had sustained the fewest casualties in the previous four days of fighting with E and F Companies following along with H and M Companies from 3rd Battalion. The first objective was the village of Moreuil-en-Dôle, about two and a half miles to the north, and to secure a line three hundred yards to the west of that village. The French and the 165th moved in parallel to the left and right, respectively, covering the regiment's flanks. As the men advanced up to the crest of the ridge, the German machine guns opened fire from the Forêt-de-Nesles, but soon they stopped firing as the Germans quickly retreated.[52]

The leading skirmish lines of G Company reached a point about four hundred yards south of Moreuil-en-Dôle and reported the enemy could be seen evacuating the village. The advance of the rest of the attacking Americans picked up the pace of their advance. As G Company cleared the ridge, the Germans saw them and let loose with a massive artillery barrage. Despite the carnage caused by the shelling, the regiment's four companies pressed the attack. Dana Daniels wrote that "this was the worst shelling" the men had been through thus far, which was saying something.[53]

The attack was proceeding so fast now that contact with the French on the left was lost. G and E Companies halted and dug in until the flanks were secure again. Dana Daniels said that, as he came over the hill, he saw everyone else in the company digging in, so he jumped into a shell hole with another man from Marysville, Private Wood Carter. The two men took out their trenching shovels and began to make the hole a little deeper, just to be on the safe side. At that point, the advance on Moreuil-en-Dôle stopped, as the men enjoyed the sight of the enemy running about the village, burning supplies, and preparing for a hasty departure.[54]

While the men waited in their trenches and shell holes, the steady rain made things pretty miserable. But for many soldiers, the rain proved to be an unexpected blessing. Peter Weiss, a twenty-year-old G Company sergeant from Columbus, later recalled, "Their artillery was firing point-blank—we could see the flame belch from their 77's on the opposite hill." But as the shells came screaming in and struck the ground at a ninety-degree angle, the soft, soggy mud cushioned their impact with the ground, causing many of them to be duds.[55]

LATE THAT AFTERNOON, the regiment received news that the entire 42nd Division would be relieved that night by the American 4th Division. When Colonel Hough heard this news, he ordered the forward assault elements to withdraw to the reverse side of the ridge so they could avoid any further artillery fire from the enemy. Around 9:30 p.m., the first units of the 4th Division arrived, and all of the 166th was on their way out of the area by midnight. They camped that night back in the Forêt-de-Fére, where they would remain until August 11.[56]

Unfortunately, the forest was a miserable place to rest and recover. "Flies and mosquitoes abounded, dirty pools of stagnant water gave forth terrible odors, and the stench from dead bodies of German and American alike" made the place almost unbearable. But the men of the regiment seemed not to care. As these exhausted soldiers made their way into the dense woods, they sank to the ground and went to sleep. Many of them slept for almost twenty-four hours straight. The salvage and burial details began their work on August 4, and the Supply Company was able to furnish a fresh supply of razors, brushes, soap, combs, and towels. However, with no clean clothes available and no place to bathe, the regiment's leadership decided that a proper cleanup could wait. Besides, there was a rumor that the regiment was going to pull back for a thirty-day rest, which caused the men to rejoice.[57]

The eight days the regiment spent in the "pest-hole" of the Foret-de-Fére were as miserable as one might expect. After the men had gotten some initial rest, the conditions in the forest led to many weakened men developing dysentery. Raymond Cheseldine would write that, when the regiment finally left, "It was a dirty looking regiment, a sick regiment in fact, that swung down the road toward Château-Thierry that morning of August 11th."[58] When they reached Château-Thierry, many men, including Dana Daniels, made straight for the Marne River and a chance at last to get a much-needed bath.[59]

The regiment had much to be proud of as they rested briefly in Château-Thierry. They had been part of an effort that had pushed the vaunted 4th Prussian Guard Division, commanded by the kaiser's son, Prince Eitel Friedrich, as well as the 201st German, 10th Landwehr, and the 6th Bavarian Divisions back a distance of over seven miles. But the cost had been terrible. In five days of vicious fighting, the 166th Infantry had lost just over one thousand men killed, wounded, and missing, almost double the number of casualties they had suffered in the five months from mid-February to mid-July at Lunéville, Baccarat, and Champagne. Worst of all, perhaps, was the fact that most of the new draftees the regiment had received just before they reached the Ourcq, men who were untrained and had been in the army less than a month, were among the dead. As Raymond Cheseldine would write most emphatically, "They didn't have a chance."[60]

At one point in the battle for the Ourcq, an officer from the Supply Company was on the road heading to the Regimental Headquarters. Up ahead, he saw a soldier slowly coming toward him. The young man was covered in blood and was trying to make his way to the nearest aid station. The officer noticed that the soldier was gripping his abdomen with both hands, and he called out to him saying, "What's the hurt, Buddy, can I help?" The soldier replied, "I'm shot through here, sir. If I take my hands away, everything will fall out. I haven't far to go now, I'll make it."[61]

The fight for the high ground at the Ourcq River would prove to be the bloodiest of the war for the 166th. But there was more fighting to be done, and it was coming very soon.

American soldiers armed with French automatic rifles early in the morning of the first day of the assault upon the salient of Saint Mihiel. (*National Archives*)

On the Offensive—Saint Mihiel

"We have had another little rumpus with the Dutch and chased them quite a ways. We got a lot of their big guns and a little of everything else."—Private Austin Dewitt "Dusty" Boyd, letter of September 19, 1918

As the September rains poured down on them, the men of I Company crouched low among the trees, observing the village of Saint Baussant and trying to take the measure of the place. The company commander, Captain "Hell Roarin' Henry" Grave, was also watching the village, perhaps even more carefully than his men. Since moving across the deep mud of no man's land at 5:00 a.m., there had been no signs of any Germans except those who emerged enthusiastically from their dugouts to surrender.

Suddenly, he saw movement at the edge of the village, and this was followed by the clattering sound of fire from a German Maxim gun. The captain and all his men flattened themselves on the ground as the bullets went whizzing by above them. Captain Graves had no intention of trying to rush these gunners, so he sent word to the men with the Stokes mortars to set up and open fire on the gun's position. Within minutes, mortar rounds came arcing overhead from a few yards to the rear, crashing into the machine gun emplacement in a series of small explosions.[1]

With that, those machine guns became silent, but another set opened up on the opposite side of the village. Grave ordered more supporting fire while sending a few men led by Corporal William Jones, a farmer from Newark, Ohio, to flank the guns. Jones took part of one squad on a rapid flanking maneuver toward the gun position. After carefully deploying his men so that they surrounded the machine guns, they opened fire and tossed grenades toward the emplacement. As soon as the grenades exploded, the German gunners called out and raised their hands in the air to surrender to Jones and his men.[2]

At that, Captain Grave shouted for his men to storm the village. As the men of I Company went house to house kicking down doors, they found nothing but hurriedly abandoned meals and supplies, as well as more Germans anxious to surrender. One building, however, proved to be an exception. There, the men found Private George Dennis, the battalion's medic who was from Cardington, Ohio. Dennis had left the rear early that morning, driving the battalion's medical cart forward. In the dark and the rain, he apparently had lost his way and ended up going down the road to Saint Baussant. At one point, Dennis saw other soldiers from the regiment waving their arms and shouting at him in an attempt to tell him he was heading into German territory. But the noise from the American rolling artillery barrage was so loud that he could not hear them. As a result, Dennis continued driving ahead until he found himself at Saint Baussant. Seeing no one else around, including any menacing Germans, he unloaded his cart at the entrance to one building, went inside, and set up a dressing station a full thirty minutes ahead of I Company's arrival.[3]

What became known in the regiment as the "One Hundred Yard Dash toward Metz" was on.[4]

THE FRENCH REFERRED to the Saint Mihiel salient as "l'Hernie," meaning "the Hernia." This bulge in the lines along the Western Front about twenty miles northwest of Nancy had the town of Saint Mihiel as the apex of a right triangle, with a southern face that ran across open, flat terrain toward the Moselle River. The salient was twenty-five miles wide at its base, and it protruded fifteen miles deep into the Allied lines. The base, which was the shorter leg of the triangle, ran from east to west between Saint Mihiel and Pont-à-Mousson on the Moselle River.[5]

Since the initial German advance of 1914, the Germans had been fortifying the salient with a series of defensive lines. At the base of the salient was a line called the Michel Stellung, which included a reinforced first line and a less-developed second line running between the towns of Haudiomont and Pont-à-Mousson. Within the salient, they constructed an outer defensive line called the Wilhelm zone and an inner line known as the Schroeter zone. The town of Montsec sat at the approximate center of the salient about ten miles east of Saint Mihiel on high terrain that rose more than 2,500 feet above the surrounding countryside. From there, the Germans could observe any activity along the Allied lines and far to their rear.[6]

In September 1918, the Germans manned the defenses in the salient with eight full divisions and two separate brigades along the forward face of the salient. This group of forces was known as Army Detachment C, and the Germans put General George Fuchs in command. Army Detachment C was organized in groups that defended specific geographic sections of the line. The Gorz Group, which included the 77th and 10th Divisions of the I Bavarian Corps, was stationed along the German left flank. Meanwhile, the Mihiel Group, which was composed of the 5th Landwehr Division and the 31st Division, also of the I Bavarian Corps, was assigned to the forward tip of the salient. The Combres Group, consisting of the 35th Austro-Hungarian and the 8th and 13th Landwehr Divisions, was positioned along the German right flank. Finally, the Metz Group was placed in the rear and exercised as a strategic reserve with the 195th Saxon and 123rd Divisions.[7]

Now that General Pershing was able to create the American First Army, it was time for that army to plan, command, and act as an independent force. Collapsing the Saint Mihiel salient seemed like a natural objective for the First Army's initial operation. The French had tried repeatedly to reduce the salient but without any success. Pershing believed the First Army might be able to take the salient and then continue an offensive to the northeast to seize the strategic city of Metz. This, in turn, might threaten the Briey Iron Basin, an area critical to German war production, as well as the site for crucial rail networks leading to the coalfields in the Saar.[8] Therefore, throughout the period from July into late August 1918, the First Army staff worked diligently on a plan for an offensive into the Saint Mihiel salient that would seek to capture Metz.

The elaborate plans for the Saint Mihiel offensive proved a challenge for the inexperienced AEF headquarters staff. To execute the offensive as planned would require over five hundred thousand American troops, more than one hundred thousand French soldiers, nearly three thousand pieces of artillery, two hundred thousand tons of supplies, and fifty thousand tons of ammunition. The majority of these men, guns, and matériel would have to be sent to the area using the few available roads, so the transportation and logistics plan was very daunting. Then there were the issues of how many units to deploy and what should be the timing of the attacks and artillery support.[9]

However, as Pershing's staff developed their plans, they were unaware that Fuchs was already planning a withdrawal from the salient. Even though the French had been so unsuccessful in trying to reduce the salient, the Germans knew the position was highly vulnerable to a pincer attack. While the French had not had the manpower to make a coordinated, multifront attack, Fuchs and the other German generals could see that the massive infusion of American forces could very well make a difference. Moreover, the Germans had suffered severe losses in their spring and summer offensives in the Marne, and they needed to shorten their defensive line wherever possible. So, in June 1918, they began planning a troop withdrawal from the Saint Mihiel salient named Operation Loki. Under this plan, they would keep their forces in place so long as the sector remained quiet. However, as soon as any signs of an Allied offensive were detected, Fuchs would withdraw his forces to the Michel Stellung line along the base of the triangle and make a stand there.[10]

On August 30, the First Army officially assumed responsibility for the Saint Mihiel sector. However, on that very same day, Foch arrived at AEF headquarters to tell Pershing the situation had changed. Field Marshal Haig and Marshal Foch had decided that the Allies should concentrate their forces for an offensive in the area between the Argonne Forest and the Meuse River. To do that, they needed as many as fourteen American divisions for an attack scheduled to start on September 15, which meant the Saint Mihiel offensive would have to be canceled or reduced in scale. While Pershing was dismayed, he could see the strategic sense of what Foch was proposing. However, at the same time, Pershing also saw the crucial need for the American First Army to have an opportunity to operate on its own.[11]

The next day, August 31, Pershing went to see Marshal Pétain, the French commander-in-chief, and plead his case. For the most part, the two men found themselves in agreement. Pétain thought Foch had overstepped his authority. But Pétain also thought that Pershing's plan should drop the idea of capturing Metz for the time being. Instead, the French general suggested that Pershing's attack stop along the base of the salient. He also proposed that, once that was accomplished, Pershing should assume responsibility for the entire line west from Saint Mihiel to the Argonne Forest, an addition of almost fifty miles.[12]

Marshal Foch (left) and General Pershing meet before the Saint Mihiel offensive. (*National Archives*)

On September 2, Pétain, Foch, and Pershing met at Foch's headquarters in Ligny. In their discussions, Foch agreed to Pershing and Pétain's ideas and decided to postpone the offensive in the Meuse-Argonne sector until September 25. This delay would allow Pershing to execute his limited offensive at Saint Mihiel and then shift the First Army to participate in the Meuse-Argonne offensive. Pershing's operation would begin around September 10 and attack both the southern and western faces of the Saint Mihiel salient. Instead of driving toward Metz, the First Army's objective would be to advance to a line from Vigneulles to Thiaucourt and Regniéville in just three to four days.[13]

With this agreement in place, Pershing returned to his headquarters, where his staff now faced the challenge of altering their plans with only a week until the proposed start of the offensive. Luckily, not much would need to be changed. Pershing would use four corps comprised of four French divisions and eight and one-half divisions from the American First Army. The American I and IV Corps would execute the primary attack along the salient's southern boundary while the V Corps would attack in the west. The 42nd Division with the 166th Infantry would be part of the IV Corps and were given the objective of reaching the ruins of the village of Maizerais on the first day, the town of Pannes on day two, and the final line in the Bois de Thiaucourt by nightfall on the third day of the offensive.[14]

AFTER A BRIEF STOP in Château-Thierry on August 12, the 166th made a short five-mile march to Corrpru before hiking on to Charly-sur-Marne on August 13. This small city was hidden in the Marne Valley with hills that had protected it from German artillery fire. As a result, there was little damage in the town, and it was a peaceful, quiet place. When the men of the regiment went to sleep in their billets that night, it was the first night they had not heard artillery fire and feared the arrival of enemy shells since they went into the line at Baccarat the previous March. This was exactly the sort of place the men needed to rest and recover from their ordeal along the Ourcq, and a few even managed to get forty-eight-hour passes to visit Paris.[15]

Interestingly, the quiet in Charly-sur-Marne actually caused some men a few sleepless nights. The first night in the town, an officer returning to his camp discovered fifteen of his men lounging under a hedge in their underclothes while they conversed in hushed tones and smoked their cigarettes. The officer paused when he heard one of the soldiers say, "Ain't it Hell? There ain't been a sound for three hours except that damned mule hee-hawin'. If a battery don't cut loose somewhere pretty soon, I reckon I'll stay awake all night."

To that, one of his buddies replied, "This man's army don't know how to rest. We been fighting so long that we can't quit all of a sudden. It's just like cigarettes or booze—you got to quit slow, and here they stop us short after about five months. We'll get used to it in time, but this night sure is Hell. I can't sleep with that mule making such a racket."

The officer decided not to intrude and continued on his way to his tent in the camp. But when he tried to sleep, he also found that the quiet was just too "loud." He could not get to sleep, when, ironically, he had struggled for hours to keep his eyes open during his nights along the Ourcq amid the constant sounds of artillery and machine gun fire.[16]

After only three days of rest, the regiment received orders to march back to Château-Thierry, where they were to board trains for an undisclosed location. However, rumors persisted that this unknown destination would involve thirty days of rest in a rear area. At Château-Thierry, the men groaned when they saw they were to once again be shipped like cattle in the hideous "Hommes 40, Chevaux 8" boxcars. As they departed, they were told the regiment was headed to the Bourmont area, where they would take part in a period of intensive training.[17]

The regiment arrived in Bourmont on August 18 and marched immediately to the training area. Once there, the Regimental Headquarters,

Headquarters Company, Supply Company, Machine Gun Company, and A Company went to billets in Sommerécourt while the remainder of the 1st Battalion went to Outremécourt, the 2nd Battalion to Soulaucourt, and the 3rd Battalion split up among Nijon and Vandrecourt.[18]

After the regiment had settled in, they began a new training regimen on August 22. The course of instruction included close-order drill, athletic games, range practice, bayonet and gas drill, practice marches, and open warfare tactics. Once the training began, Colonel Hough received word that five hundred draftee replacements would arrive on August 27, and he hoped this new period of training would last long enough to whip these untrained men into shape. Unfortunately, that was not to be the case. No sooner had the replacements arrived than the regiment was ordered to break camp and begin a march toward the Toul area. Once again, the replacements might go into battle with minimal training.[19]

The orders specified that the march must take place only at night to maintain as much secrecy as possible. So, the 166th left the night of August 27, and, after two nights of marching a total distance of about twenty-five miles, they went into camp at Dolaincourt and Balléville, where they continued their training.[20]

Here, they joined the mass of American forces gathering for Pershing's Saint Mihiel offensive. However, no one in the regiment was aware of the complex discussions and negotiations that had been happening at higher headquarters, and, thus, they did not know that an attack date of September 12 had been finally determined. All they knew was that, on September 4, they were ordered to move again, this time to the vicinity of Tranqueville and then onward to Barisey-au-Plain, where they arrived in the early morning hours of September 6.[21]

But there was no time given to rest, and the regiment moved out again the night of September 7 to the vicinity of the Colombier Farm, which they reached around 2:00 a.m. on September 8. The last leg had been brutal. Night marches were always trying, but this one was performed in a driving rainstorm. When the men went into camp, they were soaked to the bone, and those bones ached from packs made even heavier by the rain. To everyone's surprise, the regiment was ordered back on the road only a few hours later—in broad daylight. This made the seemingly urgent need for the previous night marches appear genuinely idiotic. Every sane member of the regiment questioned why they had marched at night when they were in the rear areas but now traveled in daylight when they were only a few miles from the enemy. One angry Ohioan was heard to shout, "Hell's bells, now I know why they call us the AEF! It means Ass End First!"[22]

To make matters worse, the First Army's orders for the September 8 march sent the regiment and the rest of the 42nd Division to campsites deep in the Bois-de-la-Reine forest beside a dismal swamp lake called the Etang-Rome. The men had seen some damp campsites before but nothing like this one. It was so wet as to put the regiment "permanently in a state of ooziness."[23] It was an inauspicious beginning to the first great American offensive.

As THE REGIMENT MOVED into its soggy position in the Bois-de-la-Reine, the final details of the plans for the offensive were being completed, and there was one more issue to resolve—artillery preparation. Some officers were arguing that, to achieve surprise, there should be no pre-attack artillery fire. Others, however, stated that preparatory artillery fire was needed to damage enemy trenches, gun emplacements, and barbed wire as much as possible, while also providing encouragement to American troops and damaging enemy morale. Pershing, who still clung to some aspects of pre-war American doctrine, agreed that there should be no artillery preparation. However, he reconsidered his position, and, on September 10, he ordered a four-hour artillery barrage on the southern face of the salient and a seven-hour barrage on the western face.[24]

With that decision, the plan was complete. The six divisions on the south side of the salient, including the 42nd Division, would start their attack at 5:00 a.m. on September 12, and the assault on the western face would begin at 8:00 a.m. The opening artillery fire on both sides of the salient would start at 1:00 a.m. that day, and, once concluded, the guns would switch to a rolling barrage as the infantry moved forward.[25]

However, the complex set of orders for the entire offensive did not arrive at the 166th or any other unit until late on the morning of September 11. These orders contained every possible detail in what Raymond Cheseldine described as "a great pile of battle plans with annexes covering the use of every conceivable auxiliary arm, tanks, smoke screens, wire cutting devices." It would have taken several days for Colonel Hough and his staff to break down the orders and learn all they needed to know, but they barely had eighteen hours until their men were scheduled to advance against the Germans. All Hough could do was dissect the orders for the most important details, such as where his battalions were supposed to go

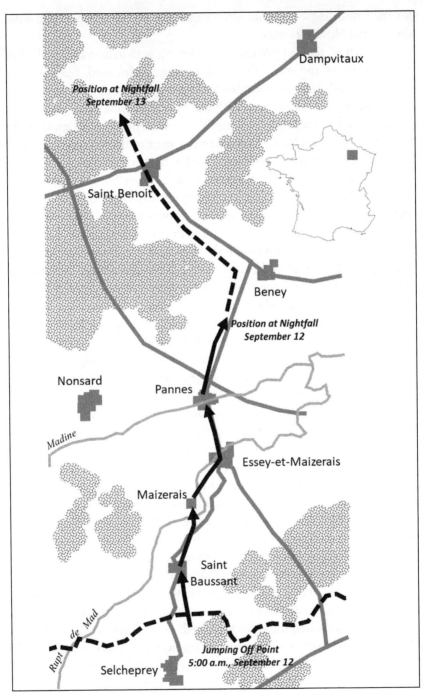

The 166th Infantry's attack in the Saint Mihiel Salient. (*Author*)

for their jumping-off points, what time they would advance, and what their initial objectives were.[26]

Meanwhile, the Supply Company swung into action doing all they could to secure and move the required supplies forward. But it was an impossible task. The steady rains had turned the roads into quagmires, and those roads were clogged with trucks and wagons from every other regiment that was trying to accomplish the same hopeless assignment. By the time set for the attack, the leading elements of the regiment only had a partial supply of what it was supposed to have for the attack.[27]

In the early evening hours, the 3rd Battalion, which was assigned to lead the regiment forward, began moving through the downpour, which seemed to only increase in intensity as the hours ticked by. The roads were virtually impassible and were choked with trucks, wagons, and artillery, all moving forward, which meant the men of the regiment had to march in the ankle-deep mud of the forest. Once they approached the jumping-off points, they found a maze of muddy, disused front-line trenches.[28]

The artillery, which had arrived first, discovered that there was nothing in front of them except a few isolated German sentry posts. So, they rolled their guns forward and established a skirmish line in front of their guns to protect against any possible German patrols. As the regiment's men came forward, they lay down between the old trenches as telephone lines were run back to Regimental Headquarters. [29]

Now it became clear that the Germans knew something was up. As the 3rd Battalion approached the jumping-off point, shells came screaming in, exploding near the roads leading to their position. However, despite the artillery fire, the 3rd Battalion made it to their advance position and waited in the soaking rain for the American artillery to open fire at 1:00 a.m. Major Haubrich placed I Company and the Machine Gun Company in the lead with L and M Companies directly behind them.[30]

As the rain continued to fall, Haubrich and his officers were likely thinking about the obstacles that lay ahead of them. First, two streams cut through the terrain to their front, the Rupt de Mad and the Madine. The Rupt de Mad cut diagonally across the center lane of the attack, while the Madine flowed from east to west, cutting straight across the 3rd Battalion's path once they cleared the ridge just north of the Rupt de Mad. Given all the rain that had fallen, they wondered how difficult those streams would be to ford. Further, they knew that large bands of barbed wire were out there ahead of them, but they did not know exactly where they were or what kind of resistance they might anticipate from the German infantry.[31]

Barbed wire obstacles erected by the Germans in the Saint Mihiel Salient. (*National Archives*)

At precisely 1:00 a.m., three thousand American and French guns opened fire with a massive volley that lit the night with what was described as "a huge sheet of flame."[32] As the Allied shells began to rain into the German positions, the enemy was surprised. They had observed the American and French units moving into the area for several days and had anticipated an attack was probably coming. General Fuchs began moving two of his divisions back to the secondary defensive line, as called for in his plan for Operation Loki. However, Fuchs apparently thought it would be several days before the Americans and French could mount an assault against the salient. As a result, these divisions had only just begun their withdrawal when the Allied artillery opened fire. In the confusion that followed, the commander of Fuchs's 77th Division misinterpreted his orders and left two-thirds of his men in their old positions virtually without any German artillery support.[33]

At 5:00 a.m. the Allied artillery shifted from a long-range barrage to a rolling barrage, signaling that it was time to go "over the top." Major Haubrich looked at his watch, then at the barrage, then back at his watch, and gave the signal to advance. It was still twenty minutes until daybreak on that foggy morning when the men of the 3rd Battalion, stiff from lying in the rain for several hours, stood up and followed Haubrich forward into the muddy no man's land before them. The battalion advanced steadily, unopposed until they reached the first bands of tangled barbed wire.[34]

Under the usual attack approach, the men of the battalion would have counted on Allied artillery to blast paths through the wire. But this time the artillery had focused on the positions of German artillery batteries. So, instead of counting on the artillery, the regiment sent teams of men with wire cutters along with groups of engineers armed with Bangalore torpedoes ahead of the first infantry wave. The torpedoes were composed of empty pipes about six feet long that, once filled with explosives, were shoved forward into the wire, and then set off to blast a hole in the obstacles. This new approach worked to perfection, allowing the battalion to quickly advance through the wire.[35]

With the cloudy skies and heavy rain and fog, the dawn was slow to arrive. Still, once it did, the advancing infantry saw billowing clouds of smoke rising from the German rear areas where the enemy was hurriedly destroying ammunition dumps. While there were a few incoming enemy artillery shells and some rifle fire from the trenches ahead, it proved to be little more than an annoyance. The only thing that began to appear in large numbers were German soldiers who emerged from their dugouts and trenches to surrender with "the utmost docility."[36] The 3rd Battalion immediately passed these prisoners to the 1st Battalion that was following close behind in support.

Once I Company approached the village of Saint Baussant, they encountered their first real resistance. Two sets of machine gun emplacements opened fire, but Captain Grave had them quickly subdued with Stokes mortar fire and a flanking attack by a half-squad of men who captured the gunners. His men then stormed the village and began a house-to-house search for the enemy. Those German soldiers they found quickly surrendered and seemed happy to do so. Major Haubrich assigned M Company to continue the search for prisoners as I Company pressed ahead to cross the Rupt de Mad and their first day's objective, the ruins of the village of Maizerais.[37]

As M Company was mopping things up in Saint Baussant, Lieutenant Harry Christopher was once again in action, busily setting up a small field hospital and aid station in the basement of a house. As he and his assistants tended to their work, a small group of the company's men entered the basement from the far side and found twenty-five German soldiers hiding. These enemy soldiers immediately surrendered and were taken to the rear.[38]

German prisoners being marched to the rear in the Saint Mihiel Salient. (*Library of Congress*)

The attack continued to sweep forward slowed only by token resistance and hundreds of surrendering Germans. Whenever resistance was met, the men of the 3rd Battalion played it safe, calling for fire support from the Stokes mortars to quickly push the enemy aside. As for the prisoners, most of them seemed to be mere boys or middle-aged men who had no desire to fight. In fact, most of them seemed to be waiting for the Americans, hiding in safety until they were surrounded and could meekly give themselves up.[39]

In one case, two soldiers from the 2nd Battalion were guarding about thirty German prisoners and escorting them back to the rear for processing. As they passed through a small village, one German soldier climbed out from the cellar where he had been hiding, and, without saying a word or even making a gesture, he fell right in with the other prisoners as they marched down the road. In fact, there were some Germans who gladly went to the rear without any guards. In another case, a wounded soldier from the regiment, whose head was bandaged and his arm tied in a sling, escorted five German prisoners to captivity armed only with a stick.[40] As

Dusty Boyd wrote home, "German prisoners go back to the prison camp without any guard and seemed tickled to death to go."[41]

When I Company reached the Rupt de Mad, the stream was badly swollen from the rain. Luckily, Captain Grave soon found a makeshift bridge over the water, and his men began to move across the raging stream. A few men were too impatient to wait their turn at the bridge, and one of them, Lieutenant Joseph Smith, jumped directly into the stream to wade across as his entire platoon dutifully followed their commander. Just ahead of them about three hundred yards to the left was Maizerais, which they immediately moved to capture. By 11:00 a.m., only six hours into the offensive, the 166th had taken its objective for the first day.[42]

The 3rd Battalion paused at Maizerais to await instructions, and they were not long in coming. At noon, Major Haubrich received orders to continue the advance toward Pannes and the Bois de Thiaucourt without any further hesitation. The only reasons to stop were if contact was lost with units on their flanks or if they found themselves outpacing American artillery. The latter was becoming an issue, and the entire regiment had to halt several times to wait for the artillery to lift its fire.[43]

The 3rd Battalion moved out and soon arrived at Essey-et-Maizerais, about one mile north of Maizerais. Once more, as they approached the village, there was almost no resistance, but they found several hundred German prisoners. In this village, however, the men of the 166th experienced something new as rejoicing French villagers surrounded them, cheering, crying, and offering their profuse thanks for this liberation from German occupation. However, the men had no time to enjoy the celebration as they began to press on toward Pannes, about one mile to the north.[44]

The advance continued until German troops in Pannes offered some resistance around 3:00 p.m. The 3rd Battalion coordinated an attack with New York's 165th and Alabama's 167th while calling up support from American tank units. The battalion and the New Yorkers slowly but steadily moved up the road and into the village as the men from Alabama flanked the German garrison with a sweep to the right. In less than thirty minutes, the village was secured, and the regiment had achieved its objective for the second day of the offensive in less than eleven hours.[45]

During the advance into Pannes, as I Company tried to locate a machine gun emplacement that was firing on them, Captain Grave decided to help by stepping into the open and drawing the gun's fire. As it fired in his direction, the men saw where it was placed and were able to quickly subdue it. A few minutes later, Captain Grave noticed that his sidearm only had two rounds remaining. So, as the company paused briefly, he fired both rounds at a tin can lying on the ground a few feet away. Before Grave could insert a new clip into the pistol, two Germans jumped up from a shell hole just beyond the tin can. Apparently, they thought Grave was shooting at them, so they put their hands up and shouted, "Kamerad!" The thoroughly surprised captain took them prisoner, while covering them with an empty gun.[46]

As Pannes was captured, more prisoners were taken, and the men seized a German quartermaster's storehouse. The Germans had left the town so quickly many of their soldiers did not have time to gather up their equipment and personal belongings. So, naturally, the doughboys began grabbing up items as souvenirs. "Pistols, spurs, hats, blankets, boots, underwear, musical instruments—the town was a regular Woolworth Store," wrote Raymond Cheseldine. The men even found a billiard table and a shower bath, as well as food in the German kitchens that was still steaming hot. They were also amazed to discover dugouts lined with wood paneling, equipped with electricity and running water, and containing elaborately furnished dining and recreation rooms.[47]

Perhaps the most interesting souvenir came from the capture of a German major and his orderly. A patrol from I Company came upon the two men as they were about to mount their horses and flee the area. They quickly took the two Germans prisoner and appropriated the major's mount with all its equipment. The horse was sent to the rear, where I Company presented it as a gift to Colonel Hough. The colonel was delighted with the mare, whom he named Gretchen, and rode throughout the regiment's remaining months in Europe.[48]

During the advance on September 12, the speed at which the regiment moved forward proved challenging for Regimental Headquarters. Given the planned objective for the day and the expected rate of advance, everyone at the headquarters assumed they would end up in Maizerais at the end of the day. Not long after the attack began, Colonel Hough and his staff moved to Siecheprey, which was near the jumping-off point. But as they set up operations at 7:45 a.m., they learned the regiment's units were already moving past Saint Baussant toward Maizerais, so they relocated the headquarters to Saint Baussant, arriving there at about 11:30 a.m. Of course, they had not been there very long before they received word from Major Haubrich that the 3rd Battalion had taken Maizerais at 11:00 a.m. Shortly after Hough sent the order back to Haubrich to continue the advance, he and the staff began to pick up their gear so they could move forward to Maizerais. The biggest problem with these moves was the need to keep running new telephone lines between the headquarters and the advancing units. At this point, the wires had not caught up, and communication had to be performed using runners. At 4:30 p.m., the Regimental Headquarters arrived at Maizerais only to learn that Pannes had fallen, and the attack was continuing toward the Bois de Thiaucourt. With that news, the staff packed up again and moved to Pannes, where they arrived around 9:40 p.m.[49]

By nightfall, the advance elements of the 166th reached the outskirts of the Bois de Thiaucourt. Here, they received orders to hold for the night and continue the attack at 6:00 a.m. the following morning. The men dug in for the night and rested after what had been a "mad gallop."[50]

During that night, C Company, which had been assigned the job of maintaining liaison with the 1st Division on the regiment's left, experienced problems maintaining contact. As the 42nd Division stopped its advance, the 1st Division kept moving forward, requiring C Company to stretch its line by using a system of patrol groups to communicate with the 1st Division. As one of the patrol groups approached the other division's lines in the dark, the men from the 1st Division thought they were Germans and opened fire. Charlie Cryder, a twenty-three-year-old corporal from Irwin, Ohio, who had been awarded the Distinguished Service Cross for saving Captain Koeppel at Champagne, was leading the patrol. Before Cryder could stop the firing, he was hit and killed.[51]

The next morning, the men rose from their foxholes and began to move into the forest. Unknown to them, the Germans had continued their mad dash toward their final defensive line, the Michel Stellung. As a result, the attack of September 13 ended up being an uneventful walk in the woods. By 8:30 a.m., the regiment arrived at its final position opposite the German defenses at the base of the salient. I and K Companies were withdrawn to support positions, and L and M Companies took over the front line around 10:00 a.m. Here, they found more gifts left by the Germans, this time in the form of a garden containing all kinds of vegetables. Taking advantage of this discovery, L Company roasted potatoes and onions, which they ate along with hot coffee for lunch.[52]

BY NOON ON September 13, the Saint Mihiel salient was gone. The regiment, along with the rest of the 42nd Division, had advanced twelve miles in less than twenty-nine hours, which was about thirty-six hours ahead of schedule. In the process, the 3rd Battalion captured over seven hundred German prisoners while the Allied total for the offensive included twenty-three hundred Germans killed and sixteen thousand captured.[53] Also, the 166th had captured huge amounts of enemy stores and equipment including fourteen large narrow-gauge railroad freight cars, one large water tank car, two carloads of engineering tools, three carloads of engineering material, five carloads of narrow-gauge track sections, one carload of wagon parts, two carloads of machinery, twenty Maxim machine guns, two hundred rifles, and two carloads of machine gun ammunition and spare parts, as well as stoves, practice ammunition (wooden bullets), one bowling alley, boots, masks, and packs. In the minds of the soldiers, however, the most important war material taken was four kegs of German beer. To this day, no one is quite sure why the beer was officially listed as captured since, for some unknown reason, the kegs were never turned in as war material.[54]

From September 14-17, the new front line was reasonably quiet. The only hostile activity came from German aircraft and long-range artillery. German bombers came overhead, especially at night, to drop bombs on the campsites and villages but did very little damage. As for the enemy artillery, they apparently did not want to lose any of their guns to counterbattery fire, so they employed long-range pieces deployed far behind the front. These did not do much physical damage, but their fire was somewhat unnerving. At regular intervals, the Germans would use one gun to fire a shell to the left, one to the right, one in the center, and one to the rear, while always mixing the targets and ranges. This practice continued as the men "grew almost crazy wondering where the next would hit." As Raymond Cheseldine pointed out, "In a heavy bombardment, this curiosity is not evident, but in the dead of night a lone gun can cause great anxiety."[55]

On September 17, the 166th was relieved by the French 146th Infantry Regiment, and the Ohioans pulled back to a campsite on the southern edge of the Bois de Nonsard. This location turned out to be a simply fabulous place for a bivouac. During their long period occupying the area, the Germans had established permanent camp facilities that, based on what the regiment had seen up to this point, bordered on the luxurious. The Germans had paved the roads leading throughout the camp area with cinder, and the roads were lined with "rustic cottages completely furnished and equipped with electric lights." The men took advantage of all these facilities, but there was one disadvantage to them—the Germans, of course, knew about these campsites and seemed to take special delight in shelling them every night.[56]

However, there was one other problem related to the luxurious quarters the regiment had found, and it offers yet another example of rank having its privileges and how some officers can abuse that privilege. The 166th's Supply Company was the first group to occupy these camps. They had moved in and made themselves quite comfortable, when General Lenihan, commander of the 83rd Brigade of which the 166th was a part, decided he wanted to be billeted in the cottages at the campsite. The general and his staff were given the most luxurious of the cottages, but, while there was more than enough room for everyone, including the Supply Company, the general decided he did not like all the activity around the nearby ration dumps, fearing they might attract shelling or an airstrike. So, Lenihan told the Supply Company that they had to find other accommodations.[57]

The Muleskinners immediately started to scout for another spot in which to camp the company and quickly found another site back from the main road. It was just as nice as their first set of quarters. But no sooner had the company moved in than General MacArthur, commander of the 84th Brigade, arrived. He and his staff had been billeted at the Chateau Benoit near the front lines, which MacArthur found too hot given the occasional artillery fire. So, he decided he liked the Supply Company's new location and ordered them out.[58]

Undaunted and undeterred, the Muleskinners once again set out to find a new home. This time, they found a clearing deep in the forest with what they called a "model village" of bungalow cottages in a lovely clearing. At the center of the clearing, there stood a wonderful single-story log building with four bedrooms and a big living room that had a large stone fireplace. Surrounding the large log building were several smaller houses and stables where the men could keep their mules and horses. It was perfect, and, of course, their occupancy did not last very long.[59]

After two days there, Major General Menoher, the 42nd Division commander, arrived. He and his staff found quarters in a bungalow park in the Forest of the Lovely Willow, just a short distance from the Supply Company's camp. While Menoher was perfectly happy with the arrangement, his chief artillery officer, General Gately, insisted that he needed to have his own set of cottages to use as the Division Artillery PC. Seeing the Supply Company's camp and finding it ideal for his purposes, he ordered the men to leave.[60]

This time, the Supply Company commander asked his veteran stable sergeant, Red Waggoman, to find a new campsite. Waggoman used his keen understanding of headquarters' staff officers to seek and find a good campsite that was "too damned close to the front for any generals!" The company moved there, set up, and remained undisturbed until the regiment moved again. However, the Supply Company said they could rightfully claim to be "the best billeting party the Division Generals ever had."[61]

On September 27, the regiment received orders to move back into the front line near Saint-Benoît-en-Woëvre and relieve the 167th Infantry. The men moved forward, and the relief took place quietly and without any incident. The 1st Battalion took the forward positions along with the Machine Gun Company, while the 2nd Battalion occupied the support positions, and the 3rd Battalion acted as the reserve. Unfortunately, there were no complex trenches or deep dugouts, only foxholes, and the Germans had decided not to remain quiet for very long. The enemy shelled these positions, and the foxholes provided little cover from the high explosives, shrapnel, and even mustard gas. The Supply Company carried food up to the line every night, but the men lived in misery.[62]

The division also ordered patrols to go into no man's land to scout enemy positions. These patrols went out every night, but on September 28, a rare set of daylight patrols were ordered. The two patrols consisted of twenty men from A Company led by Lieutenant Reppy and twenty more men from B Company led by Lieutenant DeLacy. Their objective was to determine whether or not the Germans had withdrawn from the village of Haumont, about two miles away across no man's land. They were to make this determination by actually making contact with the enemy.[63] In other words, they were to find the Germans and start a firefight, a foolproof method for learning if the enemy was still in the village but one fraught with obvious danger.

The patrols set off at 5:30 a.m. and were preceded by a three-hour barrage by American artillery. Reppy's patrol was to approach the village from the left while DeLacy split his men into two groups that would attempt to enter the town. As DeLacy's men approached Haumont, they saw a large group of Germans on the northern edge of the town who opened fire on one group of the Americans. The corporal leading the other group got close enough to the village's church to hear a telegraph being operated inside. However, the telegraph was apparently being used to call in artillery support, as a German barrage was soon pouring down on DeLacy and his men. Meanwhile, the Germans had detected Reppy's patrol and opened up on them with machine gun fire.[64]

The Germans fired red flare rockets into the air to warn their nearby comrades of the Americans' presence as the artillery barrage crashed into Haumont and to the right of DeLacy's position. Then two three-star white rockets were fired from the American lines behind Reppy and DeLacy, signaling American artillery to provide supporting fire. Within seconds, American shells came screeching overhead, landing in enemy positions about 150 yards northeast of the village with several striking the enemy's machine gun emplacements. One of DeLacy's men was hit and killed, but no one could reach his body to recover it. Another man was wounded, and Sergeant David Russell went forward under heavy machine gun fire to retrieve the soldier and carry him back to American lines.[65] The two patrols then withdrew with definitive information that the Germans were still in Haumont but did so with what should have been seen as an unacceptable loss given the limited value of the intelligence.

On September 30, the regiment received orders to fall back as units from the 89th Division arrived to relieve them. As they headed to the rear, they were still hoping for that rumored thirty-day rest period, but the final great Allied offensive of the war had begun, and they were needed elsewhere.

8

The Big Push—
The Meuse-Argonne to Sedan

"For my part, the only thing I want to take back to the States is myself safe and sound."—Private Enoch Williams, October 1, 1918

As K Company of the 3rd Battalion moved forward, German artillery was raking the road that led north from the village of Chéhéry toward Cheveuges and then on to the critical French city of Sedan. Despite the shells raining down, the company made good progress until heavy machine gun fire suddenly brought them to an abrupt halt. The company commander, Captain Reuben Hutchcraft, moved forward to the leading edge of the company's advance to see what was happening. "Hutch," as he was known to his close friends in the regiment, was a thirty-two-year-old attorney from Paris, Kentucky, who had served three terms in the state legislature representing Bourbon County before war was declared.[1] Hutchcraft had also enjoyed a prosperous legal career, and the University of Kentucky had invited him to take a position as a law professor.[2] He was described by Colonel Hough as "honest, chivalrous, and fearless." Hough saw him as the very epitome of a soldier and an officer and a gentleman. Hutchcraft was also somewhat diminutive and slight in stature, so much so that, when he first arrived as a new lieutenant, the men of his platoon referred to him as the "Boy Scout."[3] However, his men soon came to admire and respect him as a leader.

Crouching low to the ground, Hutchcraft could see that the German machine guns were well hidden in emplacements atop a knoll covered in pine trees just north of Cheveuges and about one hundred yards away from K Company's position. Rather than send any of his men forward, Hutchcraft decided to advance on the guns himself. He ordered his men to stay down, rose up, and began making a series of short dashes up the slope toward the German position. The Germans focused their fire on him, but he managed to elude their aim as he closed in on them. But his final rush would be his last. Now only thirty yards from the enemy, he rose to make another run forward, but they cut him down and he fell, "his body riddled with bullets."[4]

Seeing his captain go down, Private Eli Mutie, a young immigrant from Mos, Austria, got up and tried to run to Hutchcraft's aid. He only got a few feet before the German machine guns killed him. Corporal John Allen, Private Earl Dempsey, and Private Bobell Purdy each made the same attempt but were also killed by the withering enemy fire. Finally, Private Werner Eich, a nineteen-year-old soldier from Mount Washington, Ohio, began to crawl forward toward Captain Hutchcraft. After slithering along the ground for seventy yards, Eich finally reached the captain, who, while mortally wounded, was still alive. Eich tried valiantly to stem the bleeding from Hutchcraft's wounds as the German bullets swept above him, but to no avail. Grasping Eich's hands, Hutchcraft showed himself to indeed be a Kentucky gentleman of the "old school" by saying, "They've got me, boys, but don't give up."[5] Then he died.

Four men had been killed in action while trying to clear a path to Sedan. However, their deaths and those of many other men that would occur over the next few days would come to seem even more tragic and meaningless because, in only four days, the war would be over.

ON SEPTEMBER 26, as the 166th maintained its positions at the new line in Saint Mihiel, the Allies opened the final great offensive of the war in the area between the Meuse River and the Argonne Forest. When General Pershing agreed to provide American forces to Foch's planned offensive, he must have had many misgivings. First, the scale of the American role in the attack was stupendous for an army that just eighteen months before had numbered less than two hundred thousand men but now numbered over one million.[6] The logistics alone proved overwhelming, but the terrain and German defenses would be worse.

The terrain where the 166th Infantry would have to advance in the Meuse-Argonne. (*National Archives*)

On the right boundary of the battlefield was the Meuse River, which was unfordable, and a series of ridges that provided the enemy with a clear viewpoint of Allied movements and excellent positions for their artillery batteries. Twenty miles away, the left boundary went through the dense woods of the Argonne Forest. Filled with heavy growth and deep ravines, the Argonne was difficult to even walk through on the best of days much less under fire in combat. Also, steep bluffs overlooked the Aire River at the eastern edge of the forest, providing excellent observation and gun positions similar to those along the Meuse on the right.[7]

In between these dominating terrain features was the defile through which American forces would be expected to attack. Worse, perhaps, that defile had its own challenges in the form of the Montfaucon ridge and the surrounding dense woods. The Germans, being the skilled tacticians that they were, made good use of these features by establishing four layered lines of defense. The first two lines covered the initial ten miles of the defile. After passing those two lines, any attacker would run into the main line of defense, the Kriemhilde Stellung or Hindenburg Line. This formidable line of fortifications extended from the right boundary at the Meuse River north of Brieulles, then passed through the Cunel Heights before crossing the left boundary north of the Argonne near Grandpré.

If an attacker made it through these first three defensive fronts, they would confront the final line, the Freya Stellung, along the Barricourt Ridge. A member of Pershing's First Army staff later said, "This was the most ideal defensive terrain I have ever seen or read about. Nature had provided for flank and crossfire to the utmost in addition to concealment."[8]

The objective of the offensive was the French city of Sedan, which lay about twenty-five miles away. The city was a key strategic position because it was the major center for rail lines that might be critical to the Germans if they had to retreat behind the Rhine River. However, Sedan also had great symbolic value to the French because the city was linked to their humiliation in the Franco-Prussian War of 1870-1871. It was in Sedan that Napoleon III was forced to surrender to the king of Prussia, who would become Kaiser Wilhelm I, the father of the current kaiser.[9]

The Allied plan involved making two deep penetrations into the German lines on each side of the high ground at Montfaucon using turning movements to envelop enemy forces. Once those movements were complete, the Allies would mount an attack against the Hindenburg Line in the area around Romagne-sous-Montfaucon and Cunel. Unfortunately, while this plan seemed to pose numerous risks, the terrain provided few options, as there was no room to maneuver. Furthermore, any attack had to move quickly, as planners hoped to penetrate the Hindenburg Line on the second day of the offensive. This would require American forces to advance ten miles in one day, which was twice that planned in the Saint Mihiel salient.[10]

The offensive did not get off to an auspicious start. Many of the problems for the Americans involved the divisions that made up the initial attack force. Some of them were new to France, were filled with draftees, and were brought straight from their training areas to the front. Then they were sent over the top directly into German defenses that had been carefully prepared over four years. It was the same issue the 166th had experienced with its draftee replacements but much worse by orders of magnitude. These divisions went into the maelstrom as ordered and did manage to push four miles into the German lines in the first two days. Of the nine American divisions that began the offensive on September 26, however, several had to be pulled out of the attack after only three days because of the severe casualties they had suffered.[11] By the time the 166th received orders to begin their move to the Meuse-Argonne on September 30, the offensive had only made it halfway to the objectives planned for the first two days of the attack, and, furthermore, a renewed attack that began on October 1 was making very slow progress.

So, as had become the pattern of American operations, the 42nd Division and other more experienced units were now called upon to assume the primary burden of the offensive. In a way, this was something of a backhanded compliment. On the one hand, it was a recognition of how far the 166th Infantry and the 42nd Division had progressed in their combat capabilities, while, on the other, it meant more suffering and death for the men who would bear that burden.

ON SEPTEMBER 30, Colonel Hough received word the regiment was being relieved by units from the 89th Division. As had so often been the case, the relief was to take place at night so that it would not be observed by the Germans. But getting organized and creeping quietly in the dark is never easy. Roy Bailey, a twenty-year-old platoon sergeant in D Company from Marion, Ohio, wrote in his diary that he "had a time getting [the] platoon together," but he had them off the line by 10:00 p.m. He added to his entry for the day by writing, "Don't know where [I] am taking platoon, but on my way."[12]

Except for the 3rd Battalion, the regiment was off the line by midnight, and they hiked about six miles to a bivouac on the western edge of the Bois-de-Pannes, getting there around 1:00 a.m. The next morning, the 3rd Battalion arrived in camp, but it would not be for long. Orders soon came, telling the regiment to begin marching toward Saint Mihiel that afternoon. Before they departed, however, the regiment had a mail call, which was the first they had seen in several weeks since the offensive in Saint Mihiel had begun.[13]

"Feverish preparations" for the march started, and at 12:30 p.m. on October 1 the regiment started its hike to Saint Mihiel. When they arrived there around 6:00 p.m., they found trucks waiting to begin their journey to the west of Verdun, where they would join the new Allied offensive. Once the men were loaded, the trucks drove off and traveled all night. Around 7:00 a.m. on October 2, after a drive of about thirteen miles,[14] the column of trucks came to a stop near Neuville-en-Verdunoi, the men unloaded, and the regiment went into bivouac.

However, their stay proved to be a short one. At 9:00 a.m. on October 4, they began a fourteen-mile march northeast to Jubécourt, which was followed the next day by a twelve-mile hike deep into the Bois de Montfaucon, which took them over the ground recently captured by the US 37th Division. As they marched through the forest, the fall rains so typical of France resumed, and as the sun set it became windy and much colder. As the regiment marched in the driving rain, the night sky to the north was lit by red flashes of artillery, and a "deep, reverberating murmur at intervals kept alive the fact that the war was no myth, no dream, but terribly real."[15]

The rains made the road north from the village of Avocourt turn into a quagmire of deep, sticky mud, which made life for the Supply Company's mules and Muleskinners very difficult. When the wagon train reached one steep hill, things became particularly challenging. The mules were exhausted and needed human assistance to make it over the ridge. One by one, the wagons were pulled by mules and pushed by soldiers over the hill. Then one wagon arrived that was obviously overloaded. The poor mules managed to get the wagon halfway up the hill before they could pull it no farther. Six men moved to the rear of the wagon and began pushing it, but soon it was stuck firmly in the mire.[16]

The muleskinner in charge was cursing softly but "prayerfully." As the men caught their breath, the muleskinner looked about him in the dark, rain-filled night for some more help. He soon spotted a large, bulky figure by the roadside and shouted to him, "Come on, you big stiff, and give us a hand. How do you get to loaf?" The man quietly moved to the wagon, grasped the spokes of one of the wagon's wheels, and said, "Let's go, all together." With a mighty lift of his shoulders and a steady pull and push by mules and men, the wagon began to move up the hill until, at last, it reached the crest.[17]

With the wagon moved successfully, the large, dark figure walked away to where a horse could be seen waiting for him. He mounted the horse and called out, "Is that the last of the big wagons?" The men replied that it was. As the rider and his horse rode off into the night, the muleskinner realized just who that dark figure he had called a "big stiff" was—it was Colonel Hough. In a hushed voice, he said, "My Lord, that was the Old Man," and then, in evident admiration, he added that the colonel had "out-pushed the whole crowd."[18]

About 4:30 a.m. on October 6, the regiment turned onto a plank road built by the Germans and went into bivouac. When the sun finally rose, it revealed a scene of devastation like nothing the men had seen thus far in the war. "Literally, every inch of the ground had been torn by shells," recalled Raymond Cheseldine. There were craters fifteen feet deep and

The ruins of the town of Montfaucon. (*National Archives*)

just as wide as far as one could see, and what had once been a dense forest filled with trees and undergrowth was now "a mere graveyard of broken limbs and splintered stumps." The men set up their pup tents between the shell holes and shattered trees as the October rains continued.[19]

It was quite a grim campsite. As the rain continued and the temperatures continued to fall, the men huddled together. They were still wearing uniforms that had been issued during the heat of August, had only one blanket, and most did not have an overcoat. The kitchens did their best, but fresh foods, even meat, were in short supply. At night, German artillery pounded the town of Montfaucon, just a few miles away, and sent shells screaming into every corner of the woods. Along with marauding German bombers in the dark skies, the big German guns made sleep all but impossible. For four days and five nights, the regiment lay in these wet, soaked woods, "doggedly waiting." Morale also began to suffer. "Men were sick in mind and body," wrote Raymond Cheseldine, as "each day saw ambulances start back with new loads of human freight."[20]

On August 10, the regiment was ordered to begin its move to the front lines. The inexperienced units of the American First Army needed relief after repeated attempts to break the Hindenburg Line. In some ways, the men of the 42nd Division were now seen as "shock troops" from an elite, combat-hardened unit. The tag of being unreliable National Guard citizen-soldiers seemed to be gone at last. Even the Germans had come to respect these Guardsmen. Just a day before the 166th began to move up to the front, the headquarters of the German group of armies in the Meuse-Argonne issued an analysis that said, "The engagement of the 42nd Division is to be expected soon. It is in splendid fighting condition and is counted among the best American divisions."[21] But this newfound reputation had come at a terrible cost in dead and wounded from Champagne to the wheat fields above the Ourcq River.

The regiment initially marched about eight miles before camping near a little knoll that had been the scene of desperate fighting just a few days before. Dana Daniels walked over to the small hill to take a look. The burial details had not been able to visit the site yet, and the dead still littered the ground. Daniels recorded that he counted the bodies of thirty-four Germans and thirty-five Americans on the knoll.[22]

The next morning, October 11, the 166th marched about four miles through the rain to positions near Exermont. The regiment halted so the officers and noncommissioned officers could go forward to the front lines and make a reconnaissance of the regiment's new positions along a line near Sommerance that had been designated as Hills 240, 263, and 269. That night, the men quietly advanced to relieve the exhausted soldiers of the 1st Division and were in position by dawn. The 2nd Battalion under Major Geran took the regiment's forward positions southeast of Sommerance, with the 3rd Battalion in support on the southwestern side of Hill 240 and the 1st Battalion in reserve in the Bois de Montrebeau. On Major Geran's left was the 325th Infantry of the 82nd Division, while the old reliable New York Fightin' Irish of the 165th Infantry were aligned on the right of the regiment. [23]

As the sun came up, the men of the 166th found the sights surrounding their foxholes anything but comforting. Alison Reppy later recalled that the scene "on that cold, wet and foggy morning was one that can never be forgotten."[24] Groups of dead Americans lay scattered everywhere, and German machine gunners still lay dead in their gun emplacements. Dana Daniels wrote in his diary that "there were many dead lying around here, all the horrors of war."[25] And this carnage was not limited to human beings. The fields around them were filled with dead horses and mules who had been either killed by artillery fire or died in their harness of physical strain and starvation. "The stench arising from the bodies of these poor, dumb beasts added the last element of grimness," wrote Alison Reppy. "Strew the field with rifles, packs, machine guns, and ammunition, and you have the picture."[26] Leon Miesse, now commanding C Company of the 1st Battalion, speaking of the new American units that had been so badly used on this part of the front, added, "The sights which met our eyes are too sad to relate, but somebody blundered."[27]

As the men surveyed the surrounding terrain, they could see why these positions had been so difficult to take from the Germans. The ground would also make it hard to resupply the men of the regiment and the entire 42nd Division. It was a rugged landscape, marked by four large conical-shaped hills with two in perfect alignment from front to rear in each of the division's brigade sectors. The only access to these hills was via deep valleys and ravines over muddy roads so rudimentary that they barely qualified for the term "road." The mud in them was a foot deep, and water filled the pathways, making them more like canals than roads. The conditions were so bad that no form of animal transport could pass. This also meant that ambulances could not get to the front lines. Therefore, everything from food to ammunition to wounded men had to be carried by the soldiers.[28]

The first day in the lines proved to be quiet, as the regiment's men sat in their foxholes with the rain continuing to douse both their bodies and spirits. The next day, October 13, the Germans opened a heavy barrage on the 166th's positions in the late morning. Around 3:45 p.m., the artillery fire increased in intensity, and German infantry could be seen advancing across the open ground to the regiment's front. Any chance for enemy success, however, quickly ended when American artillery laid down its own barrage on the German infantry. The attacking waves immediately came to a stop, and the Germans fell back to their trenches.[29]

While the regiment was sitting in their soggy foxholes and fending off the weak enemy infantry attack, the operations planners at the First Army were hard at work devising a new plan to break the Hindenburg Line. They decided that a double-enveloping pincer movement similar to their original attack plan for September 26 might break through the formidable German defensive line. While the plan involved all seven American divisions currently deployed at the front, the American 5th Division and the 42nd Division would draw the critical assignments for the attack.

The idea was to break the German lines between Saint Georges and the ridges just west of Romagne in a single attack on October 14. The American V Corps, including the 42nd Division, would advance through the enemy lines and swing to the right toward the Bois de Bantheville behind the Hindenburg Line while the American III Corps did the same and pivoted to their left, enveloping German forces. As the 42nd Division attacked toward the villages of Saint Georges and Landres-et-Saint Georges, the 82nd Division would also move forward covering the 42nd's left flank. While this pincer attack was taking place, the 32nd Division was supposed to attack in the center to prevent the Germans from shifting forces to support either of their flanks. The hope was that, once these forces had seized the heights at the center of the German lines, the Hindenburg Line would become untenable, forcing a German withdrawal.[30] Like many such plans, it looked logical, sound, and executable on paper. The reality, however, showed otherwise, as almost nothing went right from the very beginning.

The regiment received its orders for the attack just after midnight on October 14. They called for an attack by the 166th Infantry and 165th Infantry on the German trenches between Saint Georges and Landres-et-Saint Georges. The 166th was to advance directly toward Saint Georges on the far left while the 165th moved forward on their immediate right. Meanwhile, the Alabama 167th Infantry and Iowa 168th Infantry would attack on a line to the right of the Ohioans and New Yorkers. The Alabama and Iowa regiments' position at the front was slightly to the rear of the 166th and 165th, so they would begin their attack at 5:30 a.m. Once they had advanced forward to the same line as the 166th and 165th, the entire division would attack around 8:30 a.m. G Company and H Company would make up the 166th's first wave with E and F Companies right behind them.[31]

The problems the regiment faced in this attack were overwhelming. It was just over two miles from the jumping-off positions to the German trenches between Saint Georges and Landres-et-Saint Georges, and the ground was completely open. From the moment the men left their foxholes, the Germans could observe every move they made. The only cover from enemy fire would be the shell holes that pockmarked the terrain. Also, the Germans had managed to lay down belts of barbed wire across no man's land.[32] Anyone trying to clear pathways through the wire would be an easy target for German machine guns.

The other problem in the attack was a familiar one: a lack of artillery support. While the plan for employing American artillery was sound, many felt there were simply not enough guns available to do the kind of damage needed to overwhelm the Hindenburg Line. The Germans had

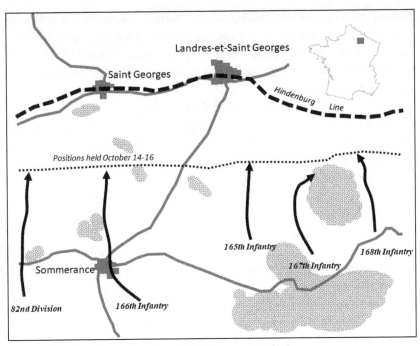

The 166th Infantry's attack against Saint Georges. (*Author*)

four years to make this defensive line into a formidable barricade to any attacker. Therefore, the ability to concentrate heavy artillery firepower would be critical. Once again, it looked like the pre-war American doctrine that minimized the importance of artillery support was adversely impacting the infantry's probability of success.

At 5:30 a.m., the 167th Infantry and 168th Infantry advanced as planned, and, at 8:30 a.m., the men of the 166th saw a rocket rise into the sky, indicating those two regiments were in position. As the appointed time for the division's general advance arrived, American artillery laid down as heavy a barrage as it could on the German positions, and the regiment moved forward to the attack. The men picked their way across the field under comparatively light German artillery fire. An hour later, they had advanced about 1,300 yards to Hill 230 just southeast of Sommerance, where enemy artillery fire increased, including gas rounds, and German resistance became much stiffer.[33]

The first two waves pressed on, and just before 11:00 a.m. they had reached the woods immediately west of Sommerance, and the 3rd Battalion entered the village right behind them. At noon, they were ordered to keep moving, so the 2nd Battalion started advancing toward Saint Georges. But within an hour, progress slowed as machine gun fire from nine different enemy emplacements swept the ground ahead of them. Not long after that, the advance came to a complete halt a few hundred yards south of Saint Georges.[34]

A few hours later, it was decided that another artillery barrage on the German trenches between Saint Georges and Landres-et-Saint Georges would begin at 3:30 p.m. and continue for an hour. In an attempt to make up for the lack of guns, every artillery piece was ordered to use a maximum rate of fire of one hundred rounds per hour. The American artillery opened fire as planned, but it clearly was not making any difference. So, just after 4:00 p.m., orders came for the barrage to continue until 5:00 p.m. An hour after the artillery lifted its fire, the assaulting companies moved out with patrols in the lead. These patrols were told to advance until resistance was met. That resistance came very quickly, and, despite the artillery support, no further advance could be made. After only moving about a mile, the attack bogged down completely, and the men of the 2nd Battalion dug in. Later that night, orders arrived for the 3rd Battalion to relieve the 2nd Battalion and for the 1st Battalion to move up into a support position.[35]

The day had proved to be something of a small disaster. Only the 32nd Division had any success, while the 42nd and 5th Divisions were lucky to have made any progress at all.[36] But at no point was the Hindenburg Line pierced by the attack. The 166th, meanwhile, had suffered 267 casualties, with 105 killed, 28 wounded, and 134 missing in action, a great price to pay for less than a mile of ground. Most of the losses came in H Company, which had 123 casualties.[37]

At the end of the day, First Army Headquarters decided that, despite casualties and the lack of success, both the 5th and 42nd Divisions must resume their attacks on October 15 and continue until the originally planned objective points had been reached. As a result, 83rd Brigade Headquarters issued a field order at 1:00 a.m. directing the 166th to resume its assault on Saint Georges at 7:30 a.m., preceded by fifteen minutes of artillery fire on the enemy's wire barricades. The artillery fire would lift temporarily to allow the men of the 3rd Battalion to get through the wire. Then the artillery fire would resume with a rolling barrage that would move forward at a rate of one hundred meters every six minutes. This time, L and M Companies would make up the first wave of the assault, with I and K Companies in the second wave.[38]

Machine gunners advance in some of the dense woods at the Meuse-Argonne. (*National Archives*)

A new and potentially important element was also added to the October 15 attack plan: tanks. The First Army had used tanks, mostly French-built Renault FT light tanks, from the outset of the offensive, but they had proved ineffective primarily because of mechanical breakdowns. At one point in the offensive, over half of the First Army's tanks were inoperable. For the day's attack, the First Army planned to provide sixteen tanks from the US 3rd Tank Brigade, which was commanded by Lieutenant Colonel George Patton, who would later lead the American Third Army's tanks across France in July 1944.[39]

As the sun began to rise, the men from the 3rd Battalion waited for their tank support to arrive and prepared to advance. The Germans must have anticipated the attack because, at 6:20 a.m., they began to send both high explosive and gas shells into the regiment's positions around Sommerance. This was followed by a German infantry counterattack an hour later. At 7:30 a.m., the time to go over the top arrived, but the regiment still had no tank support. So, despite the lack of tanks and the enemy infantry counterattack, the regiment moved forward with its assault, as scheduled.[40]

Not long after the 3rd Battalion started to move forward, the regiment received messages saying that the tanks were on their way and would arrive soon. Meanwhile, the regiment's men crept forward across no man's

land, and M Company sent patrols forward into some woods to clear out
any German infantry that might be taking cover there. The men entered
the woods, where they engaged a considerable number of German infantrymen. In a brief firefight, they inflicted heavy casualties on the
enemy, who quickly withdrew. However, M Company lost twenty men in
the process.[41]

Meanwhile, the rest of the assault was getting nowhere, and, at 8:55
a.m., word was received that there would be no tank support. Apparently
so many of the sixteen tanks allocated for the attack had broken down
that the tank commander had to withdraw and reorganize.[42]

At 9:35 a.m., an artillery barrage was called for to sweep the entire zone
of enemy trenches, and, at 10:15 a.m., the barrage began. The artillery
would maintain their fire until noon when the infantry from the regiment
would once again try to move forward. As the American artillery struck
the German positions, L and M Companies waited to renew the attack.
But when they did so, they discovered that the 165th was not covering
their right flank and, as a result, enemy machine guns on the right were
raking their positions. The New Yorkers had been unable to move forward
and, without their presence on the right, the 166th's assault waves could
not advance. Despite this, M Company kept trying. By 1:30 p.m., however,
they had made four unsuccessful attempts to advance and had lost sixty
men.[43] By nightfall, all further attempts to advance were halted.

During the attack that day, I Company took heavy casualties among
its officers. Not only were Lieutenants Christenson, Smith, Wooley, Stutz,
and Belhorn hit, but the company commander, Captain Grave, was also
severely wounded. Just before Lieutenant Belhorn was put in an ambulance, he sent a message to the 3rd Battalion commander, Major
Haubrich, requesting the much-needed tank support. His message said,
"Please send tanks at once. Excuse holes in this message blank, but it's the
only one I have." Later, it was learned that the holes in the message paper
were caused by German machine gun bullets that went through Belhorn's
dispatch case before wounding him.[44]

H Company, which was part of the first assault wave on October 14,
sent one of its platoons on an advanced patrol toward the regiment's left.
As they moved forward, the platoon's two leaders went down with
wounds and went to the rear. That left Sergeant Irvin Dresbach in command. Dresbach was twenty-three years old and a house painter from
Hallsville, Ohio. He had joined the old 4th Ohio in June 1916 just in time
to make the trip to the Mexican border and had risen to the rank of cor-

The 166th attacked across the open ground between Sommerance, above, and Saint Georges. (*State Historical Society of Missouri*)

poral by the time the regiment went into federal service in August 1917. Even though Dresbach had been severely gassed during the morning's barrage by the Germans, leaving his eyes and throat burned and swollen, the young sergeant took command without hesitation and pushed the platoon forward. When they encountered the Germans southwest of Saint Georges, he ordered an attack that broke the enemy who fled west into the waiting arms of the 82nd Division.[45]

On October 16, the regiment remained in its positions as the 82nd Division on their left was ordered to make an assault. If they were successful in advancing, K Company was told to send out strong patrols to link up with the 82nd and then try to enter Saint Georges from the west. If K Company was able to enter the town, M Company would make an attack on the flank of the enemy trenches east of Saint Georges.[46]

At noon, Captain Hutchcraft, commander of K Company, left the regiment's positions near Sommerance and took his patrol to the western edge of Saint Georges, believing that the 82nd was making its advance as planned. However, not long after the patrol had left friendly lines, the 3rd Battalion PC in Sommerance received word that the 82nd was not advancing but, instead, had merely been ordered to keep pace with the 78th Division on its left. Captain Hutchcraft soon discovered this error on his own when he advanced and found that the 82nd was a considerable distance down the road south of Saint Georges. He tried to make contact with the 82nd, but before he could do so, a German observation plane spotted his patrol and directed heavy enemy machine gun fire on his men. Realizing there was no way for him to gain entry to Saint Georges, he withdrew his patrol with the loss of two men killed and four wounded.[47] With that, the regiment's efforts to break the Hindenburg Line were over.

After the failure to take Saint Georges and Landres-et-Saint Georges, the V Corps commander, General Summerall, decided that someone must be blamed. As is often the case, even though no one individual was responsible for the failure, Summerall had to assign blame to ensure neither he nor his staff was found at fault. On the night of October 17, Summerall relieved both General Lenihan as 83rd Brigade commander and Colonel Mitchell as commander of the 165th Infantry.

In relieving both officers, General Summerall also indicated that he thought Colonel Hough should be relieved, but he left that decision to General Menoher, the 42nd Division commander. Menoher called Hough to Division Headquarters for a meeting in which the division commander told Hough of Summerall's opinion. Menoher also commented on what he saw as a problem involving low morale in the 166th, apparently blaming that for the regiment's inability to take Saint Georges. To say that Colonel Hough took issue with Menoher's views would be an understatement. He told the general that his men's morale was not low but that they were physically worn out. He roared at Menoher, shouting, "No one man can take [the] fatigue out of men who have been living in water-filled holes in the ground with no overcoats and but one blanket seeing their comrades killed by shell fire or dying from pneumonia. The men want action. If you hold me responsible for the condition which you allege to be true, then remove me now."[48]

Menoher immediately backed down, which was a good thing as the men of the regiment might have mutinied had Hough been relieved. Most of the men in the 166th believed a lack of strong artillery support was the primary reason they had been unable to advance. Lacking that, any infantry attack would have been "sheer suicide."[49]

But there may have been at least some element of truth to Summerall's beliefs about low morale. By October 15, rumors were rampant among the men that peace talks were underway and that an end to the fighting might be in the offing. There was some factual basis for the rumors, as the German government had been exchanging messages with President

Wilson since October 5 regarding his proposed "Fourteen Points" as a basis for peace. Dana Daniels wrote in his diary on October 15 that the men were "very anxious about peace talk."[50] There was little doubt then that, given that the war might end very soon, at least some portion of the regiment's men had little appetite for facing enemy machine gun fire in what might eventually amount to nothing but a meaningless gesture.

In the early morning hours of October 18, the regiment received reports that the enemy might be falling back from their trenches. So, at 3:00 a.m., a patrol was sent out to ascertain the facts. The patrol pushed forward to Hill 230, about five hundred yards north of the regiment's positions outside Sommerance, and a small detail was sent ahead to a point about one hundred fifty yards south of the road leading into Saint Georges. Almost immediately they encountered heavy machine gun fire from the German lines, which clearly demonstrated that the enemy had not abandoned their trenches.[51]

That same day, however, Colonel Hough's comments to General Menoher seemed to pay off. Suddenly, as if by magic, a shipment of new uniforms, underwear, blankets, and overcoats from the division stockpiles arrived at the Supply Company. To men who had been living in filthy, wet clothing for over three weeks, this was a godsend. But while improved, the supply situation was far from perfect. Hot, fresh food was still unavailable, and the men living in their foxholes continued to subsist on a steady diet of canned meat, dehydrated potatoes and onions, and hard bread.[52]

Little happened for the next five days. There was an attack planned for October 20, but it was canceled when one of the staff officers from 42nd Division Headquarters got lost and was captured while carrying all the orders and maps for the assault.[53] Instead, the men sat in their foxholes on the hill outside Sommerance and tried to take cover from enemy artillery fire. In fact, every entry in Sergeant Roy Bailey's diary for October 16 through October 23 said the same thing: "Still on hill, shelled."[54]

As the men waited in the rain and mud, Enoch Williams was able to secure a scrap of YMCA paper to write home and tell his mother about the delights of living in a foxhole dugout. "Am in the lines now but expect to be relieved soon as we have been in about 14 days," he wrote. "Say, you ought to see my home. It's a hole in the ground [with] a few boards and dirt on top. The entrance is just big enough to crawl in and runs enough inside for two to lay squeezed up close together. But that don't matter as long as we are dry and warm. Gee, but I would like to sleep in a real bed once."[55]

On October 26, a new field order arrived from Division Headquarters that, in the words of Raymond Cheseldine, "aroused the mingled feelings of relief and disappointment." The order stated that the entire 83rd Brigade was coming off the line at last and being replaced by the Marine Brigade of the 2nd Division. The men of the 166th would finally get out of their watery, mud-filled holes for the first time in more than two weeks. However, the order also provided details on the hundreds of new artillery pieces that were coming on the line to support a renewed attack. The Ohioans had endured, attacked, lost hundreds of men, and attacked again to no avail because there was not enough artillery to support them. But now the guns were arriving, and someone else would get to make the breakthrough.[56]

On October 31, the 166th pulled back from the front and made camp near the village of Charpentry. Meanwhile, on the morning of November 1, the war's greatest concentration of American artillery opened fire, and the final phase of the offensive began. The marines and 2nd Division smashed through the Hindenburg Line and drove the Germans back toward Sedan. As the men of the regiment listened to the massive barrage, one soldier was heard to say with disgust, "They had us up there S.O.L. ['shit outta luck'] for two weeks, and now listen to what they're givin' them Marines. I ain't hankerin' fer no more fighting than's necessary, but somebody's always takin' the joy out of life."[57]

THE REGIMENT HAD BEEN at their new camp in Charpentry only three days when orders came to prepare to move forward again. With the Germans in a general retreat, they and the rest of the 42nd Division were needed to help keep pushing the enemy backward, not allowing them the time to dig in and establish a new defensive position. On November 3, the 166th broke camp and marched eleven miles to Verpel, where they bivouacked for the night and had a meal of canned meat and coffee.[58]

The men arose from their pup tents, packed up, and were on the road again at 6:00 a.m. the next morning, this time marching eight miles north to the village of Authe. As the men approached the town, they could see that the villagers had placed white flags atop many of the houses to let them know the Germans were no longer there. As the regiment made camp for the night, they sent out patrols, but this time, the patrols went out in trucks because the Germans were retreating so fast.[59] That night the men hoped for some warm food, but the Supply Company got held up in the clogged roads behind them. So, it was another night of eating canned beef in the cold rain.[60]

That night, the 166th was joined in Authe by a battalion from 6th Division, known in the AEF as the "Sight Seeing Sixth" because they always seemed to somehow avoid combat. The men from the 6th camped just across the road and, to everyone's surprise, proceeded to light numerous campfires and fire up their kitchens. Everyone in the 166th looked on in shock. They were only a few miles from the Germans, and everyone except neophytes like the "Sight Seeing Sixth" knew you did not show any light at night when so close to the enemy. The regiment's Muleskinners, always an outspoken lot, went across the road to tell the 6th's men to douse their lights, but no one would listen, and their "lights burned merrily."[61]

As fate would have it, the pulsing sound of approaching German bombers soon filled the night, and the Muleskinners made one last attempt to avert disaster by yelling across the road for them to put out their fires. No one listened. So, the regiment's Muleskinners decided to at least try to save some of the 6th's animals. They dashed across the road, unhitching mules from their carts and wagons as fast as they could and taking them back to safety with the 166th's mules and horses. Everyone in the regiment took cover as the men from the 6th laughed at the sight of everyone scrambling to get to a safe place.[62]

A few minutes later, the bombers saw all the lights and turned toward this fat, tempting target. They descended to a low altitude to make sure their bombs would not miss and began to pulverize the 6th's campsite. At least twelve bombs fell on the camp, killing several men and destroying equipment. Once the bombers were gone, the Muleskinners took the mules they had saved back across the road and hitched them to their wagons, barely able to disguise their disgust for the officers and men who refused to listen to the advice of experienced front-line soldiers.[63]

On the morning of November 5, the 166th took to the road with orders to catch up to the 78th Division and leapfrog it to become the lead unit for the advance. So, the objective for the day was to reach the towns of Brieulles-sur-Bar and Verrieres, about four miles away. However, when the regiment arrived in Brieulles-sur-Bar, they discovered the Germans had destroyed the causeway leading to Verrieres. The causeway had been about one thousand feet long, spanning the Biévre River and a marsh creek, and had stood fifteen feet above the valley floor. Nothing, not man or mules, could make it across with the causeway gone, and Dana Daniels noted that the "holes in the road were so big an ordinary horse could be dropped in very easy."[64] The engineers were called forward to make repairs while the regiment rested and waited.

As the engineers built a corduroy bridge over the holes in the causeway, Dana Daniels and E Company waited in Brieulles-sur-Bar. Much of the village had been damaged by artillery fire, and only a few houses were left standing. With the Germans now gone, some of the villagers were returning to see what was left of their homes. Daniels saw one elderly woman on her knees in front of her home. She was sobbing and moaning as she looked at what once had been her family's home for generations but now was nothing more than a pile of rocks and bricks.[65]

The people of this village and others told the Americans the same tragic story. During the last few weeks before they had evacuated their village, the Germans had rounded up all the young women and men between the ages of seventeen and fifty and sent them to Germany as slave laborers. Also, before they retreated back toward Sedan, the Germans had taken all foodstuffs and livestock, leaving nothing for the villagers to eat.[66]

After a few hours, Colonel Hough decided they could not wait any longer for the engineers to finish their work. He ordered the regiment to move out and slog through the knee-deep waters of the river and the marsh beyond. They made it across, moved through Verrieres, and arrived in the Bois du Mont Dieu about four miles beyond the town at 2:30 p.m. Here, they passed the lines of the 78th Division and assumed the lead, throwing out patrols toward the village of La Neuville-á-Maire. The patrols ran into German resistance near the town and withdrew for the night to the northern edge of the Bois du Mont Dieu.[67]

It proved to be far from a restful night due to the incessant rain and enemy artillery fire. Leon Miesse wrote in his journal, "I never spent a more miserable night. Between the rain and shrapnel, we had a lovely time."[68]

During the night of November 5, Division Headquarters issued a new field order designated as F.O. No. 53. The order directed its regiments to continue the pursuit of the enemy at 5:30 a.m. on November 6 with the objective of "defeating the enemy's rear-guards and capturing or destroying his troops and transports before a crossing [of the Meuse River] is affected." The order concluded by saying that the pursuit must be "pushed with the utmost vigor" and that the "opportunity presented to the Division is one of the most brilliant of the war."[69]

This field order exhibited a shortcoming that was becoming disturbingly common in the weeks since the Meuse-Argonne campaign had

Road congestion that slowed the progress of the advance toward Sedan. (*National Archives*)

begun. It asked men to achieve challenging if not impossible objectives by declaring the pride and reputation of their units were at stake while, at the same time, providing none of the resources required to actually perform the mission. In this case, the critical resource was, once again, artillery support.

With the infantry advancing so quickly, artillery batteries could not keep up because of the terrible road conditions. To make matters worse, even when artillery support was available, not enough ammunition had made it forward for the guns to provide an effective barrage. Finally, if a few guns made it to the front and had ammunition, the maps provided to both the infantry and artillery units were so bad that they could not be used to safely provide target coordinates. Therefore, to achieve the field order's objectives, the regiment's men would have to surround and silence enemy machine guns all on their own.[70]

As F.O. No. 53 was being issued by the 42nd Division, two other division headquarters in the I Corps to the 166th's immediate left flank were issuing the same orders. In a colossal mix-up that remains a mystery, all three divisions were told to race to Sedan using the same roads and ignoring each division's assigned sector boundaries.[71] Given the lack of artillery support and the mass confusion that these orders were bound to produce, a quick and easy advance into Sedan was highly unlikely.

At 6:00 a.m., the 166th moved out of the Bois du Mont Dieu and began to advance up the main road to La Neuville-á-Maire and Chémery-sur-

Bar. As the main body of the regiment departed the woods, a patrol led by Lieutenants Sinclair Wilson and Thomas Freeman crept up to the outskirts of La Neuville-á-Maire. As they cautiously entered the village, they found that the Germans had left just ahead of their arrival. Moving to the northern edge of the town, the patrol came under machine gun fire from enemy positions just southeast of Chémery-sur-Bar. But the Germans quickly retreated through the town, going over the hills near Chéhéry, about three miles away from La Neuville-á-Maire.[72]

The regiment picked up the pace of their march and entered Chémery-sur-Bar. When the regiment arrived in the village, they were greeted with cheers, flowers, and embraces from the villagers. The people provided them with warm billets for the night in their homes, where Dana Daniels said the men dried out their clothes and blankets and "hunted cooties." They also found one German soldier whom they took prisoner but not before one of the French villagers took the opportunity to pummel the hapless German. Once he was saved from this vicious assault, he apparently was very willing to talk, saying that the Germans were massing to make a stand just south of Sedan.[73]

Around 9:00 p.m. that night, as the regiment camped in and around Chémery-sur-Bar, a new division field order, F.O. No. 54, reached Colonel Hough. This order told the colonel that the pursuit of the Germans must continue immediately without any further pauses, even to rest. Finally, the order said that the Meuse River must be crossed and Sedan taken by the end of the next day, November 7. The entire order was ludicrous. Colonel Hough wisely decided to ignore the "continue immediately" part of the order, as the men were already bivouacked for the night. However, he ordered the 3rd Battalion to move out at 2:30 a.m., followed by the 2nd and 1st Battalions once the men had a hot meal that would be served at 3:00 a.m.[74]

The lead patrols from the 3rd Battalion reached Chéhéry by 4:00 a.m. and quickly moved through the town, where they captured some Germans who were trying to drive two trucks away.[75] As the 3rd Battalion moved forward, German artillery and machine gun fire increased, but the men pressed on. As the rest of the regiment moved through Chéhéry, patrols from the 28th Infantry of the 1st Division showed up right behind them. This came as a surprise to Colonel Hough, who did not realize as yet that the 1st Division had received similar orders to take Sedan. So, they had not only entered the 42nd Division's sector, but they had also cut across the 77th Division's boundaries to try to get ahead of the 166th.[76]

Shortly after that, General Parker, commander of the 1st Division, arrived in Chéhéry. He set up a command post and told Colonel Hough and Colonel Reilly, the 83rd Brigade commander, that he was going to advance on Sedan no matter what orders the 166th had received.[77]

The 28th Infantry marched out of Chéhéry right beside the men from the 2nd Battalion on the highway to Sedan and began to try to overtake the 3rd Battalion in the advanced position. However, Major Haubrich kept the 3rd Battalion moving in what had become a race for Sedan. It would have been a complete farce had not the lives of so many men been at risk from this sort of competitive stupidity. As enemy resistance increased near Cheveuges around 9:20 a.m., Major Haubrich called for 2nd Battalion to move forward to his left while the 1st Battalion came forward on his right. He planned to envelop both flanks of the German defenses, but the 1st Division troops refused to follow his orders. They moved up on his line of advance and would not withdraw, preventing him from conducting his attack.[78]

By 2:00 p.m., the situation deteriorated to the point that no further progress was possible. Haubrich ordered all the regiment's men on the line of attack to dig in. They were about a half-mile south of Cheveuges and only about four miles from the Meuse River and Sedan, with the Germans positioned on a hill just two miles below the riverbanks.[79] But nothing could be done because there was no artillery support, and the units from the two different American divisions refused to cooperate.[80]

During the fighting at Cheveuges on November 7, the regiment's new chaplain, Father George Carpentier, distinguished himself. Carpentier, a Dominican priest who had been a teacher at Aquinas College High School in Columbus, Ohio, before the war, had joined the 166th during the Saint Mihiel offensive and quickly endeared himself to the men. He might have been a soft-spoken, gentle man, but he was not a chaplain who did his work in the safety of the rear.

During one of his first days with the regiment, he heard a dangerous patrol was heading out into no man's land. He immediately went to Lieutenant Rankin, the patrol's commander, and, without hesitation, asked to go out with the patrol. When Rankin asked him why he wanted to go, Carpentier said that he thought the men might need spiritual aid. While he was clearly puzzled by such an unusual request from a chaplain, Rankin shrugged and agreed. Rankin later said, "It was as good an excuse as any. I let him go because he wanted to go, and I liked his nerve. Of course, he knew I wasn't responsible for his safety, he just went because he felt he should go."[81] After that, Carpentier's "Ohio Boys" called him the "chaplain who went over-the-top."[82]

As the 3rd Battalion was trying to fight their way into Cheveuges, Father Carpentier was with them. Carpentier was a native of France, having been born in Rennes. His family immigrated to America when he was a boy, but he spoke fluent French, a skill that came in very handy when trying to get information on the enemy's positions from the local populace. But when the battalion met resistance and took heavy casualties, Carpentier switched his job to medical support. Despite having been wounded twice himself, the chaplain set up an aid station where he provided both medical treatment and spiritual comfort to the wounded and dying even as heavy shell fire came down on the village, an act for which he would later receive the Distinguished Service Cross for valor.[83]

Late on the afternoon of November 7, new orders arrived from Division Headquarters that stated all American units within the 42nd Division's boundaries would now be under the direct command of the 83rd Brigade. While this might end the confusion, the orders also told the 166th to fall back and make camp in La Neuville-á-Maire. The lead position would now be given to the French 40th Division, allowing the French to take Sedan. This was intended to show respect for the long-suffering French and was seen by everyone as very appropriate.[84]

The 166th fell back and made camp somewhat disappointed that they would not get to capture Sedan but also relieved to be out of the fighting. However, the next morning, they received a surprise when the commanding general of the French 40th Division asked that a company of the 166th Infantry accompany his men into Sedan. No other American unit was requested to provide a company, which was a sign of the deep respect the French had for the men from Ohio. D Company, now led by Captain Russell Baker, was chosen by Colonel Hough to represent the regiment, and they set out for Sedan at 7:00 a.m. on November 8.[85]

Baker and his men arrived in Frenois, where the French division was camped around noon. They were immediately assigned to a French infantry regiment, reporting to Lieutenant Colonel Ludoric Abel de Ville. That night, Baker and the other officers attended a lavish dinner served in the high-ceilinged, candle-lit hall of a grand chateau. Afterward, two platoons from D Company were sent out with a French patrol to enter the suburbs of Sedan. They made it to the west bank of the Meuse opposite the city. Crawling forward, they found themselves so close that "they could throw pebbles onto the roofs of the silent houses" in the city. They also were so close that the Germans discovered them and opened fire. The patrol withdrew, but no other American unit would come so close to the city, and the regiment could rightfully say they had reached "the coveted goal of Sedan."[86]

WHILE THE FRENCH and Americans observed the city of Sedan across the Meuse River, they were unaware that active and serious peace negotiations were underway. On the night of November 7, a German armistice delegation crossed the French lines to meet and make final terms for an armistice with the Allies. Not long after the meetings began, the kaiser abdicated and a revolution broke out in Germany. Marshal Foch gave the German representatives until 11:00 a.m. on November 11 to sign the agreement.[87]

On November 9, the 166th moved to La Petites Armoises and then on to Sommauthe and finally Verpel on November 11. All the while, the men in the regiment were unaware of anything official regarding the negotiations. To be sure, rumors about peace talks had been floating about for several weeks, but no one from the AEF down to the regiment had uttered a word that might confirm the rumors.

At 5:10 a.m. on November 11, the Germans signed the armistice agreement, which would take effect at 11:00 a.m. The first hint of anything official came to the regiment later that morning, and that news was confined to Raymond Cheseldine's ears. Cheseldine, now a captain on Colonel Hough's staff, was riding with the colonel in the Supply Company wagon train as it passed through the village of Buzancy, about four miles from their final destination in Verpel. At 10:57 a.m., Hough glanced at his watch and said quietly to Cheseldine, "In three minutes, the war may be over."[88]

Within moments of this, Chaplain Halliday rode up to the head of the column. "The Germans have accepted the Armistice," he blurted out. "The artillery has orders to cease firing at 11 o'clock. The war is over, Colonel." Hough merely nodded and made a sound in his throat, intended to acknowledge the information. He likely was more than a little overwhelmed by the news that meant he could now set down the burden of command he had carried so ably for the last eighteen months.[89]

A few minutes later, the distant rumbling of artillery that had been a daily fact of life in France for the last four years abruptly ended. Sergeant Roy Bailey noted in his diary, "Noise stopped at 11a.m."[90]

At 4:00 p.m., shortly after the regiment had arrived in Verpel, Colonel Hough called a meeting of his officers, where he gave them each a copy of the official order declaring an armistice. The officers then met with the men in their respective companies and gave them the news. Surprisingly, there were no cheers, no open expressions of emotion. Most of the men had one simple question: When do we go home?[91]

The answer to that question would come shortly, but the answer would be "Not anytime soon."

9

War's End

"Old Girl, if you ever expect to look me in the face again, you'll have to turn the other way, 'cause I'm never leavin' this country no more!"
—Soldier of the 166th Infantry Regiment on seeing the Statue of Liberty, April 25, 1919

IT WAS A WARM SPRING EVENING, and the sun was setting on Camp Sherman, Ohio, the huge complex of barracks and office buildings that had been built outside Chillicothe to serve as a wartime military training facility. It was May 17, 1919. The last few days had been sunny, which seemed to match the spirits of the men from the 166th Infantry who had arrived on May 12.[1]

They were at Camp Sherman to perform what Raymond Cheseldine referred to as the final "paper war" phase of the Great War. Company by company, one by one, the men were processed. They received a physical examination and a $60 bonus payment before filling out final paperwork and then being formally discharged.[2] It was a happy, even fun process for the most part. But as the men made their final marches for the camp gate where trucks waited to take them to the train station or waiting family members, their happiness was tinged with sorrow and regret.

After all, while they were headed back for the simple joys of civilian life, their discharges also meant saying goodbye to comrades with whom they had shared what Supreme Court Justice and Civil War veteran Oliver

Wendell Holmes had once referred to as "the incommunicable experience of war." They had fought together, lived in filthy trenches and foxholes together as enemy artillery rained down on them, and seen friends, many of whom they had grown up with in their hometowns, cut down by enemy machine gun fire, gassed, or riddled with shrapnel. As a result, they were bound together by an experience that someone who had not been there could never understand.

As the final group of newly discharged soldiers marched past the small Regimental Headquarters building on this soft, pleasant Thursday evening, they saw their colonel, their dedicated leader, Ben Hough, standing in the doorway. As usual, his face was expressionless. But each of his soldiers could sense the deep pain, love, and pride he felt as he watched the last of his boys march away. Many of their eyes filled with tears because they felt the same love for this man who had led them throughout the most terrible days of their young lives.

As for Colonel Hough, when the sounds of his men's footsteps had faded, and the last man had disappeared, he turned to go back inside and whispered to one of his officers, "The greatest fighting unit in the world is now but a memory."[3]

ON NOVEMBER 13, 1918, only two days after the armistice was signed and the war had ended, the 166th was told to start marching toward Germany, where it would become part of the American contribution to the occupation of the region bordering the western side of the Rhine River, what was known as the Rhineland. On hearing this, one soldier growled, "Germany, hey! How many kilomets [sp] is that?"[4] To him, it was just another march that took him farther from home and family.

Unbeknownst to that soldier or anyone else in the regiment, planning for the occupation of the Rhineland had begun in October 1918 immediately after the Germans appealed to President Wilson for negotiations on an armistice. The French, who were the staunchest proponents for the idea of occupation, made the initial proposal to Great Britain and the United States. The French feared and hated the Germans and believed they might either refuse to abide by the final terms of any future armistice or peace treaty. Therefore, they believed that, at a minimum, the Allies needed to establish bridgeheads across the Rhine to pressure the Germans into following any agreements with the Allies, while providing a base of operations should fighting resume.[5]

Opinion within American leadership was divided on the issue of occupation. Major General Henry Allen, a member of Pershing's staff and the man who would eventually command American forces in Germany, told the AEF commander he believed that the AEF should not return to the United States without having entered German territory. After an October 26 meeting of Pershing, Foch, Pétain, and Haig, Pershing reported to Edward House, Wilson's envoy to the armistice negotiations, that he could not guarantee Germany's acceptance of "reasonable conditions of peace . . . without the occupation by the allied armies of the territory west of the Rhine."[6]

However, at the same time, General Tasker Bliss, the American representative to the Allied Supreme War Council, had the exact opposite opinion. He told President Wilson and Secretary of War Baker that any occupation of Germany would lead to an Allied form of militarism just as dangerous as the German variety. He argued that this, in turn, would "keep the world in turmoil for many years to come." Wilson and Baker agreed with the fears Bliss expressed. Wilson went so far as to write a note to Baker that said the occupation of Germany amounted to a virtual invasion of German soil under the proposed terms of the armistice.[7]

But Wilson and House were prepared to acquiesce on the issue of occupation if it would lead to the cessation of fighting. Therefore, all they asked for was a French guarantee that all French forces would withdraw from Germany as soon as the Germans met the terms of any future peace treaty. French premier Georges Clémenceau concurred with the American request, and Wilson backed down. Unfortunately, the French failed to perceive Wilson's reluctance to have any American forces participate in the occupation, and, by November 1, Foch had convinced Pershing and Haig that a joint Allied occupation force was a necessity. On November 5, Wilson had to inform the German government that the Allies would occupy the Rhineland until a final peace was negotiated.[8]

The German reaction to the concept of occupation was not surprising. Matthias Erzberger, the leading German representative to the armistice negotiations, was adamant in rejecting the entire idea. At the final negotiations on November 8, he argued strenuously against any occupation of German territory. But the Allies would not back down. However, fearful of a potential Bolshevik uprising in the Rhineland, Allied negotiators did agree to allow German administrative control on both banks of the Rhine, while Foch continued to insist on his bridgeheads with no limits on the size of the occupying army. As the pressure from battlefield setbacks and angry riots at home increased, Erzberger had no choice but to accept the Allied terms, and he signed the armistice three days later.[9]

The final armistice agreement required Germany to turn over five thousand artillery pieces, twenty-five thousand machine guns, seventeen hundred aircraft, and five thousand locomotives to the Allies. Furthermore, Article V of the armistice said that the lands on the west bank of the Rhine would be administered by local German governments who would conduct their business under the control of Allied forces from France, Great Britain, Belgium, and the United States. But if this occupation was not a stinging enough rebuke to the Germans, Article IX stated that the German government must pay all support expenses for the occupying forces.[10]

These harsh terms were just the beginning of a process that led to the Treaty of Versailles and, eventually, deep resentment among the German people that would lead to the rise of Adolf Hitler and national socialism. But neither the British nor the Americans could stop the French from exacting their revenge on Germany. Their hatred, while understandable, knew no bounds. Had Wilson and British prime minister David Lloyd George not tried to soften the terms as much as possible, the French might have completely broken Germany into small pieces with each one under the control of France.

Under the terms of the armistice, Marshal Foch was to direct the division of more than nineteen thousand square miles of occupied German territory along the Rhine. He carved the area up into six zones with a total population of seven million people. One zone was assigned to the Belgian Army, another went to the British Second Army, one was reserved for the American Third Army, and three were given to the French Fifth, Eighth, and Tenth Armies. The British zone included the critical bridgehead at the city of Cologne, which was the heart of German industry along the Rhine. The three French zones incorporated the Saar, Palatinate, and Mainz regions, while the American zone fell between the British to the north and French to the south.[11]

The American zone, where the 166th would be stationed, covered a total of approximately four thousand square miles between the border with Luxembourg and the Rhine bridgehead at Coblenz. This area had a population of nearly nine hundred thousand people in 1919, with Trèves and Coblenz being its largest cities. For the most part, this sector of the Rhineland consisted of small villages where agriculture was the main industry.[12]

Interestingly, however, while some in the American leadership harbored deep reservations about participating in the occupation of the Rhineland, there were practical considerations that made it advantageous to the government. First, as negotiations on the armistice began in October, no one in the War Department had done any planning for the demobilization process. At that time, the planners were still deeply involved in continued efforts to increase industrial support for the war. The basic problem was that, as the negotiations began, no one expected the Central Powers to collapse so quickly. One post-war analysis concluded that "democracy shakes down to an effective fighting machine slowly and wastefully. It reaches its peak when hostilities cease, and the enemy, for which it was fully prepared to fight, is nonexistent. Thus, when peace comes, the country is unprepared." Therefore, the War Plans Division did not start to even study demobilization until October 14 and did not deliver an initial draft plan until November 14. As a result, sending a large number of troops to Germany took some of the pressure off the need to quickly demobilize.[13]

On November 7, four days before the armistice was signed, Pershing and his staff developed the concept for how they would organize their part of the occupation force. They created the idea of the Third Army, composed of the III and IV Corps and numbering over two hundred thousand men. Following the armistice, as the first American units were already making their way toward Germany, Pershing appointed Major General Joseph Dickman as the commander of the new Third Army and assigned the 2nd, 32nd, and 42nd Divisions to III Corps. Pershing issued orders to the Third Army to enforce the terms of the armistice, which required the German army to evacuate France, Luxembourg, and the Alsace-Lorraine region within fifteen days. The official advance to the Rhineland would begin on November 17 with the III Corps on the left or northern flank of the American zone of occupation. The 2nd and 32nd Divisions would take the lead while the 42nd Division followed in support.[14]

Once the armistice was signed, German commanders issued orders for their armies to retreat into Germany in a disciplined process. For the most part, their men complied and left a substantial amount of military stores and weaponry behind them. There was very little pillaging as the Germans moved through France, Belgium, and Luxembourg, keeping a distance of about six miles between themselves and the advancing American Third Army.[15]

—————

WHILE THE PLANS for the occupation and the march to the Rhine were being finalized, the 166th Infantry camped amid the mud and filth of the ruins of what was once the village of Verpel. At first, the men seemed to barely take note of the fact the war was over. As Raymond Cheseldine noted, conditions had not improved noticeably, and "the cooties refused to recognize the Armistice."[16] So, when they heard the news that they would be going into Germany as part of the Army of Occupation, their response was more than a little muted. They would have preferred to have been told they were headed home, but at least this new assignment offered the prospect of something new, and it did not involve going over the top or being shelled day and night.

On the morning of November 13, the regiment broke camp and began the march to the Rhine somewhat oddly by moving southeast to Saint Georges, the same village they had fought unsuccessfully to capture only a month before. The town had been reduced to a pile of rubble, so the men camped on a nearby hillside. The regiment stayed in bivouac for three days, and, despite the cold weather, they were finally able to celebrate the end of the war. For the first time in months, with no fear of artillery or roaming German bombers, they could light campfires, and the hillside was dotted at night with hundreds of brightly burning fires. To men who had been living in cold, wet darkness at night for months, it felt like "Broadway, New York, with all its lights, had been transported to the battle area."[17] That alone raised spirits. But even better, one doughboy found an abandoned German signal rocket dump, and, within minutes, the men were shooting rockets skyward where they exploded, lighting up the night sky like it was the Fourth of July.[18]

On the morning of November 16, the 166th turned northeast and began the direct march toward Germany. After a fifteen-mile hike, they arrived in Stenay on the afternoon of November 17. This city on the Meuse River had been the site of a large French garrison before the war. So, the men stayed in French barracks that the Germans had occupied for four years. Not only were there beds to sleep on, but, more impor-tantly, there were showers where the men could bathe for the first time in over a month. Every soldier was deloused so they could bid their cooties goodbye and then wash off the mud and dirt they had accumulated in the Argonne.[19]

While in Stenay, the AEF made a rather humorous attempt to supply the regiment with fresh clothing. Headquarters wanted the men to look

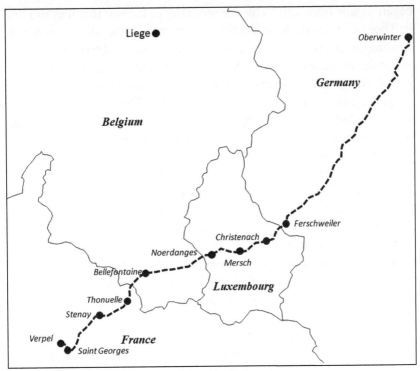

The 166th Infantry's march to the Rhine. (*Author*)

their best as they marched into Belgium and beyond, but the initial supplies of clothing they sent were ridiculously inadequate. All the shoes and shirts were the same size and, while there were undershirts, there were no underdrawers. But perhaps worst of all, the new pants would only fit a regiment filled with overweight men, not soldiers who were thin from marching hundreds of miles while they subsisted on canned meat and coffee.[20]

The division sent most of the clothing back while the regiments waited. New clothing did arrive, but it still was not adequate. Trying to issue new clothing to over thirty thousand men in three days was an impossible task to begin with, and once the supplies provided were found to be all wrong, not much could be done. So, the regiment looked like a rather motley crew when they left Stenay on November 20.

The march was a short one, only about ten miles to the village of Thonuelle. Leon Miesse wrote to his wife that the country was beautiful and that as they moved farther away from the front, any signs of the war began to fade from sight. The one reminder of the war that they did find in Thonuelle was six large-caliber artillery pieces abandoned by the retreating Germans. Since they were supposed to surrender such war material to the Allies, the Germans decided to turn the guns over to the village priest, who gave them to the regiment when it arrived in the town.[21]

The regiment camped for only one night in Thonuelle, but the short stay provided the opportunity for Captain Miesse to learn a little about what life had been like during the German occupation. He and other officers from C Company were billeted with an old French couple who welcomed them into their home with open arms. A couple of the officers spoke reasonably good French, and after dinner as they sat by the fire, the couple told them that the Germans had carried everything of value away when they left. As a result, they had very little food except for a few vegetables from the garden. So, Miesse gave them some supplies of sugar, salt, flour, and bacon for which they were decidedly grateful.[22]

The couple also said that their son had been taken prisoner three years ago and sent to a prison in Germany. They had received letters from him through the Red Cross during the first two years of his captivity but had no word from him since. The Germans told the people of the village that their submarines had sunk all the ships carrying American troops, that both Britain and Russia had been defeated, and France would be next. But when the Germans began their retreat, they told the people that Germany had decided to quit simply because they were tired of killing the French and British and that, unfortunately, France was determined to continue the war.[23]

They also related that the Germans made them virtual prisoners in their own homes. They were prohibited from leaving the village for any reason and were not even allowed to speak to their neighbors. They were fined for every infraction of the Germans' rules, and the Germans made levies on the villagers for milk and eggs, levies that were always designed to be for far more than the people could possibly provide. When the village did not meet its quota for milk and eggs, the Germans added to the people's fines.[24]

On the morning of November 21, the regiment moved out of Thonuelle and passed through the village of Fagny, which was the last village in France on their route to Germany. They marched out of the village and down into a small valley where a stone bridge crossed over a little stream, the Ruisseau des Courvées, which marked the border with Belgium. On either end of the bridge was a large evergreen tree decked out in ornaments, and the flags of France and the United States flew on the near side while the Belgian and American flags had been raised on the far side.[25]

Less than one hundred yards north of the bridge was the Belgian village of Limes, where all the inhabitants had come out to the road dressed in their finest attire to cheer the 166th as it marched through. The regimental band struck up a tune as the people waved American flags in a demonstration of their joy at being liberated. The regiment did not pause but continued to march toward Bellefontaine. Along the way, they were cheered wildly in every village as they passed under triumphal arches with inscriptions such as "Honor to Our Liberators" and "Welcome to the Allies." Children strew the roadways with flowers, and every house in every village flew either the French, British, Belgian, or American flag from its windows.[26]

That night, the regiment made camp in Bellefontaine, a neat, clean town that the Germans had not ravished as they departed. Apparently they had been surprised by their sudden orders to retreat and only had a few hours to prepare and march out of the town and, as a result, did not have enough time to steal everything that was not nailed down.[27] As was the case everywhere the regiment went in Belgium, the people of Bellefontaine opened their homes and hearts to these Americans. "Talk about treatment," Enoch Williams wrote to his mother. "We sure were treated great in Belgium. The people took us right into their homes. And cooked us meals and didn't want to take pay for it. The first night in Belgium, I had the best meal I had since I came over."[28]

On November 23, the regiment made a short march of eleven miles, during which they crossed the border into Luxembourg. They stopped in the Noerdange area, where they were told to make camp for the next week. The area was beautiful, and the men were housed in the towns of Noerdange, Niederpallen, and Rippweiler, where they would spend Thanksgiving Day. Unlike the Belgians, the people here were a bit more reserved. While happy to be liberated, they did not care for the idea of being a campground for the foreign armies crossing their little country. However, when they saw that, unlike the Germans, these Americans were more than willing to pay for whatever they needed, they happily threw open the doors of their stores and shops.[29]

Thanksgiving Day was, without doubt, a vast improvement over the one the regiment's men celebrated the year before. This time, there were clean, warm billets and lots of hot food. The officers of the 1st Battalion organized dinner and entertainment for the day, substituting roast young pig for turkey.[30] But as the men made the best of this Thanksgiving far from home, their futures seemed uncertain. "News is scarce, but we have 'beaucoup' rumors," Leon Miesse wrote to his wife, "everything from going to Germany to being back in the States by Xmas." To make matters worse, the men had not had any mail in weeks. Miesse told his wife, "I sure am anxious for a letter. They tell us they have 12 trucks full of mail back 60 kilometers in the rear and no way to get it to us. Such is life in the Army, the things you want most you never have."[31]

On December 1, the 166th began the final leg of their march to the Rhineland with a hike to Mersch, Luxembourg, which was about thirteen miles from the German border. On that day, Pershing and Foch both issued proclamations to the people of the Rhineland. Foch told the German citizens that their laws would remain in place, but he also warned that there must be no acts of hostility, either direct or indirect, toward Allied forces. Pershing, meanwhile, assured the people that American forces had no ill intentions, and he promised that his men would protect the lives, homes, and property of everyone that followed the Army of Occupation's rules and regulations. Lastly, Pershing expressed his desire that the people of the Rhineland "regain their normal mode of life" and reestablish their schools, churches, and hospitals.[32]

At the same time, General Pershing issued his orders for the soldiers of the Third Army. His tone was much like the proclamation in that he stressed their mission was to protect the civilian population. He reminded his men that they came to Germany "as instruments of a strong, free government whose purposes towards the people of Germany are beneficent." Above all, he stressed that the Third Army did not come to Germany as conquerors or oppressors, that everyone must maintain a "dignified and reserved attitude," and that any acts of violence or pillage would be punished by the maximum penalties allowed under military law. To demonstrate respect for local authorities, Pershing ordered that all commanding officers contact the local mayor, the Bürgermeister, before entering any town and inform them that all rights and personal property would be respected. They were also to make any requests for billets or supplies to the Bürgermeister. However, given that the area was suffering from food and fuel shortages, the Third Army had decided not to make any requests for foodstuffs, forage, coal, or wood.[33]

At 8:00 a.m. on December 3, the 166th left camp in Christnach, Luxembourg, and, at about noon, the regiment crossed the bridge over the Saar River at Bollendorf and marched into Germany.[34] They followed the river for a few miles and then turned north to make camp at the village of Ferschweiler, which Alison Reppy described as small and dirty.[35] Many of the men had expected an openly hostile reception from the German people, but, instead, they were met with quiet, dutiful obedience that reflected both a deep resentment of the presence of foreign troops as well as a clear understanding that the German populace was in no position to oppose that presence. Leon Miesse wrote to his wife about the regiment's arrival in Germany saying:

> Entry into Germany was without ceremony. The people were out to watch us pass, there was no hostility, but all seemed aware that Germany had been defeated and that it was up to them to receive us with good grace. It gave me a peculiar qualm to see the little Boche kids running around with Boche caps on and thought how just a few short weeks before men who wore those very same caps, were doing all within their power to do us harm.[36]

On the morning of December 5, the regiment was marching again, and on December 15 they reached their first duty station in the Rhineland. In between, however, was some of the hardest marching they had experienced to date. The men and the animals were already tired when they set out, and soon a cold rain began. Then, as the men trudged onward, the shoes they had been wearing for months began to wear out, and many men were soon marching in their bare feet. Worst of all, the roads, which wound through deep forest and up steep hills, were not particularly good to begin with. Now the steady rains made it almost impossible for either men or vehicles to navigate them.[37]

One officer from the division staff referred to the roads as "mudholes" that "looked like the 'before' photographs in advertisements of paving material." Both men and vehicles had to be careful to avoid the edges of the roadway where the mud became like "sticky strawberry jam, with no limit to its depth." The center of the road was not much better. There, the deep ruts made in the mud by wagons from the retreating German army served as a snare in which to entrap the Supply Company's carts, wagons, and trucks. To add to the problems, bridges were out in several places, requiring the regiment to backtrack and march many miles off course to find a usable bridge, making what should have been an eighty-mile journey even longer.[38]

This long hike took the 166th from Ferschweiler through Biersdorf am See, Schönecken, Dollendorf, Reifferscheid, and Höningen before finally reaching the Rhine River at Oberwinter on December 15. Here, the regiment would be part of the Third Army's Coblenz bridgehead. The Regimental Headquarters, Headquarters Company, and Supply Company set up in Rolandseck, a summer resort site downriver from Oberwinter, where the 3rd Battalion made camp. The 1st Battalion, meanwhile, was stationed in Rolandswerth, which marked the far left of the Coblenz bridgehead area, with the Machine Gun Company billeted in the Ernich Schloss, a magnificent chateau perched on the heights above the Rhine about a mile northwest of Remagen. Finally, the 2nd Battalion was scattered among the villages of Unkelbach, Leimersdorf, Birresdorf, and Niederich, all of which were a few miles back from the banks of the Rhine.[39]

Upon arrival, the regiment began the process of identifying housing for officers and men. In Rolandswerth, where C Company and the rest of the 1st Battalion were stationed, there was some resistance to finding billets for the Americans. Leon Miesse wrote in his journal:

> We expect to be here about 30 days, so we are trying to make ourselves as comfortable as possible for it is a pretty poor village, and the people are very hostile and hold rooms out. But this morning, we are making the rounds of the village, and if there is a good room, we tell them to have it vacated for an Officer who will be around at one o'clock to take possession. They try to argue, but we tell them we have no time to argue, and they know what they have to do.[40]

After much negotiation and, in some cases, direct orders, the regiment found themselves in the best billets the area could provide. They were able to take advantage of the many hotels and mansions that lined the western bank of the Rhine. Best of all, no matter where they were quartered, the men had a decent bed, clean sheets, and a real bath to use.[41]

Leon Miesse and the men from C Company did particularly well, eventually finding billets in the Haus Rolandshohe au de Rhin about three miles from Unkelbach. He put one platoon in the railroad station. The station had an upper floor that had housed a restaurant and café, was very spacious, and even offered a wide terrace with a beautiful view of the Rhine. He placed his 2nd and 3rd Platoons in a large house while the 1st Platoon and his Company Headquarters and mess were located in another smaller home. Naturally, however, the officers once again had the best billets. Miesse and the other company officers had a villa all to themselves. It sat perched on a hill overlooking the Rhine and had been "some

Dana Daniel's postcard photo of Coblenz. (*Union County Historical Society*)

Rich Dutchman's Summer Home." He added in a letter to his wife that "we have the whole place as the boys would say 'We're sitting on top of the World.' We have a billiards room with a table in it, a music room with the biggest grand piano I ever hope to see."[42]

As for their relationships with the German populace, the men were supposedly under strict orders from General Pershing not to fraternize with local citizens. However, the realities of life along the Rhine made that impossible. It is difficult to not fraternize when you are living in a German home and sharing your meals with German civilians. Still, because a state of war still technically existed with Germany, the army had to ban all "intimate personal associations" between soldiers and civilians.[43]

JUST TWO DAYS before the 166th arrived on the Rhine, the AEF created the Advance General Headquarters, known as the Advance GHQ, to preside over civil affairs in the American occupation zone. The Advance GHQ's first order was the basic charter for the American military government apparatus. This order created five different departments within Advance GHQ to handle issues related to public works and utilities, fiscal affairs, sanitation and public health, schools and charitable institutions, and legal problems. While this structure seemed logical at first glance, time would prove it to be somewhat impractical because many problems that arose did not neatly fit into any one department.[44]

The Army of Occupation's challenge in governing the Rhineland was exacerbated by the fact that the Wilson administration, State Department, and War Department provided virtually no guidance on how the Third Army and the Advance GHQ should manage their operations. Colonel Irvin Hunt, the Third Army's Officer in Charge of Civil Affairs, later said, "Military government under even the most favorable circumstances is a formidable task." But in this case, the AEF had been focused on field operations right up to the moment the armistice took place and had spent almost no time figuring out how to perform a military occupation mission. This problem was made even worse because the period between the end of the fighting and the initial crossing of the German border was less than three weeks.[45]

One of the issues faced by the Third Army, and one the 166th had already encountered during their march to the Rhine, was securing German war material. Article VI of the armistice stated that any property abandoned by the German army, in addition to that turned over to the Allies under Article IV, became the property of the Allied armies. But, demonstrating the abilities that would later help them hide their resumption of military activities in the 1930s, the German army tried to circumvent this rule by selling off military equipment to civilians, thus making it private property that was excluded from seizure. In some cases, this meant that German soldiers sold off their horses for only twenty-five marks and their rifles for less than five marks. The Third Army saw this scheme for what it was and insisted that the Americans could take military equipment into their possession no matter who might own it.[46]

This led to an order that all units in the Army of Occupation search their areas for military equipment. Any equipment found was to be placed into one of three categories: materiel abandoned by the German army, materiel transferred by the German army to a third party before the armistice, and materiel transferred to a third party following the armistice. American soldiers, including those from the 166th, were to immediately seize all property in the first category, while civilians were allowed to keep anything they purchased before November 11. However, once the armistice was signed, the German army had forfeited all rights to their property and, as a result, could not legally sell it. This policy produced considerable resentment among German civilians, especially local farmers who had purchased horses or wagons from the German army as it retreated beyond the Rhine.[47]

As the occupation continued, the relationship between the 166th's soldiers and the German population did not change. For example, Enoch Williams wrote to his mother, saying, "There isn't much to tell about the people here. They seem friendly enough and treat us all right. Most of the men here just got out of the army. The boy in the house where I am staying was up against us at Chateau-Thierry. He was a machine gunner."[48] However, some of the men recognized the resentment and dislike that was just beneath the thin surface of the people's congeniality.

As Major Tompkins from the 42nd Division staff recounted, while the people would hurl curses and "kaputs" toward the portraits of the kaiser, Bismarck, Hindenburg, and Ludendorff that still adorned the walls of their homes, their real reason for doing so was not the one that you might assume. The man who owned the house where Tompkins was billeted was a respected member of the community and a typical middle-class German citizen. In conversations with this man, he revealed his true feelings about the war. While he would tell Tompkins how much he hated the kaiser and the "Berlin crowd," when you pressed him about his feelings, he revealed that he did not hate them for starting the war that led to so much death and destruction and, eventually, the occupation of his town by a foreign army. Instead, he hated them for losing that war, and he hated the Allies for having prevailed.[49]

This underlying resentment was more important than Tompkins and the men of the 166th realized at the time. Once the Treaty of Versailles took effect, the harsh reparations exacted on Germany and the severe limitations on German military activities made this resentment grow even deeper and more dangerous. This, combined with the German economic collapse during the 1920s, made the German populace ripe for the rise of Hitler and the Nazi Party.

Some administrative orders also made life difficult for both the men of the regiment and the German populace, while increasing civilian resentment. At first, while German citizens could travel freely within the American zone, anyone wishing to travel to another of the Allied zones or unoccupied Germany had to first apply with their local Bürgermeister for permission. Once the Bürgermeister approved their application, it was forwarded to the Third Army for final approval. This angered many Germans, who were forced to stand in processing lines for hours, while severely hampering business activities.[50]

Perhaps even more onerous were the restrictions on alcohol and the press. First, sales of all alcoholic beverages except beer and light wine were prohibited. Next, even beer and light wine sales were restricted to three hours in the afternoon and two hours in the evening. Although some local commanders thought that all alcohol sales should be banned, the Third Army was wise enough to see that trying to stop all trafficking in alcohol would be an impossible task. As for the press, orders were issued that required local commanders to screen all newspapers before publication and suppress any articles that impugned the military government or its occupation policies.[51]

As Christmas arrived and passed on to New Year's Day, the 166th settled into a routine. Unfortunately, the regiment's leadership decided that acting like soldiers needed to be part of that routine. So, they scheduled daily sessions of close-order drill and then added field maneuvers. This sort of "soldiering" was met with howls of protest from the men. Having experienced war, having seen the real part of being a soldier, they had enough of such nonsense as close-order drill and pretend warfare. So, when they went out on field maneuvers and received harsh scores from referees, absolutely no one cared.[52]

One of the other monotonous tasks performed by the regiment was guard duty along the banks of the Rhine. This assignment was intended to deter anyone from crossing the river while going to or from unoccupied Germany. But, for the most part, this job quickly became more than a little pro forma. In one example, Major Volka of the 1st Battalion was given responsibility for guarding the ferry crossing at Rolandsworth. He tried to run his operation in strict compliance to orders until one night when he and his men discovered the ferry going across the river to Honne was filled with his fellow officers from the battalion. At that point, Volka threw up his hands, let the officers go, and simply gave up trying to stop anyone from crossing the river.[53]

But with the end of the war and the move to Germany, discipline had definitely suffered to some degree. Raymond Cheseldine recalled a couple of instances of this phenomenon. In one case, an officer in the regiment passed a soldier on the street who did not offer a salute. This young soldier was a recent replacement draftee who clearly had not paid much attention to his training in military courtesies. The officer then passed by him several times as the soldier stood on a street corner. Finally, the officer confronted him and said, "Look here, man, didn't you see me pass?" The young soldier looked at the officer somewhat dismissively and replied, "Hell, yes! You've passed so often I'm sick [of] lookin' at you."[54]

In another instance, a soldier failed to salute an officer, which caused the officer to turn and stop the young man. When he asked why the soldier had failed to salute, the soldier said, "Why should I salute you?" When the officer said the soldier should salute because he was an officer, the soldier smiled genially and said, "Well, you lucky son-of-a-gun."[55]

In early March, rumors were rampant that the regiment would be headed home soon. These rumors increased when the regiment received word that General Pershing was coming to inspect and review the 42nd Division, which many believed might be the first event in a process that would send them back to Ohio. The regiment began practicing, and on March 8 Dana Daniels recorded that they had "an inspection of short packs, mess gears, bayonets, rifles, helmets, shoes, and clothes" in preparation for the review.[56]

On March 16, 1919, the review by General Pershing took place. It was a cloudy day with occasional snow and rain falling as the men stood for inspection at the foot of the Ludendorff Bridge in Remagen.[57] Ironically, twenty-six years later, this exact spot would see some of the fiercest fighting of World War II, as American troops battled with the German Wehrmacht to seize the bridge, which would be one of the last ones still standing across the Rhine.

At precisely 2:00 p.m., a shrill bugle call rang out, and the men snapped to attention as General Pershing rode around the division on his white horse. He then dismounted and inspected the 166th first, since they were formed on the right of the division. Pershing approached Colonel Hough, who saluted and gave the general a brief report on the regiment and its battlefield accomplishments. Then the general walked up and down the ranks, speaking to the battalion and company commanders, as well as some of the individual soldiers. Once the inspection was concluded, men who were to receive medals for valor marched to the front of the formation to get them from the AEF commander-in-chief. After that, the division marched past Pershing in review, and then the general gave an address in which he thanked the men for all their accomplishments on the battlefield.[58]

As it turned out, the rumors about the review having some significance in terms of going home proved to be true. Shortly after Pershing departed, the division received orders to begin preparations for a departure for home on April 6, 1919.

THE FIRST ELEMENTS of the regiment to start for home on April 6 were the Regimental Headquarters and Headquarters Company. The 1st Battalion, 2nd Battalion, and Machine Gun Company followed on April 7, with the 3rd Battalion and Supply Company departing on April 8. For all of them, the route and process were the same. The men first went to Oberwinter,[59] where they boarded the train, which would spend three days taking them to Brest in Brittany on the northwest coast of France. The final leg of the journey was especially sentimental because Brittany was the home of the regiment's stalwart French interpreter, Peter LeGall, the brave French soldier who learned his English while a waiter at Delmonico's in New York City. LeGall had left for home ahead of the regiment, and as their trains went past his house he went into the yard and, with tears in his eyes, waved his final goodbye to the comrades he had come to love so deeply.[60]

Each train arrived in Brest around 8:00 p.m., where the men unloaded and marched about six miles to Camp Pontenazen. The regiment prepared for embarkation in the camp by being inspected and deloused and receiving both new clothing and pay. The transportation officers made up the passenger list, and all property was packed and labeled for shipment. On the morning of April 15, the men moved to the docks on a cold, windy day. There, the giant passenger ship *Leviathan* awaited them.[61]

The ship had once been a German-flagged luxury liner called *Vaterland* but had since been adapted for use as a military troop transport. She was too large to use the docks at Brest, so the ship remained anchored in the harbor, and small boats ferried the men of the 42nd Division out to the ship. Everyone was ready to depart, but they then learned that the ship had not received all the coal it would require for the journey. When the men were told that it might take days to get enough men to coal the ship, hundreds volunteered to take on the task themselves. They donned blue denim overalls and went to work. By April 17, the *Leviathan* was ready to sail. She pulled up her anchor and set off across the Atlantic for New York.[62]

The journey across the ocean was far more comfortable than the one the men made to France on the *Mallory* and *Pastores* and, for the most part, was uneventful. The only unpleasant incident involved a remark made by a woman who was traveling as part of a group accompanying the US ambassador to France, William Sharp. During the trip, senior officers and dignitaries such as the ambassador and his party took their

The men of the 166th Infantry arrive in New York Harbor aboard the *Leviathan*. (*National Archives*)

meals in the elegant dining halls above decks while the troops ate in large mess facilities below decks. At some point, one of the women in Ambassador Sharp's group commented that she and the other ladies ought to go below decks to "watch the cattle feed." Since there was no livestock onboard, everyone knew she was referring to the soldiers of the division. This unseemly remark eventually filtered down to the men, who became more than a little indignant. To insult men who were coming home in such a fashion was beyond reprehensible. Each regiment formed committees who met and then held a meeting with the troop commander demanding action. The troop commander promised an investigation, and that seemed to calm tempers.[63]

On April 25, 1919, the *Leviathan* sailed into New York Harbor, where the ship was greeted by hundreds of small boats, ferries, and tugboats that escorted her into the bay. One of the tugboats carried a delegation led by the governor of Ohio, James Cox. They displayed a large greeting sign, and Governor Cox shouted a boisterous "welcome home" to the men of the 166th Infantry. When the ship passed the Statue of Liberty, many of the men were moved to tears.[64]

When the giant ship docked, the men disembarked and boarded trains for Camp Merritt in Bergen County, New Jersey. When the trains arrived, the men formed up to march to the camp amid a late spring snowstorm. As Colonel Hough waited impatiently for instructions, a lieutenant from the camp headquarters arrived to act as a guide. A line of freight cars stood blocking the road, and the lieutenant told Hough the regiment could not cross the road until the freight cars had left. As the men grew restless and colder, the colonel noticed that there was no locomotive attached to the freight cars and decided he was not going to make the men wait any longer. Despite the lieutenant's protests, he led the men around the freight cars and into camp, where they were soon quartered and warm.[65]

Hough's common-sense approach for marching through the rail yard led to the one unpleasant incident that occurred during the stay at Camp Merritt. The next morning, Colonel Hough left camp to go into New York City to meet his wife, whom he had not seen for nearly two years. While he was away from camp, the camp commander sent out orders for Hough to report to him immediately. The camp commander was also a colonel, but, unlike Hough, he was a colonel who had never heard a shot fired during the war, which he had spent comfortably at Camp Merritt. He heard about Hough's conduct at the rail yard, and apparently this stateside-duty desk officer intended to dress down a combat veteran.[66]

When Hough returned from New York City the next morning, his staff told him he had orders to report to the camp commander. Hough went to the camp headquarters as requested, but exactly what happened in the camp commander's office remains unknown. The camp commander reported that Hough entered his office, still wearing his cap and with a cigar stump in his mouth. Hough later said he did not remember if he was wearing his cap, but he most definitely had a cigar in his mouth. Cap or no cap, the cigar stub, and what he saw as Hough's cavalier regard for his orders, set the camp commander off on a tirade. He proceeded to "comment caustically" about the cap and cigar and then launched into a dissertation about Hough not listening to the lieutenant's guidance about the freight train.[67]

Up to this point, Hough had listened politely, but as the camp commander finished Hough became furious. He informed the camp commander in no uncertain terms that he was not overly concerned about such petty details as caps, cigars, or freight trains. Hough continued saying that he was just getting home from a war with his men, who all wanted nothing more than to go home. Hough said he felt the same way, having been away from his wife and home while the camp commander had sat happily at his desk at Camp Merritt and went home to his family every night. Therefore, Hough said, the camp commander could not appreciate his situation and had no business lecturing him.[68]

When Colonel Hough finished, the camp commander placed Hough under arrest and ordered that he be restricted to his quarters. Not surprisingly, when the officers and men of the 166th heard about their leader's arrest, they rallied to his cause, threatening to hang the camp commander or burn down his headquarters. Hearing about Hough's situation, the commanding officers from the other regiments in the division went to see the camp commander and indignantly dressed him down. After being criticized so fervently, the camp commander said he would forget the matter if Hough apologized. When Hough heard this, he laughed and said that, while he had nothing to apologize for, he would go see the camp commander.[69]

When Hough entered the camp commander's office, he made sure he first politely removed his cap. Then he told the officer very clearly, "*If* I have broken any camp orders, I'm very sorry." The camp commander took Hough's remarks as an opportunity to save face, accepted the apology, and dropped the charges against Hough.

The work of getting the men of the regiment ready for transportation home and discharge was expedited. First, all the men from states other than Ohio were separated from the regiment and prepared to go home. This, naturally, led to many touching goodbyes between men who had formed the sort of friendships that only being together in combat can produce. By May 9, the regiment was ready to leave Camp Merritt. The trains pulled out around 10:00 a.m., and traveling via Syracuse, Buffalo, Dunkirk, Cleveland, Galion, and Delaware, the trains reached Columbus between 3:00 p.m. and 3:45 p.m. on Saturday, May 10, where they were to make a grand parade through the city.[70]

As the trains were making their way to Columbus, seemingly every newspaper in Ohio printed the story of the 166th's return as front-page news, and people from the hometowns of the regiment's companies gathered and traveled to the state capital to see the parade. The mayor of Columbus directed that all businesses be closed when the parade began at 4:00 p.m. and that all factories blow their whistles to greet the men who were being called the "Gallant Buckeyes."[71] The streets around Union Station in Columbus were packed with relatives wanting to be the first to

K Company marches in parade in their hometown of Delaware, Ohio. (*National Archives*)

welcome their "boys" home, and conservative estimates put the crowd for the parade at twenty thousand.[72]

The parade was led by a ceremonial detachment from the police department, Spanish-American War veterans, the band from Camp Sherman, and the fire department. Following them came the men of the 166th with Colonel Hough in the lead riding a horse. When he came into sight, the applause from the crowd turned into an "intense roar." Behind the colonel came the regimental band followed by the men of the 3rd Battalion, 1st Battalion, 2nd Battalion, and the Supply Company. The regiment passed the reviewing stand twice before turning into the grounds of the state house, where all semblance of order was lost. The crowd surged into the men as relatives searched for their loved ones.[73]

The men were given passes to go home for the weekend before reporting back to be on the train for Camp Sherman at 1:00 p.m. on Monday, May 12. After a short ride to Chillicothe where the camp was located, the men were quartered, and the process of completing the final paperwork began. After a physical examination and receiving final pay, the men made their way to the front gates, still grouped as the companies in which they had fought. By Saturday evening, May 17, the final company had been discharged, making the 166th the last unit from Ohio to demobilize.[74]

The war was over at last for Ohio's 166th Infantry Regiment.

Epilogue

AFTER THE WAR, the men of the regiment went back to civilian life. Here are the post-war biographies of a few of the notable figures in this story.

Benson Hough. The regiment's much beloved commanding officer went on to attain the rank of major general in the Ohio National Guard in 1923. He returned to his law practice after the war and he became a justice on the Ohio Supreme Court in 1920. He remained in that position until 1923 when he became the US Attorney for the Southern District of Ohio. Following a two-year stint there, he was nominated to be a judge for the US District Court for the Southern District of Ohio. He was confirmed by the US Senate on January 31, 1925, and remained in office until his sudden death from a heart attack on November 19, 1935.[1]

Raymond Cheseldine. One of the two oracles of the regiment's history, Cheseldine went into the publishing business after the war with Madison Press in London, Ohio. In 1924, he returned to active duty as a lieutenant colonel in the state's militia bureau. Cheseldine went back to civilian life in 1929 and worked on the Federal Reserve Board and in the Federal Trade Commission. During World War II, he was called back to active duty and took a position in the industrial division of the Office of the Chief of Ordnance in the War Department. In 1945, he was promoted to colonel and went to Germany as an advisor to General Lucius Clay, commander of American forces in occupied Germany. Later, he became an executive assistant to the undersecretary of the army until his retirement in 1951. He passed away on December 26, 1954, and was buried in Arlington National Cemetery.[2]

Alison Reppy. Reppy was the other recorder of the regiment's history. After his discharge, Reppy returned to school at the University of Chicago, where he received a doctorate in jurisprudence in 1922. He then became a member of the St. Louis law firm of Buder & Buder. He went on to write numerous legal texts and serve as a law professor at the University of Oklahoma, Rutgers University, and New York University. He became the dean of the New York University Law School in 1950, a position he held until his death on August 20, 1958.[3]

Dana Daniels. Daniels returned home to Union County at the end of the war. He worked as a farmer and was very active in war veteran organizations. He later purchased and operated the White Swan Tavern on State Route 4 between Marysville and Marion. Daniels died on June 25, 1953, and was laid to rest at Oakdale Cemetery in Marysville.[4]

Enoch Williams. After his discharge, Williams returned home to Dennison, Ohio, where he married the girl who lived next door, Sara Edwards. He worked for Timken Roller Bearing Company in Canton until he retired in the early 1960s. He died on October 18, 1962.

Leon Miesse. Miesse returned home to his wife and eventually relocated to Salem, New Jersey, where he became a plant engineer at the Anchor Hocking factory. The men in the plant called him "Cap" for captain. He never spoke much about his wartime experiences to his children or grandchildren. He passed away in April 1979.[5]

No words can adequately express the totality of what these brave men from Ohio experienced. To be sure, the 166th Infantry became one of the best combat units in the AEF and compiled a wartime service record that might be called admirable by many. Not only had they fought in the major campaigns during the final five months of the war, but forty-six men received the French Croix de Guerre and another forty-seven were awarded the US Distinguished Service Cross, which was the nation's second-highest citation for valor at that time.[6]

But their admirable service record was achieved at a severe cost. The 166th suffered over 2,300 casualties,[7] and almost all of those listed among the missing were never seen again. The wounded, meanwhile, included many who would be permanently disabled physically and even more who had been damaged emotionally and mentally during a time when such injuries were not recognized or treated effectively.

However, what made that loss so very tragic was the futility of it all. The only true by-product of the war was yet another war, one whose global scope and destructive costs still seem unimaginable. Sadly, the political leaders of the Allied nations squandered any opportunity for a lasting peace. Beginning with the harsh punishment of Germany in the Treaty of Versailles, followed by the abandonment of support for the League of Nations by the United States, and the eventual failure of the British and French governments to confront Nazi Germany in the late 1930s, the inevitable path to a second world war was laid down. As so often happens, politicians took sacrifice and the victory it produced and turned it into defeat.

World War II was the only real legacy of the Great War. The "war to end all wars," as it was called, produced nothing but more death and destruction, rendering the sacrifices of those who fought in the 166th Infantry essentially meaningless. This seems even worse when one realizes that World War II came at a time when many of the children of the men who served in the 166th were old enough to fight in that conflict.

Perhaps all we can say of the men of the 166th Infantry Regiment was that, even though they never thought they would become soldiers and certainly never expected to fight in such a horrific and futile war, these men from Ohio went when they were called and did what they were asked to do with bravery, courage, and honor.

No one could ever ask for more.

Notes

INTRODUCTION

1. Edward M. Coffman, *The War to End All Wars: The American Military Experience in World War I* (Lexington: University Press of Kentucky, 1998), 5.

2. Adam Hochschild, *To End All Wars: A Story of Loyalty and Rebellion, 1914-1918* (New York: Houghton Mifflin Harcourt, 2011), Kindle Edition, 206.

3. Ibid., 26, 167.

4. Ibid., 231.

5. Diary entry for September 4, 1916. Douglas Haig. *War Diaries and Letters, 1914–1918*, Eds. Gary Sheffield and John Bourne (London: Weidenfeld & Nicolson, 2005), 226.

6. Coffman, *The War to End All Wars*, 6.

7. Robert B. Asprey, *The German High Command at War: Hindenburg and Ludendorff Conduct World War I* (Fort Mill, South Carolina: Quill House, 1993), 292-294.

8. Eric B. Setzekorn, *Joining the Great War, April 1917-April 1918* (Washington, DC: Center of Military History, United States Army, 2017), 12-13.

9. Woodrow Wilson, *War Messages, 65th Cong., 1st Sess. Senate Doc. No. 5, Serial No. 7264* (Washington, DC, 1917), 3-8.

10. Coffman, *The War to End All Wars*, 8.

11. Ibid., 8-9.

12. Allan R. Millett, *Well Planned, Splendidly Executed: The Battle of Cantigny May 28-31, 1918* (Chicago: Cantigny First Division Foundation, 2010), 154.

13. Millett, *Well Planned, Splendidly Executed*, 155.

14. David A. Armstrong, *Bullets and Bureaucrats: The Machine Gun and the United States Army, 1861-1916* (Westport, Connecticut: Greenwood Press, 1982), 189, 195, 204.

15. Conrad H. Lanza, "The Artillery Support of Infantry in the A.E.F.," *Field Artillery Journal 26, January-March 1936* (Washington, DC: United States Field Artillery Association, 1936), 62.

16. Coffman, *The War to End All Wars*, 10.

17. Joseph Jacques Césaire Joffre, *The Personal Memoirs of Joffre: Field Marshal of the French Army, Volume II* (New York: Harper and Brothers, 1932), 568.

18. Coffman, *The War to End All Wars*, 11-12.

19. Ibid., 13.

20. John S.D. Eisenhower, *Yanks: The Epic Story of the American Army in World War I* (New York: Simon and Schuster, 2001), Kindle Edition, Kindle Location 390.

21. Mark Ethan Grotelueschen, "The AEF Way of War: The American Army and Combat in the First World War." PhD dissertation, Texas A&M University, 2003, 10-11; American Battle Monuments Commission, *American Armies and Battlefields in Europe: A History, Guide, and Reference Book* (Washington, DC, US Government Printing Office, 1938), 501.

22. Coffman, *The War to End All Wars*, 18.

23. Ibid.

24. Ibid.

CHAPTER ONE: MOBILIZING THE 4TH OHIO

1. *Official Roster of the Soldiers of the State of Ohio In the War with Mexico, 1846-1848* (reprint edition) (Mansfield: Ohio Genealogical Society, 1991), 453.

2. *The Army Lineage Book, Volume II: Infantry* (Washington, DC: US Government Printing Office, 1953), 477-490.

3. Cheseldine, *Ohio in the Rainbow*, 37-41.

4. Coffman, *The War to End All Wars*, 13.

5. Thompson, David G. "Ohio's Best: The Mobilization of the Fourth Infantry, Ohio National Guard, in 1917," *Ohio History Journal*, Volume 101, Winter-Spring 1992 (Columbus: Ohio Historical Society, 1992), 40.

6. Coffman, *The War to End All Wars*, 13.

7. Cheseldine, *Ohio in the Rainbow*, 42.

8. Ibid.

9. Thompson, "Ohio's Best," 41.

10. Cheseldine, *Ohio in the Rainbow*, 42.

11. *Le Bijou 1913, The Annual of Ohio Wesleyan University, Volume XVII* (Delaware: Ohio Wesleyan University, 1913), 238.

12. Cheseldine, *Ohio in the Rainbow*, 43.

13. *Ohio State Journal*, Columbus, March 4, 1917.

14. Ohio Adjutant General, *General Order No. 12, 17 April 1917*, State Archives Series 30, Ohio Historical Society, Columbus.

15. Thompson, "Ohio's Best," 42.

16. *Marysville Journal-Tribune*, Marysville, Ohio, April 4, 1917, 3.

17. Thompson, "Ohio's Best," 39.

18. *Marysville Journal-Tribune*, Marysville, Ohio, April 4, 1917, 3.

19. Thompson, "Ohio's Best," 43.

20. *Marion Star*, Marion, Ohio, May 22, 1917, 13.

21. Ibid., November 29, 1946, 1, 10.

22. Ibid., June 1, 1917, 7.

23. Ibid., June 4, 1917, 2.

24. Thompson, "Ohio's Best," 43.

25. Cheseldine, *Ohio in the Rainbow*, 44.

26. Alison Reppy, *Rainbow Memories: Character Sketches and History of the First Battalion, 166th Infantry, 42nd Division, American Expeditionary Force* (Columbus, Ohio: Executive Committee, First Battalion, 166th Infantry, 1919), 7-8.

27. Ibid., 8.

28. Ibid.
29. Cheseldine, *Ohio in the Rainbow*, 29.
30. Ibid., 31.
31. Thompson, "Ohio's Best," 43.
32. Cheseldine, *Ohio in the Rainbow*, 45.
33. Ibid., 45-46.
34. Thompson, "Ohio's Best," 46.
35. Cheseldine, *Ohio in the Rainbow*, 46.
36. Thompson, "Ohio's Best," 46.
37. Enoch Williams to his mother, August 17, 1917. Enoch Williams, *Letters Home from Somewhere in France (P.S. Send cigarettes & chocolate)*, Gary Williams, ed. Unpublished. Accessed at https://archive.org/details/EnochWilliamsWwiLettersHome1917-1919, 4-6.
38. Enoch Williams to his mother, August 22, 1917. Williams, *Letters Home*, 10.
39. Cheseldine, *Ohio in the Rainbow*, 47.
40. Ibid.
41. *Thirteenth Census of the United States: 1910–Population*, Department of Commerce and Labor, Bureau of the Census, Washington Court House, Ohio, April 19, 1910, National Archives and Records Administration (NARA), 14.
42. Ibid., 16.
43. *Marysville Journal-Tribune*, Marysville, Ohio, May 11, 1955, 1; Cheseldine, *Ohio in the Rainbow*, 49-50.
44. Cheseldine, *Ohio in the Rainbow*, 48.
45. Enoch Williams to his mother, September 2, 1917. Williams, *Letters Home*, 12.
46. Cheseldine, *Ohio in the Rainbow*, 51.
47. Ibid., 52.
48. Ibid., 53.
49. Leon Miesse to his wife, September 11, 1917. Leon Miesse, *100 Years On: WW I—Leon Miesse, Captain, 166th*, Ed. Robert Laird (Zerone Publishing, 2017), Kindle Edition, 9.
50. Enoch Williams to his mother, September 10, 1917. Williams, *Letters Home*, 23.
51. Cheseldine, *Ohio in the Rainbow*, 53-54.
52. Enoch Williams to his mother, September 10, 1917. Williams, *Letters Home*, 24.
53. Enoch Williams to his mother, October 8, 1917. Williams, *Letters Home*, 48.
54. Raymond S. Tompkins, *The Story of the Rainbow Division* (New York: Boni and Liveright, 1919), 6-7.
55. Ibid.
56. Cheseldine, *Ohio in the Rainbow*, 54.
57. Ibid., 56.
58. *Annual Report of the Adjutant General to the Governor of the State of Ohio for the Year Ending November 15, 1914* (Springfield: State of Ohio, 1915), 131-132.
59. Cheseldine, *Ohio in the Rainbow*, 57.
60. Leon Miesse to his wife, September 12, 1917. Miesse, *100 Years On*, 11.
61. Leon Miesse to his wife, October 9, 1917. Miesse, *100 Years On*, 26.
62. Tompkins, *The Story of the Rainbow Division*, 18.
63. Cheseldine, *Ohio in the Rainbow*, 59-60.
64. Enoch Williams to his mother, October 2, 1917. Williams, *Letters Home*, 45.
65. Leon Miesse to his wife, September 12, 1917. Miesse, *100 Years On*, 11.
66. Enoch Williams to his mother, October 2, 1917. Williams, *Letters Home*, 44.
67. Enoch Williams to his mother, September 20, 1917. Williams, *Letters Home*, 28.

68. Cheseldine, *Ohio in the Rainbow*, 59.
69. Enoch Williams to his mother, September 24, 1917. Williams, *Letters Home*, 31.
70. Leon Miesse to his wife, September 12, 1917. Miesse, *100 Years On*, 11.
71. Enoch Williams to his mother, October 2, 1917. Williams, *Letters Home*, 45.
72. Leon Miesse to his wife, September 26, 1917. Miesse, *100 Years On*, 34.
73. Cheseldine, *Ohio in the Rainbow*, 60.
74. Ibid., 61.
75. Ibid., 60.
76. Leon Miesse to his wife, September 12, 1917. Miesse, *100 Years On*, 12.
77. Enoch Williams to his mother, September 24, 1917. Williams, *Letters Home*, 31.
78. Enoch Williams to his mother, October 17, 1917. Williams, *Letters Home*, 52.
79. Cheseldine, *Ohio in the Rainbow*, 64.
80. Ibid., 49.

CHAPTER TWO: OVER THERE

1. Dana Daniels, *Dana Daniels Diary, 1917-1919* (Columbus: Dana Daniels Collection, Ohio Historical Society, MS 5; Box 1, Folder 6), 2.
2. Cheseldine, *Ohio in the Rainbow*, 64.
3. Ibid., 71.
4. Ibid., 64.
5. Benedict Crowell and Robert Forrest Wilson, *The Road to France: The Transportation of Troops and Military Supplies, 1917–1918-How America Went to War: An Account from Official Sources of the Nation's War Activities, 1917–1920* (New Haven, Connecticut: Yale University Press, 1921), 314-315.
6. Cheseldine, *Ohio in the Rainbow*, 64.
7. Carl F. Ebert, *A Brief History of Co. D, 166th Infantry* (Marion, Ohio: Unknown Publisher, 1939), 9.
8. Cheseldine, *Ohio in the Rainbow*, 66-67.
9. Ibid., 67.
10. Ibid.
11. Ibid.
12. Ibid., 64.
13. Ibid., 66.
14. Ibid., 68-69.
15. Ibid., 69-70.
16. Ibid., 68.
17. Daniels, *Dana Daniels Diary,1917-1919*, 1-2.
18. Cheseldine, *Ohio in the Rainbow*, 70.
19. Ibid., 67-68.
20. Enoch Williams to his mother, November 2, 1917. Williams, *Letters Home*, 53.
21. Daniels, *Dana Daniels Diary, 1917-1919*, 2.
22. The Sam Browne belt is a wide belt, usually leather, supported by a narrower strap passing diagonally over the right shoulder. It was invented by a nineteenth-century British Indian Army officer who had lost his left arm, which made it difficult for him to draw his sword because the left hand was typically used to steady the scabbard while the right drew out the sword ("Sam Browne Belts Originally Devised For One-Armed Men," *Atlanta Constitution*, July 23, 1921).
23. Cheseldine, *Ohio in the Rainbow*, 70-71.

24. Ibid., 71.

25. Enoch Williams to his mother, November 2, 1917. Williams, *Letters Home*, 54.

26. Austin Boyd to his family, letter undated. Austin Dewitt Boyd, *Austin Dewitt "Dusty" Boyd in WWI: Service in France and Germany*, Mark Boyd, ed. Unpublished. Accessed at www.markboyd.info/adboyd/war.html#mar-15-1919, 1.

27. Enoch Williams to his mother, November 6, 1917. Williams, *Letters Home*, 55-56.

28. Ebert, *A Brief History of Co. D*, 10.

29. Daniels, *Dana Daniels Diary, 1917-1919*, 2.

30. Ebert, *A Brief History of Co. D*, 10.

31. Cheseldine, *Ohio in the Rainbow*, 73.

32. Ibid.

33. Ibid., 71.

34. Ibid., 71-72.

35. Ibid., 73.

36. Ibid., 75.

37. Daniels, *Dana Daniels Diary, 1917-1919*, 2-3.

38. Cheseldine, *Ohio in the Rainbow*, 78.

39. Daniels, *Dana Daniels Diary, 1917-1919*, 2.

40. Enoch Williams to his mother, November 11, 1917. Williams, *Letters Home*, 58.

41. Austin Boyd to his family, November 11, 1917. Boyd, *Austin Dewitt "Dusty" Boyd in WWI*, 2.

42. Cheseldine, *Ohio in the Rainbow*, 77.

43. Ibid.

44. Leon Miesse to his wife, November 17, 1917. Miesse, *100 Years On*, 36-37.

45. Leon Miesse to his wife, November 28, 1917. Miesse, *100 Years On*, 39-40.

46. Cheseldine, *Ohio in the Rainbow*, 78.

47. Ibid., 79.

48. Ibid., 79-80.

49. Ibid., 80.

50. Ibid., 85.

51. Ibid., 85-86.

52. Austin Boyd to his family, November 18, 1917. Boyd, *Austin Dewitt "Dusty" Boyd in WWI*, 2

53. Leon Miesse to his wife, February 10, 1917. Miesse, *100 Years On*, 73.

54. Tompkins, *The Story of the Rainbow Division*, 21.

55. George M. Chinn, *The Machine Gun: History, Evolution and Development of Manual, Automatic, and Airborne Repeating Weapons, Volume I* (Washington, DC: US Government Printing Office, 1951), 200.

56. *History of Machine Guns and Automatic Rifles* (Washington, DC: US Government Printing Office, Small Arms Division, Office of the Chief of Ordnance, 1922), 12; *Handbook of the Hotchkiss Machine Gun, Model of 1914* (Washington, DC: US War Department, Office of the Chief of Ordnance, 1917), 25.

57. *History of Machine Guns and Automatic Rifles*, 12.

58. *Handbook of the Hotchkiss Machine Gun, Model of 1914*, 26.

59. *History of Machine Guns and Automatic Rifles*, 13-14.

60. Virgil Ney, *Evolution of the US Army Infantry Mortar Squad: The Argonne To Pleiku* (Fort Belvoir, Virginia: Technical Operations, Incorporated, Combat Operations Research Group, 1966), 20-30.

61. Cheseldine, *Ohio in the Rainbow*, 84.

62. Ebert, *A Brief History of Co. D*, 21; Cheseldine, *Ohio in the Rainbow*, 84.

63. Walter B. Wolf, *A Brief History of the Rainbow Division* (New York: Rand, McNally, 1919), 10.

64. Cheseldine, *Ohio in the Rainbow*, 86.

65. Ibid., 88.

CHAPTER THREE: "VALLEY FORGE"

1. Reppy, *Rainbow Memories*, 63.

2. Leon Miesse to his wife, February 2, 1918. Miesse, *100 Years On*, 70.

3. Tompkins, *The Story of the Rainbow Division*, 23.

4. Cheseldine, *Ohio in the Rainbow*, 87.

5. Ibid., 88.

6. Tompkins, *The Story of the Rainbow Division*, 24.

7. Cheseldine, *Ohio in the Rainbow*, 89.

8. Cheseldine, *Ohio in the Rainbow*, 93; Daniels, *Dana Daniels Diary, 1917-1919*, 3.

9. Cheseldine, *Ohio in the Rainbow*, 92.

10. Ibid., 92-93.

11. Ibid., 93.

12. Ibid., 94-95.

13. Cheseldine, *Ohio in the Rainbow*, 95; Wolf, *A Brief History of the Rainbow Division*, 9-10.

14. Tompkins, *The Story of the Rainbow Division*, 24-25.

15. Cheseldine, *Ohio in the Rainbow*, 96.

16. Ibid.

17. Ibid.

18. Ibid., 97-98.

19. Ibid., 98.

20. Ibid.

21. Wolf, *A Brief History of the Rainbow Division*, 10.

22. Cheseldine, *Ohio in the Rainbow*, 98.

23. Ibid., 99.

24. Ibid.

25. Daniels, *Dana Daniels Diary, 1917-1919*, 4.

26. Wolf, *A Brief History of the Rainbow Division*, 9.

27. Cheseldine, *Ohio in the Rainbow*, 100.

28. Daniels, *Dana Daniels Diary, 1917-1919*, 4.

29. Cheseldine, *Ohio in the Rainbow*, 102.

30. Ibid., 104.

31. Daniels, *Dana Daniels Diary, 1917-1919*, 4.

32. Cheseldine, *Ohio in the Rainbow*, 102.

33. Daniels, *Dana Daniels Diary, 1917-1919*, 4.

34. Cheseldine, *Ohio in the Rainbow*, 104-105.

35. Ibid., 103.

36. Ibid., 103-104.

37. Ibid.

38. Coffman, *The War to End All Wars*, 145.

39. Sanitary Report, 26th Division, October 1918, Box 22, *Clarence R. Edwards Papers, 1879-1937*, Massachusetts Historical Society (MHS), Boston, cited in Mark Ethan

Grotelueschen, "The AEF Way of War: The American Army and Combat in the First World War," PhD dissertation, Texas A&M University, 2003, 134.
40. Leon Miesse to his wife, February 9, 1918. Miesse, *100 Years On*, 71.

CHAPTER FOUR: IN TO THE TRENCHES—LUNÉVILLE AND BACCARAT

1. Cheseldine, *Ohio in the Rainbow*, 113-114.
2. Ibid., 105.
3. Burt Moffett, entry for February 16, 1918, *Burt Moffett Diary*, 5-6.
4. Cheseldine, *Ohio in the Rainbow*, 105.
5. Leon Miesse to his wife, February 19, 1918. Miesse, *100 Years On*, 72.
6. Coffman, *The American Experience in World War I*, 150.
7. Cheseldine, *Ohio in the Rainbow*, 105; Daniels, *Dana Daniels Diary, 1917-1919*, 5-6.
8. Cheseldine, *Ohio in the Rainbow*, 106.
9. Ibid.
10. Coffman, *The American Experience in World War I*, 150.
11. Cheseldine, *Ohio in the Rainbow*, 106-107.
12. Ibid., 107.
13. Enoch Williams to his mother, March 9, 1918. Williams, *Letters Home*, 85.
14. Tompkins, *The Story of the Rainbow Division*, 31-32.
15. Ibid., 29.
16. Cheseldine, *Ohio in the Rainbow*, 113.
17. *Richwood Gazette*, Richmond, Ohio, March 14, 1918, 1; *Marysville Journal-Tribune*, Marysville, Ohio, March 7, 1918, 2.
18. Notes on Photo from US Army Signal Corps. Subject 7659, March 3, 1918, National Archives and Records Administration (NARA).
19. Cheseldine, *Ohio in the Rainbow*, 113.
20. Leon Miesse journal entry for March 2, 1918. Miesse, *100 Years On*, 81.
21. Cheseldine, *Ohio in the Rainbow*, 114.
22. Leon Miesse to his wife, March 15, 1918. Miesse, *100 Years On*, 84-85.
23. Burt Moffett, Entry for March 9, 1918, *Burt Moffett Diary*, 15.
24. Caleb Byron Lear, *Veteran's Compensation Application, State of Pennsylvania*, September 7, 1937, Pennsylvania Historical and Museum Commission.
25. Cheseldine, *Ohio in the Rainbow*, 114-115.
26. Ibid., 116.
27. Ibid., 117-118.
28. Burt Moffett, Entry for March 11, 1918, *Burt Moffett Diary*, 16.
29. Cheseldine, *Ohio in the Rainbow*, 118-119.
30. Daniels, *Dana Daniels Diary, 1917-1919*, 7.
31. Cheseldine, *Ohio in the Rainbow*, 120.
32. Ibid.
33. *New York Times*, March 21, 1918.
34. Ibid.
35. Cheseldine, *Ohio in the Rainbow*, 119; Burt Moffett, Entry for March 9, 1918, *Burt Moffett Diary*, 15.
36. Cheseldine, *Ohio in the Rainbow*, 120-121.
37. Daniels, *Dana Daniels Diary, 1917-1919*, 7.
38. Cheseldine, *Ohio in the Rainbow*, 121.
39. Ibid., 119.

40. C. C. Lyon, "Mule Skinner's Life Isn't Wholly Dull," *Stars and Stripes*, Paris, France, April 26, 1918, 1.

41. Cheseldine, *Ohio in the Rainbow*, 120-121.

42. Ibid., 123.

43. Burt Moffett, Entry for March 23, 1918, *Burt Moffett Diary*, 21-22.

44. Cheseldine, *Ohio in the Rainbow*, 123.

45. Wolf, *A Brief History of the Rainbow Division*, 14.

46. Cheseldine, *Ohio in the Rainbow*, 124; Daniels, *Dana Daniels Diary, 1917-1919*, 9.

47. Cheseldine, *Ohio in the Rainbow*, 124; Daniels, *Dana Daniels Diary, 1917-1919*, 9.

48. Leon Miesse journal entry for March 31, 1918. Miesse, *100 Years On*, 92.

49. Wolf, *A Brief History of the Rainbow Division*, 14-15.

50. Ibid., 15.

51. Cheseldine, *Ohio in the Rainbow*, 126.

52. Ibid., 126-127.

53. Leon Miesse journal entry for April 8, 1918, Miesse, *100 Years On*, 97.

54. Cheseldine, *Ohio in the Rainbow*, 127.

55. Ibid., 128.

56. Ibid., 128-129.

57. Ibid., 127-128.

58. Ibid., 129.

59. Austin Boyd to his family, April 12, 1918. Boyd, *Austin Dewitt "Dusty" Boyd in WWI*, 7.

60. Tompkins, *The Story of the Rainbow Division*, 38-39.

61. Cheseldine, *Ohio in the Rainbow*, 133-134.

62. Leon Miesse journal entry for May 3, 1918. Miesse, *100 Years On*, 107.

63. Leon Miesse journal entry for May 3, 1918. Miesse, *100 Years On*, 107; Cheseldine, *Ohio in the Rainbow*, 134.

64. Michael S. Neiberg, *The Second Battle of the Marne* (Bloomington: University of Indiana Press, 2008), Kindle Edition, Kindle Locations 1260-1265.

65. Leon Miesse journal entry for May 3, 1918. Miesse, *100 Years On*, 107; Cheseldine, *Ohio in the Rainbow*, 134.

66. Tompkins, *The Story of the Rainbow Division*, 39.

67. Cheseldine, *Ohio in the Rainbow*, 134; Leon Miesse journal entry for May 3, 1918. Miesse, *100 Years On*, 107.

68. Davis F. Bryant, US, World War I Draft Registration Cards, 1917-1918, Registration State: Virginia; Registration County: Prince George; Roll: 1985047 (Provo, Utah: Ancestry.com, 2005), 1005; Paul Jarrett, *The Return of Paul Jarrett*, DVD, Director: Clark Jarrett. Los Angeles: Jarrett Entertainment, 1998, 34:06-36:20.

69. Paul Jarrett, *The Return of Paul Jarrett*, 34:06-36:20.

70. Cheseldine, *Ohio in the Rainbow*, 134.

71. Ibid., 130-132.

72. Ibid., 131.

73. Caroline Alexander, "The Shock of War," *Smithsonian*, September 2010.

74. *Ohio Rainbow Reveille*, May 18, 1918, 2.

75. Cheseldine, *Ohio in the Rainbow*, 137.

76. Reppy, *Rainbow Memories*, 55.

77. Reppy, *Rainbow Memories*, 55; Cheseldine, *Ohio in the Rainbow*, 138.

78. Cheseldine, *Ohio in the Rainbow*, 139.

79. Ibid.

80. Cheseldine, *Ohio in the Rainbow*, 139-140.

81. Daniels, *Dana Daniels Diary, 1917-1919*, 14.

82. Robert Thorn to Hillis Thorn, May 26, 1918. Author's family collection.

83. Burt Moffett, Entry for May 27, 1918, *Burt Moffett Diary*, 41.

84. Cheseldine, *Ohio in the Rainbow*, 142; Daniels, *Dana Daniels Diary, 1917-1919*, 15-17.

85. Daniels, *Dana Daniels Diary, 1917-1919*, 16-17.

86. *New York State Abstracts of World War I Military Service, 1917–1919*, Adjutant General's Office, Series B0808. New York State Archives, Albany, New York.

87. Cheseldine, *Ohio in the Rainbow*, 143-144.

88. Leon Miesse to his wife, June 26, 1918. Miesse, *100 Years On*, 122.

89. Cheseldine, *Ohio in the Rainbow*, 148-149.

CHAPTER FIVE: GUARDIANS OF THE PASS—THE CHAMPAGNE DEFENSIVE

1. Report of Captain Henry Grave, Commander, I Company, 166th Infantry Regiment, cited in Cheseldine, *Ohio in the Rainbow*, 167.

2. Henry J. Reilly, *America's Part* (New York: Cosmopolitan Book Corporation, 1928), 241.

3. Daniels, *Dana Daniels Diary, 1917-1919*, 18-19; Cheseldine, *Ohio in the Rainbow*, 151.

4. Leon Miesse journal entry for June 28, 1918. Miesse, *100 Years On*, 125.

5. Neiberg, *The Second Battle of the Marne*, Kindle Location 160.

6. Ibid., Kindle Location 171-172.

7. John J. Pershing, *My Experiences in the World War, Volume 2* (New York: Frederick Stokes, 1931), 159.

8. Daniels, *Dana Daniels Diary, 1917-1919*, 19.

9. Leon Miesse journal entry for June 28, 1918. Miesse, *100 Years On*, 125.

10. Patrick Takle, *Nine Divisions in Champagne: The Second Battle of Marne* (Barnsley, UK: Pen & Sword Books, 2015), Kindle Edition, Kindle Location 171-174.

11. Ibid., Kindle Location 175-180.

12. Ibid., Kindle Location 180-182.

13. Ibid., Kindle Location 622-645.

14. Ibid.

15. Cheseldine, *Ohio in the Rainbow*, 152.

16. Wolf, *A Brief History of the Rainbow Division*, 24-25.

17. Ibid.

18. Cheseldine, *Ohio in the Rainbow*, 152; Daniels, *Dana Daniels Diary, 1917-1919*, 20-21.

19. *Fourteenth Census of the United States, 1920.* (NARA microfilm publication T625, 2076 rolls). Records of the Bureau of the Census, Record Group 29. National Archives, Washington, DC; *U.S., Select Military Registers, 1862-1985* [database on-line]. Provo, UT, USA: Ancestry.com.

20. Cheseldine, *Ohio in the Rainbow*, 152; Daniels, *Dana Daniels Diary, 1917-1919*, 20-21.

21. Tompkins, *The Story of the Rainbow Division*, 50-51.

22. Cheseldine, *Ohio in the Rainbow*, 152.

23. Ibid., 153.

24. Tompkins, *The Story of the Rainbow Division*, 51.

25. Ibid., 153-154.

26. Ibid., 154-155.

27. Ibid., 155.

28. Enoch Williams to his mother, July 9, 1918, Williams, *Letters Home*, 110.

29. Cheseldine, *Ohio in the Rainbow*, 160.

30. Ibid., 160-161.

31. Neiberg, *The Second Battle of the Marne*, Kindle Location 1166-1171.

32. Cheseldine, *Ohio in the Rainbow*, 162.

33. Leon Miesse journal entry for July 14, 1918. Miesse, *100 Years On*, 136.

34. Cheseldine, *Ohio in the Rainbow*, 162.

35. Ibid.

36. Wolf, *A Brief History of the Rainbow Division*, 25.

37. Ibid.

38. Neiberg, *The Second Battle of the Marne*, Kindle Location 1221-1227.

39. Ibid., Kindle Location 1244-1245.

40. Wolf, *A Brief History of the Rainbow Division*, 26-27.

41. Cheseldine, *Ohio in the Rainbow*, 164; *The Official Roster of Ohio Soldiers, Sailors, and Marines in the World War, 1917-18* (Columbus, Ohio: F.J. Heer Printing Co., 1926), 525.

42. Cheseldine, *Ohio in the Rainbow*, 164-165.

43. Ibid., 164.

44. Wolf, *A Brief History of the Rainbow Division*, 27.

45. Tompkins, *The Story of the Rainbow Division*, 56.

46. Cheseldine, *Ohio in the Rainbow*, 165.

47. *American Armies and Battlefields in Europe: A History, Guide, and Reference Book* (Washington, DC: US Government Printing Office, 1938), 344; Reilly, *America's Part*, 241; Report of Captain Henry Grave, commanding officer, I Company, cited in Cheseldine, *Ohio in the Rainbow*, 167.

48. Cheseldine, *Ohio in the Rainbow*, 165-166.

49. Wolf, *A Brief History of the Rainbow Division*, 28.

50. *Thirteenth Census of the United States, 1910.* (NARA microfilm publication T624, 1179 rolls). Records of the Census Bureau. National Archives, Washington, DC; *General Index to Compiled Service Records of Volunteer Soldiers who Served During the War with Spain.* Microfilm publication M871, 126 rolls. ARC ID: 654543. Records of the Adjutant General's Office, 1780s–1917, Record Group 94. The National Archives at Washington, DC

51. Cheseldine, *Ohio in the Rainbow*, 171-172.

52. Ibid., 172.

53. Ibid.

54. Ibid., 173.

55. Ibid.

56. Ibid., 174.

57. Ibid., 169.

58. Reppy, *Rainbow Memories*, 31.

59. Cheseldine, *Ohio in the Rainbow*, 169-170.

60. Ibid., 170-171.

61. Leon Miesse journal entry for July 15, 1918. Miesse, *100 Years On*, 137.

62. Cheseldine, *Ohio in the Rainbow*, 166.

63. Report of Captain Henry Grave, commander, I Company, 166th Infantry Regiment, cited in Cheseldine, *Ohio in the Rainbow*, 167.

64. Ibid., 168.

65. Cheseldine, *Ohio in the Rainbow*, 178-179.

66. *The Official Roster of Ohio Soldiers, Sailors, and Marines in the World War, 1917-18*, 838.

67. Cheseldine, *Ohio in the Rainbow*, 175.

68. Ibid.

69. Ibid.

70. Ibid., 176-177.

71. Report of Captain Henry Grave, commander, I Company, 166th Infantry Regiment, cited in Cheseldine, *Ohio in the Rainbow*, 168.

72. Ibid., 167.

73. Leon Miesse to his wife, July 20, 1918. Miesse, *100 Years On*, 140.

74. Cheseldine, *Ohio in the Rainbow*, 183, 344.

75. Ibid., 156.

76. Ibid., 150, 190.

CHAPTER SIX: THE OURCQ——RIVER OF DEATH

1. Daniels, *Dana Daniels Diary, 1917-1919*, 25-27.

2. Cheseldine, *Ohio in the Rainbow*, 193-194.

3. Daniels, *Dana Daniels Diary, 1917-1919*, 23; Cheseldine, *Ohio in the Rainbow*, 194.

4. Leon Miesse journal entry for July 25, 1918. Miesse, *100 Years On*, 141-142.

5. Cheseldine, *Ohio in the Rainbow*, 192.

6. Daniels, *Dana Daniels Diary, 1917-1919*, 23-24.

7. Cheseldine, *Ohio in the Rainbow*,190-191.

8. Ibid., 192.

9. Ibid.

10. Ibid., 193.

11. Reilly, *America's Part*, 282-283.

12. Ibid., 283-284.

13. Cheseldine, *Ohio in the Rainbow*, 197.

14. Ibid., 193.

15. Ibid., 194.

16. Ibid.

17. Ibid., 196.

18. Neiberg, *The Second Battle of the Marne*, Kindle Location 1852-1861.

19. Cheseldine, *Ohio in the Rainbow*, 197-198.

20. Ibid.

21. Ibid., 198.

22. Ibid.

23. Leon Miesse journal entry for July 28, 1918. Miesse, *100 Years On*, 142.

24. Cheseldine, *Ohio in the Rainbow*, 199; 214.

25. Ibid., 200.

26. Neiberg, *The Second Battle of the Marne*, Kindle Location 2226-2230.

27. Tompkins, *The Story of the Rainbow Division*, 86.

28. Ibid., 86-87.

29. Ibid.

30. Cheseldine, *Ohio in the Rainbow*, 201.

31. Daniels, *Dana Daniels Diary, 1917-1919*, 27-28.

32. Ibid., 29-30.

33. Ibid., 30-31.

34. Cheseldine, *Ohio in the Rainbow*, 202.

35. Ibid.

36. Ibid.

37. Ibid., 205.

38. Ibid., 205-207.

39. Ibid., 203.

40. Ibid.

41. Daniels, *Dana Daniels Diary, 1917-1919*, 32.

42. *The Official Roster of Ohio Soldiers, Sailors, and Marines in the World War, 1917-18.*

43. Daniels, *Dana Daniels Diary, 1917-1919*, 33-34.

44. Cheseldine, *Ohio in the Rainbow*, 203-204.

45. Ibid., 204.

46. *Handbook of Artillery Including Mobile, Anti-Aircraft and Trench Materiel* (Washington, DC: Office of the Chief of Ordnance, US Government Printing Office, 1920), 51-53.

47. Cheseldine, *Ohio in the Rainbow*, 213.

48. Daniels, *Dana Daniels Diary, 1917-1919*, 34.

49. Ibid., 35-37.

50. Cheseldine, *Ohio in the Rainbow*, 209.

51. Cheseldine, *Ohio in the Rainbow*, 209; Daniels, *Dana Daniels Diary, 1917-1919*, 36.

52. Cheseldine, *Ohio in the Rainbow*, 210.

53. Cheseldine, *Ohio in the Rainbow*, 210; Daniels, *Dana Daniels Diary, 1917-1919*, 37.

54. Daniels, *Dana Daniels Diary, 1917-1919*, 37-38.

55. Cheseldine, *Ohio in the Rainbow*, 212; *The Official Roster of Ohio Soldiers, Sailors, and Marines in the World War, 1917-18.*

56. Cheseldine, *Ohio in the Rainbow*, 210-211.

57. Ibid., 211.

58. Ibid., 217.

59. Daniels, *Dana Daniels Diary, 1917-1919*, 39.

60. Cheseldine, *Ohio in the Rainbow*, 216, 212.

61. Ibid., 215.

CHAPTER SEVEN: ON THE OFFENSIVE—SAINT MIHIEL

1. Cheseldine, *Ohio in the Rainbow*, 231.

2. Ibid., 241.

3. Coffman, *The American Experience in World War I*, 279-280.

4. Cheseldine, *Ohio in the Rainbow*, 231.

5. David Bonk, *St. Mihiel, 1918: The American Expeditionary Force's Trial by Fire* (Oxford, UK: Osprey Publishing, 2011), Kindle Edition, Kindle Location 492; Eisenhower, *Yanks*, Kindle Location 3215-3223.

6. Ibid., Kindle Location 492-496.

7. Donald A. Carter, *St. Mihiel, 12–16 September 1918* (Washington, DC: Center of Military History, US Army, 2018), 14.

8. Ibid., 13.

9. Coffman, *The American Experience in World War I*, 268.

10. Carter, *St. Mihiel*, 15.

11. Coffman, *The American Experience in World War I*, 270-271; Bonk, *St. Mihiel*, Kindle Location 542.

12. Coffman, *The American Experience in World War I*, 271-272.

13. Carter, *St. Mihiel*, 20.

14. Coffman, *The American Experience in World War I*, 273-274.

15. Cheseldine, *Ohio in the Rainbow*, 219-220.

16. Ibid.

17. Tomkins, *The Story of the Rainbow Division*, 103.

18. Cheseldine, *Ohio in the Rainbow*, 224.

19. Ibid., 224-225.

20. Ibid., 226.

21. Ibid.

22. Ibid., 227.

23. Wolf, *A Brief History of the Rainbow Division*, 37.

24. Coffman, *The American Experience in World War I*, 278.

25. Ibid.

26. Cheseldine, *Ohio in the Rainbow*, 228.

27. Ibid.

28. Shipley Thomas, *The History of the A.E.F.* (New York: George B. Doran, 1920), 212.

29. Thomas, *History of the A.E.F.*, 212.

30. Cheseldine, *Ohio in the Rainbow*, 231.

31. Wolf, *A Brief History of the Rainbow Division*, 40.

32. Carter, *St. Mihiel*, 33-34.

33. Coffman, *The American Experience in World War I*, 279.

34. Thomas, *History of the A.E.F.*, 213-214.

35. Carter, *St. Mihiel*, 35.

36. Reppy, *Rainbow Memories*, 17.

37. Bonk, *St. Mihiel, 12–16 September 1918*, Kindle Location 921.

38. Cheseldine, *Ohio in the Rainbow*, 232.

39. Ibid.

40. Leon Miesse to his wife, September 16, 1918. Miesse, *100 years On*, 156-157.

41. Austin Dewitt "Dusty" Boyd to his family, September 23, 1918. *Austin Dewitt "Dusty" Boyd in WWI*, 11.

42. Cheseldine, *Ohio in the Rainbow*, 232.

43. Ibid., 232-233.

44. Ibid., 233.

45. Ibid.

46. Ibid., 235.

47. Cheseldine, *Ohio in the Rainbow*, 233; Coffman, *The American Experience in World War I*, 281.

48. Cheseldine, *Ohio in the Rainbow*, 235.

49. Ibid., 234.

50. Ibid.

51. Cheseldine, *Ohio in the Rainbow*, 235-236; *The Official Roster of Ohio Soldiers, Sailors, and Marines in the World War, 1917-18*.

52. Leon Miesse journal entry for September 13, 1918. Miesse, *100 years On*, 155-156.

53. Thomas, *History of the A.E.F.*, 217-218; Leon Miesse to his wife September 16, 1918. Miesse, *100 Years On*, 156-157; Carter, *St. Mihiel*, 58.

54. Cheseldine, *Ohio in the Rainbow*, 234-235.

55. Ibid., 236-237.

56. Ibid., 237.

57. Ibid.

58. Ibid., 237-238.

59. Ibid., 238.

60. Ibid.

61. Ibid.

62. Cheseldine, *Ohio in the Rainbow*, 239; Reppy, *Rainbow Memories*, 17.

63. Reppy, *Rainbow Memories*, 17.

64. Official Report of Lieutenant Aubrey DeLacy cited in Cheseldine, *Ohio in the Rainbow*, 239.

65. Ibid.

CHAPTER EIGHT: THE BIG PUSH—THE MEUSE-ARGONNE TO SEDAN

1. "Captain Reuben B, Hutchcraft, Jr., Makes the Supreme Sacrifice for His Country," *Bourbon News*, December 13, 1918, 1.

2. Lyman Chalkley, "Captain Reuben Brent Hutchcraft, Jr.," *Kentucky Law Journal*: Vol. 7: Issue. 1, Article 7, 1919, 42.

3. Cheseldine, *Ohio in the Rainbow*, 272.

4. Ibid.

5. Ibid., 273.

6. Maarten Otte, *The Meuse Argonne 1918: Breaking the Line* (Barnsley, United Kingdom: Pen & Sword Books, 2018), Kindle Edition, Kindle Location 427.

7. Coffman, *The American Experience in World War I*, 299-300.

8. Ibid., 300.

9. Otte, *The Meuse Argonne*, Kindle Location 307.

10. Coffman, *The American Experience in World War I*, 300.

11. Tompkins, *The Story of the Rainbow Division*, 128-129.

12. Roy Bailey, *Roy Bailey Diary, 1917-1919* (Unpublished. Accessed at www.markboyd.info/MarionsOwn/Sgt_Bailey), 67.

13. Cheseldine, *Ohio in the Rainbow*, 240; Daniels, *Dana Daniels Diary, 1917-1919*, 47.

14. Cheseldine, *Ohio in the Rainbow*, 241; Daniels, *Dana Daniels Diary, 1917-1919*, 47-48.

15. Cheseldine, *Ohio in the Rainbow*, 241, 244; Daniels, *Dana Daniels Diary, 1917-1919*, 48.

16. Cheseldine, *Ohio in the Rainbow*, 244.

17. Ibid.

18. Ibid., 245.

19. Ibid.

20. Ibid., 246.

21. Ibid., 248.

22. Daniels, *Dana Daniels Diary, 1917-1919*, 49-50.

23. Cheseldine, *Ohio in the Rainbow*, 248-249; Wolf, *A Brief History of the Rainbow Division*, 45.

24. Reppy, *Rainbow Memories*, 17.

25. Daniels, *Dana Daniels Diary, 1917-1919*, 49-50.

26. Reppy, *Rainbow Memories*, 17.

27. Leon Miesse journal entry for October 11, 1918. Miesse, *100 Years On*, 166, 177.

28. Wolf, *A Brief History of the Rainbow Division*, 45.

29. Cheseldine, *Ohio in the Rainbow*, 249-250.

30. Richard S. Faulkner, *Meuse-Argonne, 26 September-11 November 1918* (Washington, DC: Center of Military History, US Army, 2018), 48.

31. Cheseldine, *Ohio in the Rainbow*, 250.

32. Faulkner, *Meuse-Argonne*, 48.

33. *Official War Diary of the 166th Infantry Regiment* for October 14, 1918, cited in Cheseldine, *Ohio in the Rainbow*, 250-251.

34. Ibid., 251.

35. Ibid., 252.

36. Coffman, *The American Experience in World War I*, 327-328.

37. *Official War Diary of the 166th Infantry Regiment* for October 15, 1918, cited in Cheseldine, *Ohio in the Rainbow*, 253.

38. Ibid., 252.

39. Faulkner, *Meuse-Argonne*, 20, 44.

40. *Official War Diary of the 166th Infantry Regiment* for October 15, 1918, cited in Cheseldine, *Ohio in the Rainbow*, 252.

41. Ibid., 253.

42. Ibid., 252.

43. Ibid., 253.

44. Cheseldine, *Ohio in the Rainbow*, 255-256.

45. Cheseldine, *Ohio in the Rainbow*, 262; *The Official Roster of Ohio Soldiers, Sailors, and Marines in the World War, 1917-18.*

46. *Official War Diary of the 166th Infantry Regiment* for October 16, 1918, cited in Cheseldine, *Ohio in the Rainbow*, 254.

47. Ibid., 254.

48. Cheseldine, *Ohio in the Rainbow*, 256.

49. Ibid.

50. Daniels, *Dana Daniels Diary, 1917-1919*, 50-51.

51. Report from Lieutenant Alison Reppy, 1st Battalion Intelligence Officer, October 18, 1918, cited in Cheseldine, *Ohio in the Rainbow*, 256-257.

52. Cheseldine, *Ohio in the Rainbow*, 257-258.

53. Ibid., 258.

54. Bailey, *Roy Bailey Diary, 1917-1919*, 69.

55. Enoch Williams to his mother, October 27, 1918. Williams, *Letters Home*, 123-124.

56. Cheseldine, *Ohio in the Rainbow*, 260.

57. Ibid., 261.

58. Daniels, *Dana Daniels Diary, 1917-1919*, 52.

59. Ibid., 53.

60. Cheseldine, *Ohio in the Rainbow*, 266.

61. Ibid.

62. Ibid., 267.

63. Ibid.

64. Daniels, *Dana Daniels Diary, 1917-1919*, 53.

65. Ibid., 54.

66. Cheseldine, *Ohio in the Rainbow*, 268.

67. Ibid., 267.

68. Leon Miesse journal for November 5, 1918. Miesse, *100 Years On*, 187.

69. Cheseldine, *Ohio in the Rainbow*, 268-269.

70. Ibid., 269.

71. Ibid., 268.

72. Cheseldine, *Ohio in the Rainbow*, 269; Reppy, *Rainbow Memories*, 19.

73. Leon Miesse journal for November 6, 1918. Miesse, *100 Years On*, 187; Daniels, *Dana*

Daniels Diary, 1917-1919, 55.

74. Cheseldine, *Ohio in the Rainbow*, 270.

75. Daniels, *Dana Daniels Diary, 1917-1919*, 56.

76. Cheseldine, *Ohio in the Rainbow*, 270-271.

77. Coffman, *The American Experience in World War I*, 351.

78. Cheseldine, *Ohio in the Rainbow*, 273.

79. Daniels, *Dana Daniels Diary, 1917-1919*, 56.

80. Cheseldine, *Ohio in the Rainbow*, 273.

81. Ibid., 242.

82. J. Michael Finn, "The Chaplain Who Went Over-the-Top: Father George Raphael Carpentier, O.P.," *Barquilla de la Santa Maria, Bulletin of the Catholic Record Society-Diocese of Columbus*, Volume XXX, No. 11, November 2005, 279-280.

83. General Orders No. 126, War Department, 1919, cited in Finn, "The Chaplain Who Went Over-the-Top," *Barquilla de la Santa Maria*, 282.

84. Cheseldine, *Ohio in the Rainbow*, 275-276.

85. Ibid., 276.

86. Cheseldine, *Ohio in the Rainbow*, 276; Reppy, *Rainbow Memories*, 19.

87. Coffman, *The American Experience in World War I*, 355.

88. Cheseldine, *Ohio in the Rainbow*, 278.

89. Ibid.

90. Bailey, *Roy Bailey Diary, 1917-1919*, 71.

91. Cheseldine, *Ohio in the Rainbow*, 278.

CHAPTER NINE: WAR'S END

1. Daniels, *Dana Daniels Diary, 1917-1919*, 73.

2. Cheseldine, *Ohio in the Rainbow*, 333.

3. Reppy, *Rainbow Memories*, 26.

4. Tompkins, *The Story of the Rainbow Division*, 147.

5. Brian F. Neumann and Shane D. Makowicki, *Occupation and Demobilization, 1918–1923* (Washington, DC: Center of Military History, US Army, 2018), 8.

6. Neumann and Makowicki, *Occupation and Demobilization*, 9.

7. Ibid.

8. Ibid.

9. Ibid., 9-10.

10. Ibid., 10.

11. Ibid., 10-11.

12. Ibid., 11.

13. Ibid.

14. Ibid., 14-16.

15. Ibid., 16.

16. Cheseldine, *Ohio in the Rainbow*, 298.

17. Reppy, *Rainbow Memories*, 20.

18. Cheseldine, *Ohio in the Rainbow*, 298.

19. Reppy, *Rainbow Memories*, 20; Cheseldine, *Ohio in the Rainbow*, 298.

20. Cheseldine, *Ohio in the Rainbow*, 298-299; Tompkins, *The Story of the Rainbow Division*, 148.

21. Reppy, *Rainbow Memories*, 20.

22. Leon Miesse to his wife, November 21, 1918. Miesse, *100 Years On*, 192.

23. Ibid.

24. Ibid.

25. Cheseldine, *Ohio in the Rainbow*, 301.

26. Cheseldine, *Ohio in the Rainbow*, 301; Reppy, *Rainbow Memories*, 20.

27. Cheseldine, *Ohio in the Rainbow*, 302.

28. Enoch Williams to his mother, November 24, 1918. Williams, *Letters Home*, 129.

29. Cheseldine, *Ohio in the Rainbow*, 302.

30. Leon Miesse to his wife, November 28, 1918. Miesse, *100 Years On*, 199.

31. Leon Miesse to his wife, November 29, 1918. Miesse, *100 Years On*, 200.

32. Neumann and Makowicki, *Occupation and Demobilization*, 20.

33. Ibid., 20-21.

34. Leon Miesse journal entry for December 3, 1918. Miesse, *100 Years On*, 201.

35. Reppy, *Rainbow Memories*, 20.

36. Leon Miesse to his wife, December 4, 1918. Miesse, *100 Years On*, 203.

37. Official Regimental Field Returns, December 5-13, 1918, cited in Cheseldine, *Ohio in the Rainbow*, 302-305

38. Tompkins, *The Story of the Rainbow Division*, 199.

39. Cheseldine, *Ohio in the Rainbow*, 306-307.

40. Leon Miesse journal entry for December 16, 1918. Miesse, *100 Years On*, 209.

41. Cheseldine, *Ohio in the Rainbow*, 307.

42. Leon Miesse to his wife, January 12, 1919. Miesse, *100 Years On*, 222.

43. Neumann and Makowicki, *Occupation and Demobilization*, 21.

44. Ibid., 49-50.

45. Ibid., 47.

46. Ibid., 23.

47. Ibid.

48. Enoch Williams to his mother, February 23, 1918. Williams, *Letters Home*, 181.

49. Tompkins, *The Story of the Rainbow Division*, 219-222.

50. Neumann and Makowicki, *Occupation and Demobilization*, 52-53.

51. Ibid., 53.

52. Cheseldine, *Ohio in the Rainbow*, 309, 316.

53. Ibid., 310.

54. Ibid., 312.

55. Ibid.

56. Daniels, *Dana Daniels Diary, 1917-1919*, 64-65.

57. Reppy, *Rainbow Memories*, 22.

58. Ibid.

59. Daniels, *Dana Daniels Diary, 1917-1919*, 68.

60. Cheseldine, *Ohio in the Rainbow*, 324.

61. Cheseldine, *Ohio in the Rainbow*, 324; Daniels, *Dana Daniels Diary, 1917-1919*, 69-70.

62. Ibid., 325.

63. Ibid., 326.

64. Ibid., 328.

65. Ibid., 329.

66. Ibid.

67. Ibid.

68. Ibid., 329-330.

69. Ibid., 330.

70. Daniels, *Dana Daniels Diary, 1917-1919*, 71-72; *Chillicothe Gazette*, May 11, 1919.
71. *Mansfield News-Journal*, May 10, 1919.
72. *Chillicothe Gazette*, May 11, 1919.
73. Reppy, *Rainbow Memories*, 26.
74. Ibid.

EPILOGUE

1. *Biographical Directory of Federal Judges*, Federal Judicial Center, accessed online at https://www.fjc.gov/node/1382421; *Lancaster Eagle-Gazette*, Lancaster, Ohio, November 20, 1935.
2. *Times Recorder*, Zanesville, Ohio, December 27, 1954.
3. *New York Times*, August 21, 1958.
4. Biographical data accompanying archived copy of diary, Ohio History Connection, Columbus, MS 5; Box 1, Folder 6.
5. Miesse, *100 Years On*, 53.
6. Cheseldine, *Ohio in the Rainbow*, 347-349.
7. Ibid., 344.

Bibliography

Alexander, Caroline. "The Shock of War," *Smithsonian*. Washington, DC: Smithsonian Institute, September 2010.

Annual Report of the Adjutant General to the Governor of the State of Ohio for the Year Ending November 15, 1914. Springfield, Ohio, State of Ohio, 1915.

Armstrong, David A. *Bullets and Bureaucrats: The Machine Gun and the United States Army, 1861-1916*. Greenwood Press, Westport, Connecticut, 1982.

The Army Lineage Book, Volume II: Infantry. Washington, DC, US Government Printing Office, 1953.

Asprey, Robert B. *The German High Command at War: Hindenburg and Ludendorff Conduct World War I*. Quill House, Fort Mill, South Carolina, 1993.

Baily, Roy. *Roy Baily Diary, 1917-1918*. Unpublished. Accessed at www.markboyd.info/MarionsOwn/Sgt_Bailey/pages_62-70.html.

Bonk, David. *St. Mihiel 1918: The American Expeditionary Forces' Trial by Fire*. Osprey Publishing, Long Island City, New York, Kindle Edition, 2011.

The Bourbon News, Paris, Kentucky.

Boyd, Austin Dewitt. *Austin Dewitt "Dusty" Boyd in WWI: Service in France and Germany*, Mark Boyd, ed. Unpublished. Accessed at www.markboyd.info/adboyd/war.html#mar-15-1919.

Carter, Donald A. *St. Mihiel, 12–16 September 1918*. Center of Military History, US Army, Washington, DC, 2018.

Chalkley, Lyman. "Captain Reuben Brent Hutchcraft, Jr." *Kentucky Law Journal*, Volume 7, Issue 1, University of Kentucky, Lexington, 1919.

Cheseldine, R.M. *Ohio in the Rainbow: Official Story of the 166th Infantry, 42nd Division, in the World War*. F.J. Heer Printing Company, Columbus, Ohio, 1924.

The Chillicothe Gazette, Chillicothe, Ohio.

Chinn, George M. *The Machine Gun: History, Evolution and Development of Manual, Automatic, and Airborne Repeating Weapons*, Volume I. US Government Printing Office, Washington, DC, 1951.

Coffman, Edward M. *The War to End All Wars: The American Military Experience in World War I*. University Press of Kentucky, Lexington, 1998.

Cora, Paul B. and Alexander A. Falbo-Wild. *Supporting Allied Offensives, 8 August–11 November 1918*. Center of Military History, US Army, Washington, DC, 2018.

Crowell, Benedict and Robert Forrest Wilson. *The Road to France: The Transportation of Troops and Military Supplies, 1917–1918-How America Went to War: An Account from Official Sources of the Nation's War Activities, 1917–1920.* Yale University Press New Haven, Connecticut, 1921.

Daniels, Dana. *Dana Daniels Diary, 1917-1919*. Dana Daniels Collection, Ohio Historical Society (MS 5; Box 1, Folder 6), Columbus.

Duffy, Francis P. *Father Duffy's Story: A Tale of Humor and Heroism, of Life and Death with the Fighting Sixty-Ninth*. George B. Doran, New York, 1919.

Ebert, Carl F. *A Brief History of Co. D, 166th Infantry*. Unknown Publisher, Marion, Ohio, 1939.

Eisenhower, John S.D. *Yanks: The Epic Story of the American Army in World War I*. Simon and Schuster, New York, Kindle Edition, 2001.

Faulkner, Richard S. *Meuse-Argonne, 26 September-11 November 1918*. Center of Military History, US Army, Washington, DC, 2018.

Finn, J. Michael. "The Chaplain Who Went Over-the-Top: Father George Raphael Carpentier, O.P.," *Barquilla de la Santa Maria: Bulletin of the Catholic Record Society-Diocese of Columbus*. Catholic Record Society—Diocese of Columbus, Columbus, Ohio, 2005.

Grey, Edward. *Twenty-Five Years, 1892-1916*. Hodder and Stoughton, London, 1926.

Grotelueschen, Mark Ethan. "The AEF Way of War: The American Army and Combat in the First World War." PhD dissertation, Texas A&M University, 2003.

Guild, George R. and Frederick C. Test. *Pocket Field Manual: A Manual Designed for Use of Troops in the Field*. George Banta Publishing Company, Menasha, Wisconsin, 1917.

Haig, Douglas, eds. Gary Sheffield and John Bourne. *War Diaries and Letters, 1914–1918*. Weidenfeld & Nicolson, London, 2005.

Handbook of Artillery Including Mobile, Anti-Aircraft and Trench Materiel. Office of the Chief of Ordnance, US Government Printing Office, Washington, DC, 1920.

Handbook of the Hotchkiss Machine Gun, Model of 1914. Washington, DC: US War Department, Office of the Chief of Ordnance, 1917

History of Machine Guns and Automatic Rifles. Small Arms Division, Office of the Chief of Ordnance, US Government Printing Office, Washington, DC, 1922.

Hochschild, Adam. *To End All Wars: A Story of Loyalty and Rebellion, 1914-1918*. Houghton Mifflin Harcourt, New York, 2011.

Into the Fight, April–June 1918. Center of Military History, US Army, Washington, DC, 2018.

Jarrett, Paul. *The Return of Paul Jarrett*. DVD, Directed by Clark Jarrett. Los Angeles: Jarrett Entertainment, 1998.

Joffre, Joseph Jacques Césaire. *The Personal Memoirs of Joffre: Field Marshal of the French Army*, Volume II. Harper and Brothers, New York, 1932.

Lanza, Conrad H. "The Artillery Support of Infantry in the A.E.F.," *Field Artillery Journal 26*, January-March 1936, The United States Field Artillery Association, Washington, DC, 1936.

Le Bijou 1913, The Annual of Ohio Wesleyan University, Volume XVII. Wesleyan University, Delaware, Ohio, 1913.

Lyon, C. C. "Mule Skinner's Life Isn't Wholly Dull," *Stars and Stripes*, Paris, France, April 26, 1918.

The Mansfield News-Journal, Mansfield, Ohio.

The Marion Star, Marion, Ohio.

Marysville Journal-Tribune, Marysville, Ohio.

Miesse, Leon, *100 Years On: WW I—Leon Miesse, Captain, 166th*, Robert Laird, ed. Zerone Publishing, Location Unknown, Kindle Edition, 2017.

Millett, Allan R. *Well Planned, Splendidly Executed: The Battle of Cantigny May 28-31, 1918*. Cantigny First Division Foundation, Chicago, 2010.

Moffett, Burt. *Burt Moffett Diary, January 1, 1918—September 7, 1918*. Burt J. Moffett World War I Diaries Collection, Ohio Historical Society (Vol. 1425), Columbus.

Moss, James A. *Field Service*. George Banta Publishing Company, Menasha, Wisconsin, 1917.

Neiberg, Michael S. *The Second Battle of the Marne*. University of Indiana Press, Bloomington, Kindle Edition, 2008.

Ney, Virgil. *Evolution of the US Army Infantry Mortar Squad: The Argonne To Pleiku*. Technical Operations, Incorporated, Combat Operations Research Group, Fort Belvoir, Virginia, 1966.

The Ohio Rainbow Reveille. Ohio Historical Society, Columbus, 1917-1919.

Ohio State Journal, Columbus.

Otte, Maarten. *The American Expeditionary Forces in the Great War: Meuse-Argonne 1918: Breaking the Line*. Pen & Sword Books, Barnsley, United Kingdom, Kindle Edition, 2018.

Pershing, John J. *My Experiences in the World War, Volume 2*. Frederick Stokes, New York, 1931.

Reilly, Henry J. *America's Part*. Cosmopolitan Book Corporation, New York, 1928.

Reppy, Alison. *Rainbow Memories: Character Sketches and History of the First Battalion, 166th Infantry, 42nd Division, American Expeditionary Force*. Executive Committee, First Battalion, 166th Infantry, Columbus, Ohio, 1919.

Richwood Gazette, Richwood, Ohio.

Setzekorn, Eric B. *Joining the Great War, April 1917-April 1918*. Center of Military History, US Army, Washington, DC, 2017.

Takle, Patrick. *Nine Divisions in Champagne: The Second Battle of Marne*. Pen & Sword Books, Barnsley, UK, Kindle Edition, 2015.

Thomas, Shipley. *The History of the A.E.F.* George B. Doran, New York, 1920.

Thompson, David G. "Ohio's Best: The Mobilization of the Fourth Infantry, Ohio National Guard, in 1917," *Ohio History Journal*, Volume 101, Winter-Spring 1992. Ohio Historical Society, Columbus, 1992.

Thorn, Robert L. Letter to Hillis J. Thorn, May 26, 1918. Author's private collection.

Tompkins, Raymond S. *The Story of the Rainbow Division*. Boni and Liveright, New York, 1919.

Williams, Enoch. *Letters Home from Somewhere in France (P.S. Send cigarettes & chocolate)*, Gary Williams, ed. Unpublished. Accessed at https://archive.org/details/EnochWilliamsWwiLettersHome1917-1919.

Wilson, Woodrow. *War Messages, 65th Cong., 1st Sess. Senate Doc. No. 5, Serial No. 7264.* Washington, DC, 1917.

Wolf, Walter B. *A Brief History of the Rainbow Division.* Rand, McNally, New York, 1919.

Index